SOWING IN TEARS

A Documentary History of the Church Struggle against Apartheid, 1960–1990

M. John Lamola

*Those who sow in tears
Shall reap in joy.
They who continually go forth weeping,
Bearing seed for sowing,
Shall surely come again
With rejoicing,
Bringing their sheaves with them.*

Psalm 126

·PUBLISHING·

African Perspectives Publishing
PO Box 95342, Grant Park 2051, South Africa
www.africanperspectives.co.za

© African Perspectives Publishing 2021

All rights reserved

No part of this publication may be reproduced, stored in a retrieval system or transmitted in any form or by any means, electronic, mechanical, photocopying or otherwise, without the prior permission of the publisher and author.

PRINT: ISBN 978-1-990931-24-6
DIGITAL: ISBN 978-1-990931-30-7

Cover Image: Gallo Images/Getty Images
Editor: Tumelo Motaung
Proof Reader: Rose Francis
Graphic Designer: Mfundo Mthiyane
Typesetting: Phumzile Mondlani

TABLE OF CONTENTS

PREFACE   9

PROLOGUE   15

Why the Church Failed to Resist Apartheid Before 1960   15

CHAPTER ONE - The Resurrection at Sharpeville   25

D1.1 *Report of the World Council of Churches Mission in South Africa: April–December 1960*   32

D1.2 *Statement of the Cottesloe Consultation, 14-17 December 1960*   37

D1.3 *Statement from the Third Assembly of the World Council of Churches, New Delhi, 1961 [Excerpts]*   46

CHAPTER TWO - The Challenge of the Apartheid Republic   51

D2.1 *All-In Africa Conference, Pietermaritzburg, 25–26 March 1961*   59

D2.2 *A Programme of Action for the Christian Institute*   61

D2.3 *Attacks on the Christian Institute: Statement by the Executive Committee of the CI, 9 November 1963*   64

D2.4 *Statement from the WCC Mindolo Consultation on Christians and Race Relations in Southern Africa. 4 June 1964*   69

D2.5 *Press statement by iNkosi Albert Luthuli on the Rivonia Trial verdict, 12 June 1964*   73

CHAPTER THREE - Triumphant Apartheid   76

D3.1 *Statement of the Christian Council of South Africa on the Bantu Laws Amendment Bill, February 1964*   83

D3.2 *Bantu Laws Amendment Bill: a press statement of the Conference of the Catholic Bishops of South Africa, July 1964*   84

D3.3 *Statement on the End of Session Legislation, June 1964*   85

D3.4 Declaration of Church Principles as accepted by the Christian Council of South Africa, August 1965   86

D3.5 Message to Overseas Partners, June 1965   90

CHAPTER FOUR - Liberalism and Race Relations   94

D4.1 World Conference on Church and Society – 'Christians In The Technical and Social Revolutions of our time', Geneva, July 1966   102

D4.2 The Woodstock Theses, October 1967   105

D4.3 Statement from the Fourth Assembly of the World Council of Churches, Uppsala, 20 July 1968   114

D4.4 The Reformed Ecumenical Synod, Lunteren, August 1968   118

D4.5 Message to the People of South Africa, 20 September 1968   122

CHAPTER FIVE - Black Consciousness and Black Theology   127

D5.1 "Black Anger and White Power in an Unreal Society" Dr CF Beyers Naude   134

D5.2 Statement of the Black Theology Conference, Wilgespruit, 1971   145

D5.3 Black Priests Solidarity Group: Principles And Aims   146

D5.4 Desmond Tutu's Open Letter to John Vorster, 6 May 1976   148

D5.5 Resolution on the Black Confessing Church, SACC Consultation on Racism, Hammanskraal, 11–15 February 1980   156

CHAPTER SIX - Church Support for Armed Resistance?   158

D6.1 Statement of the WCC Executive Committee, Arnoldshain, West Germany, September 1970   164

D6.2 SACC Resolution on Conscientious Objection to Compulsory Military Conscription to the South African Military Forces, National Conference, August 1974   166

D6.3 South Africa: What Hope Now? December 1977   169

CHAPTER SEVEN - The State Versus the Christian Institute: Schlebush Commission   194

D7.1 A Pilgrimage of Confession   200

D7.2 *Divine or Civil Obedience: Statement Declaring Refusal to Testify Before the Schlebusch Commission by the Staff of the Christian Institute, 22 June 1973* — 203

D7.3 *Statement by The Christian Institute on the 'Police State'* — 216

D7.4 *Report of the Schlebusch Commission: Conclusions and Recommendations* — 219

D7.5 *Statement of the SA Council of Churches on the Report of the Schlebusch Commission of Inquiry on the Christian Institute* — 222

CHAPTER EIGHT - The State Versus the SACC: Eloff Commission — 225

D8.1 *SACC Statement of Theological Principles* — 230

D8.2 *SACC 1978 National Conference Resolution: Call for a National Convention* — 240

D8.3 *The Eloff Commission Report: Official Summary And Recommendations* — 241

D8.4 *SACC Response to the Findings of the Eloff Commission* — 252

CHAPTER NINE - The Demise of Afrikaner Civil Religion — 264

D9.1 *NG Kerk: Human Relations and the South African Scene in the Light of Scripture, 1974 General Synod* — 270

D9.2 *Alliance of Black Reformed Christians In Southern Africa, 1981, ABRECSA Charter* — 275

D9.3 *World Alliance of Reformed Churches, Ottawa, 1982. Statement on Racism and the South African Afrikaans Churches* — 279

D9.4 *A Statement on Rejection of Apartheid Theology By 123 Ministers of The NG Kerk, 8 June 1982* — 282

D9.5 *Nederduitse Gereformeerde Sendingkerk, 1982 Synod Statement on Apartheid: Belhar Confession of Faith* — 287

CHAPTER TEN - Call To Prayer for an End to Unjust Rule — 293

D10.1 *Pastoral Letter of the Southern African Catholic* — 297

D10.2 *The Kairos Document: Official Summary* — 301

D10.3 *A Theological Rationale and a Call to Prayer for an End to Unjust Rule, 16 June 1985* — 306

D10.4 *A Memorandum to the State President, P.W. Botha, 17 March 1986*   311

D10.5 *Urgent Message to the State President from the Southern African Catholic Bishop's Conference, 20 August 1986*   315

D10.6 *Belhar Confession of Faith, Drafted In 1982, Adopted In September 1986*   325

CHAPTER ELEVEN - Sanctions: The World's Moment of Truth   330

D11.1 *SACC National Conference Resolution on Disinvestment, 28 June 1985*   334

D11.2 *The Harare Declaration, WCC World Church Leaders Emergency Meeting on South Africa, 4–6 December 1985*   337

D11.3 *United Church of Christ (USA): 1985 General Synod Resolution*   339

D11.4 *British Council of Churches, November 1985 General Assembly Resolution on South Africa*   343

CHAPTER TWELVE - Pilgrimages to Lusaka   344

D12.1 *A Communique of the Southern African Catholic Bishops Conference, Jointly With The African National Congress, 16 April 1986*   351

D12.2 *Lusaka Statement, 8 May 1987*   352

D12.3 *Theology and Violence: A Working Document of the ICT Theological Conference, Cape Town. 26 November 1987*   362

CHAPTER THIRTEEN - Standing for the Truth   365

D13.1 *Statement by the Leaders of South African Churches, 25 February 1988*   372

D13.2 *Church Leaders' Petition to Parliament, 29 February 1988*   376

D13.3 *Statement by The SACC on the State President's Invitation to Churches, 31 January 1990*   379

NOTES   381

SELECT BIBLIOGRAPHY   390

PREFACE

This book project was birthed during the darkest time in the history of South Africa. This period, incidentally, is narrated in Chapter 13. It was 1988. I had just landed in Britain as a depressed and flabbergasted political refugee who bore what felt like an onerous moniker of a Reverend John Lamola. This, at a time when the world was gripped with the news of the arrest of a group of prominent church leaders who, under the leadership of Archbishop Desmond Tutu, had attempted to march to Parliament on 29th February 1988.

I was a young theologian who, in the five years prior, was in the employ of both the South African Council of Churches (SACC) and the Institute of Contextual Theology (ICT). The African National Congress (ANC) community in London and some well-placed leaders in the British Council of Churches had heard of my name.

At the age of twenty-four, whilst a final-year undergraduate student at the University of South Africa (UNISA), I was invited to contribute a chapter on the ethics of violent resistance for a special anthology celebrating Desmond Tutu's receipt of the Nobel Peace Prize in 1984.[1] In May 1987 I was invited by Beyers Naude to join the delegation of the SACC to a conference with the banned liberation organisations in Lusaka, at which occasion I made acquaintance with exiled leaders of the ANC and the Pan-Africanist Congress of Azania (PAC) who, all of a sudden, I found myself having to fraternise with in London. Landing in exile at that juncture of the display of the most radical and determined resolve to bring an end to apartheid by the Christian leadership associated with the SACC, I found myself overwhelmed by church activists and ANC comrades who were keen to decipher the dynamics of the church's evident leadership of the struggle in South Africa. This was in the aftermath of P.W. Botha's regime having placed all community-based opposition structures within the country under fresh draconian restrictions on 25th February 1988.

The pervasive depression that clouded my mind then stemmed largely from the agony that while I was successfully smuggled out of South Africa, several of my very close comrades were in captivity, facing torture and charges of treason in a Bophutatswana special court. On the other hand, was the angst of settling in exile in the midst of the news of the assassination Dulcie September, the ANC Chief Representative in Paris on 29th March 1988. In the darkness of those days, and the pressure of maintaining a lifestyle dedicated to the momentum of frustrating the apartheid government as an activist political theologian, I stumbled upon a treasure trove of historical documents on the anti-apartheid activities of several church institutions and individuals – most of which were in books and journals that were declared banned literature in South Africa.

The first of these was the personal library of Horst Kleinschmidt in his London home. Horst had worked with Beyers Naude at the Christian Institute prior to being forced into exile in the late 1970s. His hospitality earned me the trust of the staff at the International Defence Aid Fund of South Africa (IDAF) who had one of the most sophisticated collections of rare documents about the struggle in South Africa because they were working very closely with the ANC in granting legal aid support to persons back in the country who had fallen into hands of the security police.

At the beginning of 1989 I also discovered an amazing archive of documents on the Black Consciousness Movement at the Selly Oak Colleges library in Birmingham. At that stage, my discoveries and readings were more for my own healing and fortitude. I wallowed into the enlightenment of how the struggle against apartheid colonisation had been prosecuted by those in near-similar professional and personal circumstances as mine.

It was Tony Trew of IDAF who presented an explicit challenge and proposed that I write a book out of the material and reflections that I had progressively shared with him. He indicated that the United Nations Educational, Scientific and Cultural Organization (UNESCO) would be interested in the publication. The book would specifically be a record of a historicist interpretation of how the Christian religion, whose theology had notoriously been used to foster coloniality and explicitly nurture apartheid philosophy, had transformed itself into an intellectual force and organisational bulwark of the struggle for political change in South Africa.

A nagging complication was that at the time of agreeing to work on this, that is mid-1989, my own level of consciousness had deepened to a point where I was seriously questioning if the monstrous level of the evil and might of the Pretoria regime could effectively be countered by a religious political activism which was largely married to the ideology of non-violent direct action. In August 1988 agents of the state security apparatus had bombed and destroyed Khotso House, headquarters of the SACC where I used to occupy a little office. What the situation seemed to demand was not another book.

Besides this political pessimism which I had already converted into a theoretical platform whereby against the hype of admiring the heroism of the church-in-struggle, I saw it as my duty to contribute to the ANC's political strategy planning structures a warning that we should tactically view the church not as force of struggle, but as the 'site for struggle'. I was against the church being posited, or regarding itself as the leader of the political struggle. I contested that church leaders inherently lack the scientific attitude required for prosecuting a political struggle to an ultimate revolutionary end.[2]

At that juncture, Jack and Ray Simons of the South African Communist Party, who warmly welcomed me into their home in their curiosity to understand the social power of religion in South Africa, became an invaluable sounding board for my intellectual and spiritual agonies. I had commenced my studies at Edinburgh University, where I incidentally ended up writing a doctoral thesis that questions the efficacy of the epistemology of political theology in delivering the kind of revolutionary social change required in our kind of world. The title of the completed dissertation became "The Poverty of a Theology of the Poor: An Althusserian (Louis Althusser) exposure of the philosophical basis of Latin American theology of liberation".

Using original Marxian literature sources, I demonstrated the revolutionary limitations of what was then considered the most radical mutation of Christian theology into a political programme. Having moved away from Theology and now firm in Philosophy, my task of writing a theological appreciation of the rise of the church in South Africa as the epitome of moral radicalness of Christian thought against political injustice, as contracted with Tony Trew, became both a burden and a relished experiment.

I duly decided that instead of writing a treatise on the subject, I would package and present a resource of theological material that bears evident political content and relevance. I would let others join in, have access to the material, and draw their own conclusions. The format of this book as a documentary history was thus decided.

As the original manuscript was compiled thirty years ago, I have had to revise and update it for current publication. The original manuscript that I carried with me from exile was lost with a Johannesburg publishing house as it went into bankruptcy in 1993. Beyers Naude had graciously contributed a Foreword for that planned publication. Distraught, I completely abandoned the project for over fifteen years.

The guilt of having all these documents in private obscurity has gnawed at my conscience for all these years. I firmly believed that the potential, but seemingly aborted, book would be of some value to researchers in the field of South African political history and to students of the history of political-theological thought within the ecumenical movement.

During 2019 I started working from a back-up hard copy of the original manuscript. Our 1988-89 computer did not have sophisticated data storage capabilities. In re-reading the text, I found that I had to rewrite much of what I had originally articulated. However, in doing so, I resolved to keep the 1989 character of the book intact. I was determined to maintain the presentation of the facts as I had gathered them thirty years prior, and as reflected upon from the gloom of my cold council flat in Muirhouse, Edinburgh.

In addition, I decided that while I am now a maturing academic within the disciplinary field of philosophy, I will stick to the idiomatic quality of language from my erudition as a Masters-level student of philosophical theology in 1989. I have also resisted the temptation to update my ideological prism from what it was then: a Black Consciousness thinker who believed in and served through the African National Congress.

The implicit claim of this book is that religious political activity is patently subordinate to the wider social occurrences that take place outside of the religious arena itself. Theological proclamation takes elements from the social milieu from which it arises, whilst, it simultaneously seeks to transform that very milieu. I have thus privileged the historiographical account of what was happening in the political arena over and above the ecclesiastical statements themselves in shaping the narrative flow of the text.

Consequently, the book is a catalogue of selected statements and pronouncements with an ecclesiastical standing (emanating from a church conference or interventional writing of a leading church figure) that relate to actual evolving events during the conflict between the apartheid government and those working against it. A directed historical-political narration precedes, and thus dictates which statements have been chosen to complete the historico-political theme of a given chapter. Preference has been given to documentary statements which come from a broad multi-denominational context, that is: which are ecumenical, display seminal and novel integration of theological thought with political analysis, and have potentially perennial relevance to contemporary and future debates.

Readers will note the sparsity of statements for the Roman Catholic Church in this documentary compilation. The reason is partly due to the *modus operandi* of Catholic public witness as compared to that of protestant denominations. Official Catholic reaction to issues 'outside' the church is traditionally expressed through the pronouncements of a Bishops Conference who would issue a pastoral letter.

These pastoral letters are didactic in character. They are designed to guide individual Catholics in their personal response to the matters under consideration. Unlike the traditionally proclamatory character of Protestant documents, pastoral letters rarely make direct and categorical judgments.[3] It should, however, be noted that the Catholic Church has been an 'observer member' of the SACC from whence most of the relevant statements seem to have emerged.

This book is not meant to be a portable library of all that the church has ever said or done against apartheid. I might have omitted some critical statements or included what may be judged by some as insignificant ones. Ultimately, it is hoped that as a record of and review of the development of religious resistance in South Africa, the curation of these documents will be a reminder of both the Christian community of its historical stance against the evil of racism, and of today's generation of the tears that flowed at the blood that was spilled in the quest for a free and peaceful land.

I thank the persons I have mentioned in the foregoing genealogy of this text: Horst, Tony, and posthumously, Beyers Naude (who we affectionately referred to as Oom Bey). Yusuf Asmal of Next Communications, who is also departed, sponsored the retyping of the back-up copy of the original manuscript in 1999, rendering it into an electronic version that I could edit and present in this current format.

PROLOGUE

Why the Church Failed to Resist Apartheid Before 1960

Having lost the popular vote in the 1948 general elections but gaining the majority of only five parliamentary seats, the National Party, led by Nederduitse Gereformeerde Kerk (NGK) theologian, Dr. D.F. Malan, stepped into power and launched its political programme based on the racial philosophy of apartheid. Out of a total population of 12,671,452 (68% of which were disenfranchised Black Africans[4]), a total of 1,073,364 Whites[5] had voted. Only 401,834 voted for the National Party and 524,230 for the United Party, the main opposition.[6] Three per cent of the population decided that the country would, for the next five decades, be known as the atrocious Apartheid South Africa.

Given that the disappointed section of the White population who supported the liberal and 'British' United Party were members of the English-language churches, it was expected that the first moral reaction against the declared intentions of Rev. Malan's party would emerge from this *ecclesia*. In December 1949 the Christian Council of South Africa – formed in 1936 as a consultative forum for the White churches to strategise on how to manage their missionary relations with urbanising Black communities – held its scheduled seven-yearly conference in Rosettenville, Johannesburg. The occasion provided the first opportunity for the churches to reflect collectively on the ramifications of apartheid, and the reality of the advent of the political hegemony of Afrikaans nationalism. In an attempt at repudiation, what by then was still just an intellectual rhetoric about the meaning of apartheid by National Party leaders and their Pretoria-located NGK theologians, the churches in Rosettenville could only declare that "the real need of South Africa is not 'Apartheid' (apartness) but 'Eendrag' (unity through teamwork)."[7]

Following this ethically benign intervention at the CCSA conference, the Congregational Church, the Methodist Church, the Presbyterians, the Baptist Union and the Anglicans each issued what then amounted to cautions to the Malan regime that it should go no further in restricting the already meagre political rights of Black people. The Catholic Church bishops went further and articulated the socio-philosophical basis of this mainly-White church community in its 1952 pastoral. As discussed below, a Eurocentrist worldview and vested racially committed social class interests muted the church leadership's critical perception of the injustice apartheid was set to unleash on the lives of Black South Africans.[8]

The political conduct of the English-speaking churches during this period makes it clear that their mission-theology was heavily underlain and informed by the subtly racist philosophy of Social Darwinism.[9] This was a belief in civilisational social evolution which – in the context of the Hegelian (G.W.F. Hegel) Eurocentric view of history - deemed native Africans as the most backward of the developing human species.[10]

The 1949 CCSA conference referred to above expressed the opinion that "individuals who have progressed from a primitive social structure to one more advanced should share in the responsibilities and rights of their new status". This statement was deployed as an argument for qualified franchise rights for Cape Coloureds. It identified and proscribed a racialised class of those who were patronisingly believed to have outgrown a particular social and cultural stage and could consequently be accorded selected commensurate human rights.

In 1952, at the height of the African National Congress's mass Defiance Campaign against Unjust Laws, the Southern African Catholics Bishop Conference (SACBC) issued a pastoral letter stating that "justice demands that Non-Europeans *be permitted to* evolve gradually towards full participation in the political, economic and cultural life of the country" (own emphasis), and that "this evolution cannot come about without earnest endeavours on the part of Non-Europeans to prepare themselves for the duties connected with the rights they hope to enjoy".[11]

The 18 July 1956 issue of *Southern Cross*, a public journal of the Southern African Bishops' Conference, carried an illuminating, if not startling, article by Archbishop Dennis Hurley – then Chairman of the bishops conference and head of its portfolio on African Affairs Committee.

The Archbishop averred that whilst the church "could not under any circumstances admit the justice of the principle of white supremacy", it could at the same time not be denied that compared with the average White, Blacks were "slower in every way" and that if they wished "to gain the right to vote they had to earn it".[12] At that given point in the trajectory of South Africa's social history, it would be "impossible to consider granting it [universal franchise] indiscriminately to all",[13] the archbishop, then a child of his times, reasoned.

In a subsequent 1957 statement, the Catholic bishops added to their 1952 message an argument that "people cannot share fully in the same political and economic institutions until culturally they have a great deal in common".[14] This was in reaction to the public controversy ignited by the apartheid regime's legislation of a 'Church Clause' of the Bantu Laws Amendment Bill that effectively prohibited people of other races from worshipping in churches in White areas. The social devastation of apartheid was becoming increasingly manifest and its repression of the articulation of the grievances of the oppressed Blacks growing more unconscionable.

Further, in response to growing self-organisation and militancy among opposition groups following the events of 1955-56, the Congress of the People, the adoption of the Freedom Charter, the arrests and the 1956 Treason Trial, the Catholic bishops pleaded:

> All Social change must be gradual if it is not to be disastrous. Nor is it unjust for a state to make provision in its laws and administration for the [racial] differences that do exist. A state must promote the well-being of its citizens. If some require special protection it must be accorded. It would be unreasonable, therefore, to condemn indiscriminately all South Africa's differential legislation.[15]

The view that there was a hierarchy of ethnically linked stages of social development, to which the English churches subscribed, was also fundamental to the ideology of apartheid. Apartheid's ideologues maintained that Blacks, to whom they referred as 'Non-Europeans', were perpetually doomed by biology to be under White tutelage. When White liberalism and generosity was to be displayed towards them, it should seek to guide them into White 'European' civilisation, which logically, they would never attain.

In 1956 the NGK (Main Afrikaans Dutch Reformed Church) published a study for an *ad hoc* commission which was appointed to internally analyse the resolutions of the World Council of Churches' 1954 Evanston Assembly. In this study, titled "The Dutch Reformed Churches in South Africa and the Problem of Race Relations", the NGK set out its own position, stating that it was "the will of God that in the foreseeable future white civilisation should be maintained in South Africa, and that this can only be done by securing white supremacy".[16] One of the authors of the report was N.P.J. Steyn of Krugersdorp, who, according to an entry in the *Survey of Race Relations in South Africa* "received a double doctorate from London University for a thesis which concluded that apartheid as applied to the native races in South Africa is a God-given command and is scriptural, legal, just and fair".[17]

A year earlier, Professor B.B. Keet, a senior professor at the NGK seminary at Stellenbosch, published his book, *Suid-Afrika Waarheen* (1955)[18] translated into English as *Whither South Africa*. Keet's main thesis, which qualitatively diverged from the racial theology of his church, argued that racial differences were no longer important since the dispensation of the New Testament; that "our fight is not between black and white, but between barbarism and civilization".

Keet's location of the 'problem of race relations' on the complexities of sophistication of peoples was mere affirmation of what was by then a widespread and generally accepted view in the White-led English churches of South Africa. For this assertion, he was regarded among his NGK colleagues as not being necessarily radical, but merely *verligte* (enlightened, reformist), as his views were the political theology of the English-speaking churches, which were dismissively judged as being liberal in the sense of not taking scripture seriously. The only difference, perhaps, was that he was saying it all in the *volk se taal*.

The core of the difference between the dominant Afrikaner view – held by some of the 'enlightened' Afrikaners and the English liberals – lay in history. Having emerged from a bitter struggle with the English for self-rule, including the Anglo Boer war of 1899-1902, Afrikaners in general could not accept the idea that Blacks should be allowed to be 'civilised' to a level at which they would equal Whites; they should not be capacitated to compete for economic status with Afrikaners who were largely impoverished working-class in the late 1940s and the beginning of the 1950s.

The very terms for the establishment of the Union of South Africa in 1910 as codified at Westminster as an act of the London Parliament had to be grounded on a 'Colour Bar' clause. The majority native Africans would be kept subordinate to the 'European' South Africans. Thus, the express mission of the Afrikaans Nationalist Party government was to overtly optimise the institutionalisation of the racist laws which Jan Smuts' United Party had been unsystematic and incoherent in enacting. The entire legislative programme would be a social engineering project that would guarantee that Blacks would not rise above a social stratum that would enable them to rise above being servants to White people in general.

This difference in approaches to 'civilising the Non-Europeans' is aptly demonstrated in the debates between Hendrik Verwoerd and the authorities of the English-speaking missionary schools during the passing of the Bantu Education Act in 1953. Verwoerd charged that the missionaries were preparing Black children for a status they would never enjoy,[19] while the English church hierarchy maintained that a measure of European civilisation had to be extended to Africans as a humanitarian act of Christian charity. The 1948 Episcopal Synod of the Anglican Church posited this argument against the rationale of apartheid when it warned:

> If Europeans [white people in South Africa] seek to withhold for themselves the exclusive benefits of Western civilization, and allow non-Europeans merely its burdens, South Africans will inexorably draw apart into mutually antagonistic racial groups.[20]

This liberal prognosis of the equitable sharing of the benefits of Western Christian Civilisation persisted even after Black political protest moved from 'protest' to resistance after 1961, until it was denuded by the rise of the Black Consciousness movement.[21] Nestled within this 'politics of civilisation' was an inherent tolerance of the apartheid regime, as in any case, the

Nationalist Party guaranteed White privilege.[22] The attendant polite intolerance of the apartheid regime is epitomised in a resolution of the 1956 General Assembly of the Baptist Church which stated:

> The assembly is deeply concerned at the hardships in which many of the Non-European peoples are involved through the implementation of such Acts as the Group Areas Act and the Natives Urban Areas Act ... We humbly beseech the Government to exercise Christian charity and patience in the application of these Acts.[23]

No outright opposition to the Government is declared here, nor is the fundamental moral value of the apartheid system questioned. Viewed with the advantage of hindsight, we might well wonder what type of 'Christian charity' could be brought to bear in the application of laws as cruel the Pass Laws and unjust as the Group Areas Act.

Another factor which contributed to the theological attitude of the White non-Afrikaans churches, as social institutions of the English-speaking British South Africans, were the lingering memories of the Anglo-Boer War. Indignation at the massive scale of the brutality of the British during the war featured prominently in the Afrikaner nationalism of the late 1940s. Public expression of this indignation by Afrikaner political figures who now wielded state power was a real concern in the English-speaking churches. In response, these churches devoted themselves to a 'mission of reconciliation' between the English and Afrikaners.

English-speaking political moralists could not attack the Afrikaner establishment with bold consciences without the risk of being reminded of the British concentration camps in which thousands of Afrikaner women and children died in 1900 and 1901[24]. Though it operated largely at the level of the subconscious, this inhibition helped muffle the moral attack by the 'traditionally liberal' English churches on the blatant evils of the emerging apartheid state.

It was only in the aftermath of the success of Hendrik Verwoerd's well-orchestrated strategy of forging 'White unity' and *twee-taligheid* (bilingualism) and the fear that the 'European way of life' was under a common threat from the problem of the presence of Blacks (*swart gevaar*),[25] that a new critical shift in political perspective could develop among a small section of the White population. This dread of black power had been articulate in 1936 by the Prime Minister General J.M.B Hertzog in a speech to Parliament during his piloting of the "Representation of Natives Bill" thus:

> If the Natives get the necessary education and the necessary schooling they must eventually get the upper hand if they only have the desire to take it. And no one can ever doubt that when the Native ever gets that upper hand at the ballot box he will not omit to use it in his own favour. We must accept that, and it has always hitherto been accepted by Europeans in South Africa[26].

According to J. J. Venter, "Verwoerd extended the concept of 'a people' to include the English-speaking section of the population; he pleaded for the relinquishment of the war between brothers (the English and the Afrikaner Whites), through a unification of symbols, so that the Whites would become one 'volk' with two languages, but with a singular patriotism."[27] In his own words (translated from Afrikaans by J.J Venter), Verwoerd put it thus in a 1959 speech:

> After half a century of co-operation – difficult, at times very difficult – a stage has been reached when both groups as never before are faced with a challenge to bury the past, to let it become the combined history of a unified people ('volk'). Today we are faced with threats for the future of our civilisation, for our prosperity, for the contribution of the white man of Africa to the struggle of the white man of Europe and America to retain his hegemony in the world. Also, to make Christianity victorious, sacrifices must be made, and nowhere is Christianity more threatened than in Africa. Sacrifices of sentiment is expected of everybody. There must not only be a union of provinces in South Africa. There must also be a union of hearts.[28]

It was against this background of White religious thinking that personalities like Trevor Huddleston, Bishop Ambrose Reeves and Rev. Michaels Scott stood out.[29] In contrast to the general stereotype of the White clergy, they showed common humanity with the Black people they served and identified with them in their struggle against White political domination and cultural subjugation.

Until his enforced departure to England in 1956, Trevor Huddleston was the symbol *par excellence* of Christian witness against the apartheid system. When the ANC awarded him its highest honour, the *Isithwalandwe/Seaparankwe* Medal, at the Congress of the People in 1955 in recognition of his outstanding service to the cause of the freedom of the African people, Fr. Huddleston's actions stood in marked contrast to the prevailing theological views about Christian duty in South Africa.

Decades before the advent of liberation theology, which gave a systematic justification for Christian involvement in secular movements for political change, here was a 'European' Christian priest in the Union of South Africa being honoured together with a noted communist leader, Dr Yusuf Dadoo, for distinguished participation in political struggle against White colonial racism.

After Huddleston was recalled to England by his religious order in 1956, his mantle fell on the Anglican Bishop of Johannesburg, Ambrose Reeves. Single-handed, as if he had given up on his fellow members of the Episcopal Synod, Reeves dedicated himself to giving support to those charged in the 1956 Treason Trial, among whom were the ANC's Chaplain-General, Rev. James Calata. Also among the trialists were Rev. Walker Gawe and Rev. Douglas Thompson.

Bishop Reeves organised international publicity and raised funds for their defence. This resulted in his work with Canon John Collin on the formation of the Treason Trial Defence Fund, which developed into the International Defence and Aid Fund for Southern Africa that successfully and masterfully arranged legal succour for activists charged under the apartheid regimes security legislation well into 1990.[30] In September 1960 Ambrose Reeves was deported from South Africa after returning from a six-months-long world tour publicising the Sharpeville massacre.

It was only after December 1960, following a special World Council of Churches conference that was held at Cottesloe, Johannesburg, that a formal current of organised Christian institutional resistance to apartheid began to emerge. Even then, it is debatable whether there was an actual shift from the pattern of the 1950s when isolated individuals stood up more out of personal conviction – without formal support from their churches – to one where the church acted officially as a united institution.

Throughout the 1960s the South African history of religious political protest continued to be dominated by the selflessness of an individual, Beyers Naude – just as it was dominated in the 1950s by Trevor Huddleston. The difference between Huddleston and Naude (and one of immense historical significance) was that whereas Huddleston worked with the liberation movement outside of the institutional church, Naude decidedly worked within the church and sought to make the entire church community in South Africa – Afrikaans, English, and African Independent Churches – aware of the need to oppose apartheid.

This shift in the nature and quality of Christian protest has dictated the character of this book. Since the National Party came to power in 1948, several phases of Christian organised protest against apartheid are identifiable. As corroborated by Jim Cochrane,[31] these could be caricatured as: passive resistance between 1948 and 1960; reconciliation and multi-racialism between 1960 and 1968; Black Consciousness and Black Theology between 1968 and 1977; the challenge to legal legitimacy of the apartheid state between 1977 and 1984; and civil disobedience from 1986.

This book covers the period from the year 1960, which signalled the beginning of an identifiable Christian tradition of protest against political oppression and repression in South Africa. As elaborated in the forgoing account, its claim is that it is only after 1960 that there can be a judicious discussion of Christian resistance to apartheid. Between 1948 and 1960 the institutional church was still frozen into its European winter of White racial paternalism and the confusion of coming to terms with the puzzling phenomenon of 'primitives' trying to violate the social laws of nature by aspiring to the same standards of living and human rights as those of their 'culturally advanced' European masters.

This kind of thinking, in the church and in wider South African life, was to be demolished by the advent of the philosophy of Black Consciousness and its attendant Black Theology at the end of the 1960s. From this point on, the incompatibility of the apartheid doctrine with Christian religious faith was articulated by the victims of the system themselves, Black people. What came to be demanded went beyond pleas for the normalisation of race relations. This was the envisioning of a new political order which would bring a democratically elected non-racial government representing the views and interests of the majority of South Africa's people.

CHAPTER ONE

The Resurrection at Sharpeville

By 1960, the ruling National Party, led by Hendrik Verwoerd (who was Prime Minister from 1957 to 1967), had arrived at the climax of its campaign to reconstitute South Africa into a racialised republic, independent of the British Crown. The Union of South Africa was then a post-Anglo-Boer War amalgamation of what had been the British colonies of the Cape and Natal and the Boer Republics of the Transvaal and the Orange Free State. The National Party was intent on rendering the country totally free of British interference. The veiled anti-British and anti-Black assertiveness of Afrikaner nationalism reached its peak during this campaign.

On the wave of Afrikaner Nationalism, all White South Africans were united in their claim that South Africa was their country and that their ancestors were placed by 'God' to civilise and rule its African Native majority.[32] There was of course, the economic motive at the heart of this White supremacist complex.

Within this hubris, the National Party government announced that there would be a referendum in October 1960 in which the White electorate was to be canvassed on the question of the proposed change in the status of the country. The announcement of this referendum provoked a trenchant opposition from the African National Congress and its Congress Alliance partners. This demonstration of the resolve at cementing exclusive White political control of South Africa caught the ANC reeling from two traumas: First, the 1956 Treason Trial in which nearly all of its leadership, who were among the 155 people charged,[33] were on a protracted trial for their lives; and second, a breakaway of the Africanists faction of the party who were protesting the ANC's subscription to the 1955 Freedom Chapter, had launched the Pan Africanist Congress in April 1959.[34]

The PAC's politics of a decolonisation of South Africa along the nationalist model unfolding in Africa since the independence of Kwame Nkrumah's Ghana occasioned serious political self-examination across the protest movement on the course and principles of the anti-apartheid struggle in the face of the marshalling of Afrikaner sovereignty. The ANC responded to the announcement of the referendum with preparations for a protest campaign which would take the form of a national strike and the burning of passes on 31 March 1960.[35]

On Monday, 21 March 1960, ten days before the start of the ANC's campaign, groups of residents in several Black townships went out on a defiance and civil disobedience action called by PAC leadership, marching out of their homes without their passes and handing themselves over for mass arrest at police stations. In Sharpeville, about seventy kilometres south of Johannesburg, the police responded with the utmost brutality to a crowd that had gathered around the police station without their pass books. By the end of the day sixty-nine of the marchers lay dead and over 200 were wounded on the streets of Sharpeville. Robert Sobukwe, leader of the PAC had been arrested in Orlando, Soweto, and would spend 9 years on Robben Island. On the same day, at a concurrent protest 1 200 kilometres away in the township of Langa, outside Cape Town, two protesters were killed and 49 wounded.

Many Black communities rose in revolt as news of Langa and the Sharpeville massacre reached them. Led by the ANC's Nkosi Albert Luthuli, scores of people began to burn their passes on 27 March 1960, which had been declared a stay-at-home day of mourning for the victims of the massacre. Secondary protestant actions around the country were met with more state violence, which sparked off yet more revolts, initiating a widespread crisis of unprecedented gravity for the apartheid regime. By the end of April 1960, 83 more people had been killed[36].

It was not the first time that Black people had been murdered in this manner by the colonial Union of South Africa regime. In the case of the Sharpeville massacre, however, the sound of the shots fired by the police at unarmed and disenfranchised political demonstrators echoed throughout the world. The apartheid regime was confronted by international condemnation of a ferocity it had never encountered.

Shares plummeted in the stock market as foreign confidence in the South African economy and the future of the Verwoerd government evaporated and a panic-stricken emigration of South African Whites began. The beleaguered government responded by invoking the Public Safety Act of 1950 to declare a national State of Emergency on 31 March 1960.

Within a week of the declaration of the State of Emergency, more than 20 000 people were in detention. The detainees included two English missionaries and virtually all the grassroots-level leadership of the ANC and the nascent PAC. The freedom of the ANC's top leadership had been restricted for some time in any case – apart from Oliver Tambo and Albert Luthuli, who were living under government-imposed restrictions – they were all defendants in a Treason Trial which had by then been in progress for four years.

On 8 April 1960, both the ANC and the PAC were declared unlawful organisations under the Unlawful Organisations Act. Those deemed to be furthering the aims of the banned organisations and those claiming continued membership of such organisations after their proscription, became liable to ten years imprisonment.

Just before the declaration of the State of Emergency, the ANC's National Executive took a decision to send Oliver Tambo on an international mission as the organisation's ambassador, to solicit international support for the struggle against White minority rule. Tambo had been the acting President of the ANC since 1959 when iNkosi Albert Luthuli was put under house arrest. Smuggled through Bechuanaland on 27th March 1960, he eventually made it to London and to the United Nations headquarters in New York without a passport to present a first-hand account of the situation in South Africa.

In South Africa, a network of defence and aid committees emerged. These committees, under the presidency of Ambrose Reeves, the Anglican Archbishop of Cape Town, sought to alleviate the extreme hardships suffered by the families of detainees in consequence of the massive repression. They also strove to publicise the harsh conditions in which African detainees were held.

As an indication of the world's attention drawn to post-Sharpeville South Africa, iNkosi Luthuli was presented with the Nobel Peace Prize for 1960. This award drew unprecedented international attention to the ANC's long struggle which began 1912, waged by means of passive resistance, against the racism of British colonialism in the earlier period, and apartheid in the later period. The announcement that the ANC's President-General was being honoured by the international community for his leadership in the non-violent struggle also sparked a painful self-examination, as the ANC sought to count the achievements of this struggle through peaceful means, particularly during the preceding five years.

The revelation of the brutality of the apartheid regime against the backdrop of the history of the non-violence of the ANC flabbergasted the international community. This period led to a renewed academic and political scrutiny of the philosophical roots, structures, and *modus operandi* of the ideology of apartheid. In turn, this drew attention to the way in which Christian theology had been misused in the interests of apartheid.[37]

The World Council of Churches (WCC) in Geneva responded to the events by launching a 'Mission to South Africa' in April 1960. A delegation of six eminent persons drawn from the international Christian community spent about six months in South Africa, where they consulted with the various South African Churches and gathered first-hand information for the WCC. The mission culminated in a consultative conference with representatives from the eight churches in South Africa which were members of the WCC.

The conference was held at Cottesloe, a suburb of Johannesburg, on 14-17 December 1960. It is noteworthy that the date of the sitting of this conference straddled the national holiday of 16th December, which among the Afrikaans nationalists was observed as the Day of the Vow (*Geloftedag*), a solemn vow made by the Voortrekkers to preserve themselves as a nation in South Africa, following their victory "through Gods help" over the Zulu warriors of King Dingane in December 1838 at the Battle of the Blood River. In 1982 the holiday was renamed the Day of the Covenant, and after 1994 the Day of Reconciliation.

The first of the three documents in this chapter (**Document D1.1**) is a record of the observations of the WCC international delegation tabled at the Cottesloe Consultation. Besides being the statement of the social role of the church and the evaluation of its response to the developments described above, it provides a rare seminal attempt of a rational view of the South African society in conflict with itself by an outsider.

The Statement of the Cottesloe Consultation, the second of the documents (**Document D1.2**), was appended to the WCC delegation's report and was distributed among WCC member churches throughout the world.

The Cottesloe Conference became a watershed in the development of an anti-apartheid political theology in South Africa, even though its view of developments was rooted in the Eurocentric perspective that dominated the ecclesiastical tradition of the time. It marked the beginning of a theological tradition which was informed by a concern about 'race relations'. This developed into a pivotal conceptual framework would inform the appraisal of the ideological rationale of the apartheid regime for about a decade. It dominated the anti-apartheid theological scene until it was overshadowed by the emergence of Black Theology and the Black Consciousness Movement in the early 1970s. The Cottesloe Conference is particularly significant because of its recommendation that a South African Council of Churches be formed in order to further the process pioneered at Cottesloe. It took eight years to put this recommendation into effect.

While the Cottesloe Conference was in progress, the ecumenical and international membership of the WCC was engaged in preparations for its third General Assembly. General Assemblies of the WCC, which had by then assumed the influential status of being major international platforms for the pronouncement of unified theological thought within the Protestant churches on matters relating to the church's role in the world, are convened every seven years. The third one, taking place in the Indian capital New Delhi in 1961, was the first to be held outside Europe and North America. Issues around decolonialisation, self-determination of the indigenous peoples, and racism hovered over its agenda. The tabling of the report of the "Mission to South Africa" at this General Assembly presented a chilling concreteness to these issues, and firmly placed the liberation struggle in South Africa on the agenda of the international ecumenical movement.

The South African churches' Cottesloe Statement had given a veiled but not sympathetic consideration to Verwoerd's adumbration of the concept of 'separate development', a philosophical rationalisation of apartheid. The New Delhi Assembly departed sharply from the Cottesloe Statement on this issue, and sought to put the character of the church's response into perspective. It asserted that in developing a political language and engaging in politics, the church was not merely commenting on political developments as an external observer. Instead, it was urged to "identify itself with the oppressed race in its struggle to achieve justice". Experts from the official WCC report on the New Delhi Assembly constitute the third document in this chapter, and explains why the NGK (Dutch Reformed Church) could no longer feel at home in the World Council of Churches (**Document D1.3**).

The New Delhi Assembly gave new impetus to the WCC's 1954 undertaking to establish a Secretariat on Racial and Ethnic Relations. The establishment of this Secretariat as one of the main departments of the WCC presaged the foundation in 1969/70 of the visibly more active and programmatically more radical Programme to Combat Racism (PCR). The situation in South Africa encroached as the foundational material that would shape much of the theological praxis of international organised Christianity from the 1960s, as the following chapters will reveal.

The Roman Catholic Church globally, and in South Africa was not part of the processes outlined above due to the fact that the World Council of Churches is expressly a multidenominational association of the historical Protestant movement within Christianity. The Catholic Church has a novel governance structure, which, it must be remembered, includes the fact that the Vatican City has a status in international law that is equivalent to that of any other sovereign state, with concomitant diplomatic ramifications. This unique ecclesiastic status, in the case of South Africa, dictated that questions pertaining to social and political responsibility are judiciously dealt with through the Southern African Catholic Bishops' Conference.[38]

After two very ambiguous and largely uncritical statements on race relations in 1952 and 1957, where the latter was more concerned with the effect of the Bantu Education Act on Catholic schools, the bishops issued a pastoral letter in February 1960, a month before the Sharpeville massacre happened. As recorded in Andrew Prior's *Catholics in Apartheid Society*[39] this pastoral letter warned, *inter alia*, that,

> The problem of 'race relations' must be solved soon, and in the light of Christian principles. Otherwise there is little hope for peace and order, as antagonisms will grow, prejudices harden into intolerance, and frustration lead to outburst of disorder and violence.[40]

It further stated that all people, irrespective of race, had fundamental human rights, and called for the use of peaceful means to reclaim these rights. It condemned the migratory labour system and urged that there be equal economic opportunities for all. Discussing a 'new vision of society', the bishops said:

> While we concede that it would be wrong to allow those with a more advanced culture (whites) to be deprived at this stage of an effective part in government, and to have their economic status reduced, yet this protection need not and must not operate oppressively on the other sections.[41]

What was new in this pastoral letter was its explicit affirmation of the fact, which became one of the mantras of the newly formed PAC, that "there is truly only one race, the human race".[42] The months immediately following Sharpeville, the Catholic Church in South Africa was virtually silent on the political developments of the time. Was this partly because its global leadership was, during that same period, engrossed in the formulation and internal debates on its new 'social teachings' at the Second Vatican Council?

D1.1 Report of the World Council of Churches Mission in South Africa: April–December 1960

Prepared by the WCC Delegation to the Cottesloe Consultation of December 1960

>Dr Franklin Clark Fry, Chairperson
>Bishop Lakdasa de Mel
>Prof. Wilhelm Niesel
>Mr Charles C. Parlin
>Dr W.A. Visser 't Hooft
>Dr Robert S. Bilheimer, Secretary

The Situation in April

'Sharpeville' was a fearsome expression of basic problems in South African society, the complexity of which was little appreciated by the outside world. The world viewed 'Sharpeville', for instance, primarily as an explosion of race tension. What, however, lies behind race tension in South Africa? The answer to that question confronts one with a range of towering problems. One is nationalism, from which no country is free, which in South Africa takes the form of a particular nationalism, that of the Afrikaner people, most but by no means all of whom are united in the National Party, in conflict with other nationalisms, particularly emerging so-called 'Black nationalism'. Another is industrialisation and urbanisation, expanding rapidly from roughly World War I, with a special impetus from World War II. This depends largely upon non-white labour, brings great numbers of non-white and white people into close contact in the growing cities, and is a main stumbling block in the way of achieving the concept of apartheid idealistically understood as 'separate development'. Still another problem of large sections of the country which need both agricultural and economic development on a large scale. Further, the cultural aspects of rapid social change pose another whole set of problems. African culture and white culture in South Africa are different. How are they related? What future form of culture is best? And how shall the transition best be managed? All these factors played into the race tension and the disturbances of March

1960, and if it be maintained, as some do, that these were caused by 'agitators', it can with reason be answered that these were among the basic problems which gave ground for agitation.

Another dimension to the whole is supplied by history. The power of historical tradition cannot be underestimated in an appreciation of the situation in South Africa.

It can scarcely be denied that those who struggle with present day conditions are the inheritors of those assumptions of 'white supremacy' from which the whole 'white' world is even today scarcely yet free. The distinctive histories and struggles between the British and the Afrikaner peoples, and the historical development of the now vast African population have a powerful effect upon the present. Contemporary history in Africa and elsewhere wields a strong influence.

Strong mass emotion ran throughout the country as it was in April, raising a constant tension to a higher pitch. The fears, the anger and the aspiration which formed the content of this emotion differed from group to group in the population. This difference, however, did not neutralise the power of the emotion itself. Indeed, the presence of mass emotion adds an element of time to every problem. 'The time factor' gave to each decision, policy and event an indefinable but strongly felt urgency.

The churches were deeply involved in this scene. The membership of the WCC did not include all of the churches and Christian agencies in South Africa. As of December 1960, there were eight WCC member churches. The Dutch Reformed Church of the Orange Free State and three other Reformed churches were not members. The many missionary societies and their daughter churches were not members. Nevertheless, the member churches of the WCC constituted a large influential and representative part of the total. The English and Afrikaans parts of the population were strongly represented in them. Both white and non-white, the latter being African and Coloured and Indian, were included in the membership of the churches. Problems which are germane to these portions of the population and their relationships between them existed within the churches, and their witness and their unity was qualified by this fact. A growing multilingualism especially among church leaders, helps to bridge some of the distance between various groups. The increasing influence of non-white members and leaders in the churches is of large present and potential importance in transcending differences among the racial groups. These facts of continuing church life were all vividly prominent during the days of the State of Emergency in April.

Similarly, an aroused Christian conscience was evident among people belonging to all member churches. This was not caused only by the dramatic events of the time but had been long in developing. Under the pressure of the Emergency, Christian conscience was expressed in sometimes radically different forms, which cannot be described in detail here. Common elements in this renewal, however, can be discerned. One is the reality of fellowship between white and non-white Christians, principally leaders in the churches, which is a result fundamentally of missionary work. In the face of the emergency and its underlying problems, this fellowship worked specially to cause a quickening of conscience as well as to provide some basis for solidarity and for hope. Theological thinking has for the past decade been marked by a new search of the Scripture for its message concerning race relations. This has taken place not only in theological faculties but also among pastors and leaders of churches. Again, the full results of this cannot be described here, but that it has been the root of awakened conscience can scarcely be denied. Further, there is evident an emerging consciousness of the Church as set within the world as a whole rather than as forming merely a part of one particular civilization. This is of particular importance in view of the force which the history of different groups have in South Africa and enables Christians to view both their missionary and prophetic calling with a clearer perspective. Finally, the influence of the ecumenical movement and of ecumenical contacts may be noted as contributing to the aroused conscience which was evident in the tense days of April.

In spite of this, however, the churches were involved in a deep struggle to transcend their situation. This affected their loyalties and their witness alike. The influence of history – the history of relations between the white and non-white peoples, the history of the relations between the English and the Afrikaans – at some points gave signs of almost engulfing the distinctive witness of the churches. The pressure of social change upon white and non-white peoples resulted, even in the churches, in a tendency to identify the Christian cause with the white or non-white causes. There was, with only a few exceptions, unfavourable reaction to nearly every influence from the 'outside', and this isolation further suggested a failure to transcend merely particular loyalties.

Unity could be discerned only among those churches of close cultural or confessional similarity, and even here there were grave differences. Two crucial points of disunity were evident. The first was that between the English-speaking and the Afrikaans-speaking churches, and the second between the white and non-white parts of the Christian community. It is true that there was fellowship between white and non-white people of the same church, although that was also under strain. It would be too much, however, to speak of fellowship or unity between white and non-white Christians in general, for here the situation was one of such acute tension as to amount to disunity. This was particularly true of the churches which had no integration of both groups in their membership. The almost total ignorance on the part of Christians of other churches than their own showed lack of unity even at the level of knowledge. A general isolationism in relation to the ecumenical movement was to some degree offset by the deep ecumenical convictions of some key leaders in the South African churches. In April, even this factor, however, was sharply qualified by the conflict between justice and unity, which gave rise to the question: must the demand for justice now be the cause for a break in ecumenical fellowship?

It must be stressed, finally, that the problem of race relations was the over-arching problem. Convictions as to the proper, or even legitimate, Christian attitude towards race relations were in radical conflict. In spite of this, however, a generally uniform practice was evident. The requirements of the social situation, different languages in the churches which oppose apartheid, the 'lag' between the convictions of the general membership and those of the leaders, meant that although Christian attitudes differed, Christian practice was relatively uniform. The upsurge of the African was evident in the churches, especially in African leadership, but also in the sensitivity of some of the white church leadership to the problems and the claims of the African. The question: 'Is Christianity on trial' was openly asked and covertly feared. The problem of race relations coloured all else.

D1.2 Statement of the Cottesloe Consultation, 14-17 December 1960

Part I

We have met as delegates from the Member Churches in South Africa of the World Council of Churches, together with representatives of the World Council itself, to seek under the guidance of the Holy Spirit to understand the complex problems of human relationships in this country, and to consult with one another on our common task and responsibility in the light of the Word of God. Our worship, Bible study, discussion and personal contacts have led us to a heightened appreciation of one another's convictions and actions. Our next task will be to report to our several Churches, realising that the ultimate significance of our meeting will consist in the witness and decisions of the Churches themselves in consequence of these consultations.

The general theme of our seven days together has been the Christian attitude toward race relations. We are united in rejecting all unjust discrimination. Nevertheless, widely divergent convictions have been expressed on the basic issues of apartheid. They range on the one hand from judgement that it is unacceptable in principle, contrary to the Christian calling and ministry that is unworkable in practice, to the conviction on the other hand that a policy of differentiation can be defended from the Christian point of view, that it provides the only realistic solution to the problems of race relations and is therefore in the best interests of the various population groups.

Although proceeding from these divergent views, we are nevertheless able to make the following affirmations concerning human need and justice, as they affect relations among the races of this country. In the nature of the case the agreements here recorded do not – and we do not pretend that they do – represent in full the convictions of the Member Churches.

The Church of Jesus Christ, by its nature and calling, is deeply concerned with the welfare of all people, both as individuals and as members of social groups. It is called to minister to human need in whatever circumstances and forms it appears, and to insist that all be done with justice. In its social witness the Church must take cognisance of all attitudes, forces, policies and laws which affect the life of a people; but the Church must proclaim that the final criterion of all social and political action is the principles of Scripture regarding the realisation for all men of a life worthy of their God-given vocation,

We make bold therefore to address this appeal to our Churches and to all Christians, calling on them to consider every point where they may unite their ministry on behalf of human beings in the spirit of equity.

Part II

1. We recognise that all racial groups who permanently inhabit our country are a part of our total population, and we regard them as indigenous. Members of all these groups have an equal right to make their contribution towards the enrichment of the life of their country and to share in the ensuing responsibilities, rewards and privileges.

2. The present tension in South Africa is the result of a long historical development and all groups bear responsibility for it. This must also be seen in relation to events in other parts of the world. The South African scene is radically affected by the decline of the power of the West and by the desire for self-determination among the peoples of the African continent.

3. The Church has a duty to bear witness to the hope which is in Christianity both to White South Africans in their uncertainty and to Non-White South Africans in their frustrations.

4. In a period of rapid social change, the Church has a special responsibility for fearless witness within society.

5. The Church as the Body of Christ is a unity and within this unity the natural diversity among men is not annulled but sanctified.

6. No-one who believes in Jesus Christ may be excluded from any Church on the grounds of his colour or race. The spiritual unity among all men who are in Christ must find visible expression in acts of common worship and witness, and in fellowship and consultation on matters of common concern.

7. We regard with deep concern the revival in many areas of African society of heathen tribal customs incompatible with Christian beliefs and practice. We believe this reaction is partly the result of a deep sense of frustration and a loss of faith in Western civilisation.

8. The whole Church must participate in the tremendous missionary task which has to be done in South Africa, and which demands a common strategy.

9. Our discussions have revealed that there is not sufficient consultation and communication between the various racial groups which make up our population. There is a special need that a more effective consultation between the Government and leaders accepted by the Non-White people

of South Africa should be devised. The segregation of racial groups carried without effective consultation and involving discrimination leads to hardship for members of the groups affected.

10. There are no Scriptural grounds for the prohibition of mixed marriages. The well-being of the community and pastoral responsibility require, however, that due consideration should be given to certain factors which may make such marriage inadvisable.

11. We call attention once again to the disintegrating effects of migrant labour on African life. No stable society is possible unless the cardinal importance of family life is recognised, and, from the Christian standpoint, it is imperative that the integrity of the family be safeguarded.

12. It is now widely recognised that the wages received by the vast majority of the Non-White people oblige them to exist well below the generally accepted minimum standard for healthy living. Concerted action is required to remedy this grave situation.

13. The present system of job reservation must give way to a more equitable system of labour which safeguards the interests of all concerned.

14. Opportunities must be provided for the inhabitants of the Bantu areas to live in conformity with human dignity.

15. It is our conviction that the right to own land wherever domiciled, and to participate in the government of the country, is part of the life of the adult man and woman, and for this reason a policy which permanently denies to Non-

White people the right of collaboration in the government of the country of which they are citizens cannot be justified.

16. (a) It is our conviction that there can be no objection in principle to the direct representation of Coloured people in Parliament.
(b) We express the hope that consideration will be given to the application of this principle in the foreseeable future.

17. In so far as nationalism grows out of a desire for self-realisation, Christians should understand and respect it. The danger of nationalism is, however, that it may seek to fulfil its aims at the expense of the interests of others and that it may make the nation an absolute value which takes the place of God. The role of the Church must therefore be to help to direct national movements towards just and worthy ends.

Part III

1. *Judicial Commission on the Langa and Sharpeville incidents*

The Consultation expresses its appreciation for the prompt institution of enquiries into the recent disturbances and requests the Government to publish the findings as soon as possible.

2. *Justice in Trial*

It has been noted that during the recent disturbances a great number of people were arrested and detained for several months without being brought to trial. While we agree that abnormal circumstances may arise in any country necessitating a departure from the usual procedure, we would stress the fact that it belongs to the Christian conception of law, justice and freedom that in normal circumstances men should not be punished except after a fair trial before open courts for previously defined offences. Any departure from this fundamental principle should be confined to the narrowest limits and only resorted to in the most exceptional circumstances.

3. *Positions of Asians in South Africa*

We assure the Indian and other Asian elements in the population that they have not been forgotten in our thoughts, discussions and prayers. As Christians we assure them that we are convinced that the same measures of justice claimed here for other population groups also apply to them.

4. *Freedom of Worship*

Bearing in mind the urgent need for the pastoral care of Non-White people living on their employer's premises, or otherwise unable without great difficulty to reach churches in the recognised townships or locations, the Consultation urges that the State should allow the provision of adequate and convenient facilities for Non-White people to worship in urban areas.

The Consultation also urges European congregations to co-operate by making their own buildings available for this purpose whenever practicable.

5. *Freedom to Preach the Gospel*

The Church has the duty and right to proclaim the Gospel to whomever it will, in whatever circumstances, and whenever possible consistent with the general principles governing the right of public meetings in democratic countries. We therefore regard as unacceptable any special legislation which would limit the fulfilment of this task.

6. ***Relationship* of Churches**
    The Consultation urges that it be laid upon the conscience of us all that whenever an occasion arises that a Church feels bound to criticize another Church or Church leader it should take the initiative in seeking prior consultation before making any public statement. We believe that, in this way, reconciliation will be more readily affected and that Christianity will not be brought into disrepute before the world.

7. ***Mutual Information***
    The Consultation requests that means be found for the regular exchange of all official publications between the member churches for the increase of mutual understanding and information. Furthermore, churches are requested to provide full information to other churches of their procedures in approaching Government. It is suggested that in approaches to the Government, delegations, combined if possible, multi-racial where appropriate, should act on behalf of the churches.

8. ***Co-operation in Future***
    Any body which may be formed for co-operation in the future is requested to give its attention to the following:
    (a) A constructive Christian approach to separatist movements;
    (b) The education of the Bantu;
    (c) The training of Non-White leaders for positions of responsibility in all spheres of life;
    (d) African literacy and the provision of Christian literature;
    (e) The concept of responsible Christian society in all areas in South Africa, including the Reserves;
    (f) The impact of Islam on Southern Africa.

9. **Residential Areas**
   The Consultation urges, with due appreciation of what has already been done in the provision of homes for Non-White people, that there should be a greater security of tenure, and that residential areas be planned with an eye to the economic and cultural levels of the inhabitants.

10. **Migrant Labour System**
    The Consultation urges the appointment by the Government of a representative commission to examine the migrant labour system, for the Church is painfully aware of the harmful effects of this system on the family life of Africans. The Church sees it as a special responsibility to advocate a normal family life for Africans who spend considerable periods of time, or live permanently, in White areas.
    We give thanks to the Almighty God for bringing us together for fellowship and prayer and consultation. We resolve to continue in this fellowship, and we have therefore made specific plans to enable us to join in common witness in our country.
    We acknowledge before God the feebleness of our often-divided witness to our Lord Jesus Christ and our lack of compassion for one another.
    We therefore dedicate ourselves afresh to the ministry of reconciliation in Christ.

Recommendations

Action concerning future co-operation between Member-Churches of the WCC in South Africa

1. It is proposed that the Consultation recommend to the eight member churches in South Africa of the World Council of Churches that they create at once a South Africa Conference of World Council of Churches member churches.

2. The general purposes of this organisation would be:
   (a) to function as an organ of study, consultation and co-operation among the South African member churches of the World Council of Churches;
   (b) to function as a point of contact and co-operation between the South African member churches and the World Council of Churches and its Divisions and Departments. It is recognised that this function would not in any way impede direct relationship between the member churches and the World Council of Churches. It is also recognised that activities undertaken by this organisation in South Africa on behalf of the World Council of Churches would be decided upon by the Conference of member churches.

3. It is recognised that this organisation would have to give early attention to relationships which should be established with other co-operative organisations in South Africa. This is particularly true of its relationships with the Christian Council of South Africa. The urgency of developing these relationships is accentuated by the prospective merger of the World Council of Churches and the International Missionary Council.

   Consideration should be given to the proposed organisation assuming the work of the Continuation Committee in consultation with the Continuation Committee.

D1.3 Statement from the Third Assembly of the World Council of Churches, New Delhi, 1961 [Excerpts]

... Where oppression, discrimination and segregation exist, the churches should identify themselves with the oppressed race in its struggle to achieve justice. Christians should be ready to lead in the struggle. The revolution is taking place whether we recognize it or not, and without Christian leadership it may be tragically perverted. The churches also have a duty to the oppressor in a ministry of education and reconciliation.

Racism and the consequent affronts to human dignity in the modern world often cause oppressed people to resort to violence when they have no other option. We urge all those in power to refrain from the use of violence and to avoid provoking it. Also we must say that the Gospel of Christ specifically urges that hate be met with love, and evil conquered with good. Therefore, we call upon all Christians to encourage and support all efforts which seek through the non-violent way, to combat human indignities and to construct a community permeated by justice and reconciliation. The Church should seek to ensure that immigration laws are not based on race discrimination.

The Local Congregation

... It is not enough that local congregations should be racially inclusive in the formal sense. Members of minority groups are often hesitant about going into a Church dominated by another racial group. There is therefore a further task – the creation of a climate of warm acceptance of minority groups which may have different ways of worship, and other gifts, that will enrich the whole Church.

When communities are not involved in direct racial tensions, it is often because they segregate themselves by choice and so evade the problems of 'intergroup living'. Often, they contain the very people who by their social position could do most for racial relations.

The complacency of a secure and homogeneous community may have to be disturbed by a Christian initiative in inviting people of different races into it.

Leadership in the Church

Denominations in their own structures must give a lead to ensure that there is no race discrimination in the Church. The churches are further called to utilize people of different races in positions of leadership, on the basis of merit only. Pastors should be not be assigned only to churches of their own race and Christians should be prepared to accept a minister of another race. Missionary appointments, executive and administrative posts within the churches should be open to qualified persons regardless of race. Churches should give equal opportunity for training to all potential leaders and take special pains to foster the gifts of those less privileged. All Christian institutions should have open policies with respect to housing and employment.

Separate Development

All races, as indeed all persons, have their own unique contribution to make to the fellowship of human society, but we cannot agree that this is a reason for 'separate development'. On the contrary, it is only in community with others of diverse gifts that persons or communities can give of their best. The expression 'separate but equal' is in concrete actuality a contradiction in terms.

ASSEMBLY RESOLUTIONS

[...]

On Racial and Ethnic Tensions

The Third Assembly of the World Council of Churches meeting at New Delhi, having considered the serious and far reaching implications of racial and ethnic tensions for the missions of the church in the world, in the light of Christian unity, witness and service:

1. Calls attention of the member churches to the mounting racial and ethnic tensions which accompany rapid social change and the struggle for social justice in many areas.

2. Notes with gratitude:
   a. The witness of churches and their members in difficult situations, struggling to uphold the unity of the Christian fellowship transcending racial and ethnic divisions;
   b. The courage and sacrifice of individuals and groups, both Christians and non-Christians who, in spite of forces urging to violence, are giving leadership in the struggle for human rights in a spirit of forgiveness and non-violence;
   c. Those churches, though divided by different approaches to the question of race relations, willing to meet each other within the unity of the Christian faith, to talk to each other and to discover together the will of God for their common witness to Christ in society.

3. Welcomes the establishment of the WCC Secretariat on Racial and Ethnic Relations and urges the member churches

to give support to developing the programme of the Secretariat.

4. Reminds all the churches of the declaration by the Evanston Assembly [1954] on Intergroup Relations that 'any form of segregation based on race, colour or ethnic origin is contrary to the Gospel, and is incompatible with the Christian doctrine of man with the nature of the Church of Christ', and urges them to act more resolutely than they have heretofore 'to renounce all forms of segregation or discrimination and to work for their abolition within their own life and with society'.

CHAPTER TWO

The Challenge of the Apartheid Republic

The political crisis of the apartheid regime that had begun in 1960 continued to deepen as the post-Sharpeville State of Emergency entered its second and third years. The new vigour at the repression of political dissent, emblematised by the wide scale mass detentions, house arrests, wanton police brutality, and the banning of liberation organisations, was being refined into a systemic feature of apartheid rule. By the end of 1960 the treason trial in which the leadership of the ANC and allied organisations stood trial on capital charges had entered its fifth year. With sixty-nine of the 155 original defendants still facing charges, an unverifiable number of activists where in police custody under the state of emergency regulations.

In September 1960 the ANC Caretaker Committee, which had been constituted by the leadership while in police detention, had announced a new plan in terms of which the ANC would continue to operate clandestinely in defiance of its ban. In the meantime, sections of activists aligned with the PAC unleashed random violent attacks against elements of the apartheid regime, an underground phenomenon that soon gained the name of Poqo – the initial signs of the turn of the resistance against apartheid into armed struggle.

Following the Whites-only referendum in October 1960, Hendrik Verwoerd announced that the Union of South Africa would be proclaimed a republic on 31 May 1961, and if need be, the Republic of South Africa will not seek membership of the British Commonwealth. In response to Verwoerd's announcement, and in continuation of the protest campaign against White republicanism planned prior to the Sharpeville massacre, a group of forty African leaders held a consultation in Orlando, Soweto, on 16 December 1960. All the participants at this crisis All-In African Consultation were associated with the banned ANC and PAC, meeting as concerned community leaders to explore new avenues of meaningful opposition in the light of the banning of their organisations.

The consultation enunciated a principle of the indispensability of the unity of all Africans as the foundation for all subsequent resistance to the imposition of a White-minority Republic of South Africa. It formulated a call for the establishment of a sovereign National Convention which would work towards the creation of a non-racial democracy as an alternative to the new racist dispensation proposed by the National Party. It also resolved to call a mass conference of Africans and all democratic sectors of South African society to protest and deliberate upon the impending entrenchment of racism threatened by Verwoerdian republicanism.

This subsequent conference, the All-In African Conference, was eventually held in Pietermaritzburg on 25–26 March 1961 under the repressive conditions of the State of Emergency. It was attended by approximately 1 500 delegates from all over the country, representing 145 religious, social, cultural, sporting and political bodies and every shade of African opinion. Nelson Mandela addressed the conference. The major resolution of the conference unanimously rejected the government's decision to proclaim republican status for the country without the consent of the African majority (See **Document D2.1.)** It reaffirmed the call of the African leaders at the Orlando Consultation for a sovereign and non-racial representative National Convention.

The conference resolved that a demand be made to the government to immediately call a National Convention, failing which, on 31 May 1961 – the day South Africa was to be declared a Republic – countrywide industrial strikes and boycotts would be held. A National Action Council was elected to this end, with Nelson Mandela its secretary and sole public spokesperson.[43] He wrote a letter to the Prime Minister Hendrik Verwoerd, communicating the resolutions of the conference. In response, a warrant for Mandela's arrest was issued.

On May 5th a section introducing the power to imprison without trial for twelve days was added to the General Law Amendment Act of 1961, and political gatherings were prohibited. As 31st May approached, thousands of political activists were arrested throughout the country, and their leaders pursued. White civilians were sworn in as special constables;

while revolver stocks in gun shops were depleted as a sudden demand to arm White families surged.[44]

As grinding state repression took effect, it fell onto Mandela to execute the conference's plan of action. As he recounts, early in April 1961 he went underground to organise the May strike, and "has never been home since"[45], until February 1990. By the time the South Africa government and its supporters held Republic Day celebrations on 31 May, more than 10 000 African workers, mainly activists involved in the organisation of the three-day stay-away, had been arrested. Mixed into this number were arrests for offences under the discriminatory pass and Bantu tax regulations whose enforcement were suddenly intensified.[46] In spite of this, a press statement issued by the ANC underground was able to state the fact:

> Ever since the All-In African Conference at Pietermaritzburg, the issue that dominated South African politics and that has attracted pressmen from all over the world was not the republican celebrations organized by the government, but the stirring campaign of the African people and other non-white sections to mark our rejection of a White Republic forcibly imposed upon us by a minority.[47]

After the peaceful three-day national protest at the end May 1961 and the manner in which the regime imposed an apartheid republic on the land, there was a consensus within the Black majority in South Africa that the government would not pay attention to their grievances unless new forms of action were adopted. Sporadic and uncoordinated acts of sabotage and ambushes of the police and White families sprouted throughout the country. In May 1962 the government decreed that punishment for acts of sabotage will be the death sentence. In the words of Nelson Mandela, during the Rivonia trial in 1964:

> The hard facts were that fifty years of non-violence had brought the African people nothing but more and more repressive legislation, and fewer and fewer rights ... When some of us discussed this in May and June of 1961, it could not be denied that

> our policy to achieve a non-racial state by non-violence had achieved nothing, and our followers were beginning to lose confidence in this policy and were developing disturbing ideas of terrorism.[48]

In response to these pressures Mandela and several leading ANC activists maintained that the eagerness of the masses to engage in armed protest needed to be channelled into a regulated military formation and structures to prevent its deterioration into a directionless racial war. During November 1961, they worked on the creation of such a formation. This involved, *inter alia*, an assessment of the relations between this formation and the ANC as a mass political organisation with a policy of non-violence, an analysis of the political and economic situation of South Africa in terms of the ways in which armed force was to be used, and the formulation of operational guidelines. It was agreed that while the ANC under the leadership of iNkosi Luthuli remained an avowedly non-violently political body, members who undertook such activity under the command of an organized armed wing would not be subject to disciplinary action.[49]

On 16 December 1961, the ANC's *Umkhonto We Sizwe* (Spear of the Nation) (MK) was launched, to the great jubilation of Black people across the country. It proclaimed its existence with a series of planned attacks on government buildings in Johannesburg, Durban, Pietermaritzburg and Cape Town, and through the distribution of a manifesto which introduced MK and enunciated its strategy and policy.

Instead of large-scale guerrilla warfare and open armed revolution, the sabotage of economic infrastructure was tactically chosen as a form of armed struggle. Based on a strategic analysis of South Africa's political, state security apparatus and economic peculiarities the MK High Command noted that,

> Since South Africa is largely dependent on foreign trade and foreign capital, planned destruction of power plants, and interference with rail and telephone communications, would tend to scare capital away from the country making it more difficult for goods from the industrial areas to reach the sea ports on schedule,

and would in the long run be a heavy drain on the economic life of the country, thus compelling the voters of the country to reconsider their position.[50]

This pivotal phase in the development of resistance against apartheid was ominously ended with the arrest of Nelson Mandela on 5 August 1962, and the capture of the rest of the members of the High Command of MK on the 11 July 1963 at a farm on the outskirts of the Johannesburg suburb of Rivonia. They were brought before the Pretoria Supreme Court on 9 October 1963 on a summary charge of operating a campaign to overthrow the South African state by violent revolution. The charge sheet listed 193 acts of sabotage committed between 27 June 1962 and 11 July 1963 allegedly carried out by persons recruited by the accused in their capacity as members of the High Command of the MK.

A theologically nuanced statement could be made that as the church is the composite of the people of faith, the church was there in all the protest agonies surrounding opposition against the declaration of the republic, and that, to the extent that some of the soldiers of MK were Christians, the church was all along present in this struggle for liberation. But in a historical review that looks at the church through its institutional organisations and profile, a monumental irony in the context of South African history was to play itself out: the first Christian theological voice to rise in anguish against this institutionalization of apartheid repression was a White Afrikaner, minister of the Nederduits Gereformeerde Kerk and a disillusioned member of the Broederbond (a secret Afrikaner cultural and political organization), Dr C. F. Beyers Naude.

Naude started around August 1960 by organising study groups around Johannesburg examining the meaning of the teachings of the Christian scriptures in a post-Sharpeville South Africa. These study groups gradually attracted concerned members of the clergy from both Afrikaans and English churches. On 15 May 1962 they founded a monthly ecumenical journal which was published in both English and Afrikaans, named *Pro Veritate*, with Naude as editor. Its sharply critical tone and its synthesis of political analysis, theology and ethical argument established it as the pioneering organ of anti-apartheid political theology. Following a series of fierce disputes with the authorities of his church, in 1963 Naude resigned from its ministry.

Soon thereafter, it was decided to establish a broader institute which would stimulate Christian communal awareness of the significance of the evolving situation through a decidedly bold proclamation of the truth ('*pro veritate*') and action outside the boundaries of the institutional ecclesiastical structures. On 13 August 1963 the Christian Institute of Southern Africa (CI), was inaugurated as a multiracial and multidenominational para-church activist organization at a public meeting held in the Central Methodist Church, Johannesburg (**Document D2.2**). Naude was appointed its first Executive Director. Although finally drafted in 1972, the statement in **Document D2.2** gives a definitive statement of the objectives of the CI as pursued throughout its history.

The NGK responded with fierce attacks against the organisation and Beyers Naude. Naude and the CI were accused of being agents of Communism. Consequent to Cold War fuelled state propaganda, as far as most Afrikaners were concerned, 'communism' meant any attempt at or calls for racial unity and non-racial social harmony. What was most disturbing was that the framing of these accusations were calculated to prepare the ground for repression action against Naude and the CI in terms of the Suppression of Communism Act of 1950. Naude's response to these attacks on behalf of the CI's Executive Committee is reproduced here as **Document D2.3**.

Naude's firm convictions, which led to a break with his Afrikaner political past on grounds of conscience, and put him in the leadership of the post-1960 ecumenical movement against apartheid, are expressed in the title of an editorial article which he wrote in 1965 for *Pro Veritate*.[51] The title of the article was 'Die Tyd vir 'n Belydende Kerk in Suid Afrika is Daar' (Now is The Time for a Confessing Church in South Africa).

Just as the church was manipulated into conspiring with Nazism in Hitler's Germany, and an anti-Nazi underground church movement called the Confessing Church emerged on the fringes of the institutional church to resist Hitler, a Confessing Church was needed in South Africa. For Naude and members of the CI, apartheid was theologically immoral, and opposition against it was justified. For the fact that the mainline Churches, particularly the NGK, had so actively accorded credibility to the apartheid system, and the liberal English Churches were uncritically organised on racially discriminatory lines, there was an obvious need for a South African analogue of the Confessing Church movement which could stand out as the critical bearer of authentic Christian witness in the country.[52]

One of the most significant consequences of the activity generated in response to the Sharpeville massacre was a spontaneous appreciation of the need for inter-denominational cooperation between the churches in South Africa, as decided at the WCC's Cottesloe conference of December 1960. The fact that collaboration was occasioned by the need to respond to the post-Sharpeville crisis meant that inter-denominational cooperation would be based upon political action from the outset. Sadly, such an organised ecumenical response was to take shape only in 1968, when the South African Council of Churches was founded. In the intervening period, it was left to the Christian Institute to drive Christian social conscience among the churches of South Africa.

As the year 1964 started, South Africans were gripped by the details of the evidence of the interrupted plans for armed resistance flowing out of the then ongoing Rivonia Treason Trial. The WCC, noting the gravity of the situation in the country and Southern Africa broadly, once again sought to organise a well-informed, international and ecumenical reaction to the liberation movement's response to the establishment of the white-minority Republic of South Africa.

An International Consultation was organised by the WCC's Church and Society department in conjunction with the CI and South African Institute of Race Relations (SAIRR). This was held at the Mindolo Ecumenical Centre in Kitwe, Zambia from 25 May to 2 June 1964, and took as its theme 'Christians and Race Relations in South Africa'. It reflected deeply upon issues which had been raised at Cottesloe in 1960, political developments since Cottesloe, and the ethical problems raised by the turn to armed resistance.

Document D2.4 is an extract from the full report of the consultation and contains excerpts from its study commission on 'Christian Practice and Desirable Action in Social Change and Race Relations in Southern Africa'. The language of the document is analytic and reflective rather than declamatory, and it is circumspect in not passing moral judgement on the position adopted by the liberation movements in Southern Africa.

On 11 June 1964, a week after the Mindolo Consultation, the Rivonia trial concluded. Nelson Mandela and seven other ANC leaders were found guilty as charged and sentenced to life imprisonment. The following day, iNkosi Albert Luthuli issued a press statement addressed to the international community. Speaking in a personal capacity (since the organisation he had led since 1952 was now banned) and relying on his international renown as a Nobel Peace Prize Laureate, he urged Western governments to apply economic pressure on the South African regime to persuade it to repeal the sentences imposed at the Rivonia trial. He noted that all of those who were sentenced were respected leaders of a community which had been left with no realistic alternative for democratic self-expression. His appeal, essential to understanding the context within which organised Christianity had to define a response to apartheid repression, is reproduced as **Document D2.5**.

D2.1 All-In Africa Conference, Pietermaritzburg, 25–26 March 1961

RESOLUTIONS

A grave situation confronts the people of South Africa. The Nationalist government, after holding a fraudulent referendum among only one-fifth of the population, had decided to proclaim a white republic on 31 May, and the all – white parliament is presently discussing a constitution. It is clear that to the great disadvantage of the majority of our people such a republic will continue even more intensively the policies of racial oppression, political persecution and exploitation and the terrorization of the non-white people which have already earned South Africa the righteous condemnation of the entire world.

In this situation it is imperative that all the African people of this country, irrespective of their political, religious or other affiliations, should unite to speak and act with single voice.

For this purpose, we have gathered here at this solemn All-in conference, and on behalf of the entire African nation and with a due sense of the historic responsibility which rests upon us.

WE DECLARE that no constitution or form of government decided without the participation of the African people who form an absolute majority of the population can enjoy moral validity or merit support either within South Africa or beyond its borders.

WE DEMAND that a National Convention of elected representatives of all adult men and women on an equal basis irrespective of race, colour, or creed or other limitation, be called by Union government not later than 31 May 1961: that the convention shall have sovereign powers to determine, in any way the majority of the representatives decide, a new non-racial democratic constitution for South Africa.

WE RESOLVE that should the minority government ignore this demand of the representatives of the united will of the African people:

We undertake to stage countrywide demonstrations on the eve of the proclamation of the republic in protest against this undemocratic act;

We call on all Africans not to co-operate or collaborate in any way with the proposed South Africa republic or any other form of government which rests on force to perpetuate the tyranny of a minority, and to organize and unite in town and country to carry out constant actions to oppose oppression and win freedom;

We call on the Indian and Coloured communities and all democratic Europeans to join forces with us in the opposition to a regime which is bringing disaster to South Africa and to win a society in which all can enjoy freedom and security;

We call on democratic people the world over to refrain from any co-operation and dealings with the South African government, to impose economic and other sanctions against this country and to isolate in every possible way the minority government whose continued disregard of all human rights and freedom constitutes a threat to world peace.

WE FURTHER DECIDE that in order to implement the above decisions, conference:

- elects a National Action Council;
- instructs all delegates to return to their respective areas and form Local Action Committees.

D2.2 A Programme of Action for the Christian Institute

1. ROLE

1.1 Change
The CI is dedicated to help bring change in Southern Africa in the name of Christ. All men [sic] should have the opportunity to develop in all fields. This means seeking fundamental change in the attitudes of people, in the structures of power, and in processes of decision-making.

The CI is concerned with reconciliation, which means, to cast out the fear in our land by love; to banish violence by peace-making; to shatter despondency and pessimism with joy and hope; to drive out injustice, deceit and oppression with justice, truth and freedom.

The CI seeks deep and radical change, in repentance and faith, obedience to the will of God and transformation of society in His name.

1.2 Help
Many organisations are concerned in helping people to live through the apartheid situation. The CI shares this concern, but its primary object is to help change the situation. Change and help can be mutually supportive.

1.3. National and International Action
The CI recognises that part of its duty is to maintain its witness to a positive Christian answer of love, unity, peace and justice in Southern Africa, on a national and international level.

1.4 Activity
The activity of the CI is to encourage groups of people to seek the Way of Christ in the whole experience of living. As individuals they

might grow in love, courage and vision, and as a group they might become a living Christian community witnessing to the experience in sharing life's joys and problems.

2. MEMBERSHIP

The Christian Institute as a body is an open community without secrets and welcomes anyone who follows Christ to its fellowship.

2.1 Members of the Christian Institute adhere to its principles, but have a wide variety of emphasis, interest, and degree of involvement.

2.2 Persons, who wish to have their names on the mailing list and to enter into CI activities, but not become formal members, are most welcome.

2.3 Many CI members are involved in allied organisations, which make demands upon their time. The CI urges its members to assess their activities, decide on priorities and to concentrate upon the 'change' role wherever possible, especially where others are willing to undertake the 'help' activities.

3. GROUPS

3.1 The CI exists in a stratified society and aims to act a transforming and building agency: we begin where people are in the hope that we shall be led forward together.

3.2 It advocates group programmes with Christian study and action. Such groups, normally non-racial and ecumenical, may be based on residential proximity or on common interests. They are not expected to follow a pattern laid down by a hierarchy, but to discover and develop their own concerns. They seek to fulfil its aims in every part of the community.

3.3 The training and exercise of leadership in a group is vital, extending a pastoral concern to the members and encouraging a shared leadership pattern.

4. COMMUNICATION

The Head Office of the Christian Institute is in Johannesburg. Regional Directors have been appointed for the Cape and Natal, and other regional appointments may follow.

It is the policy of the CI to encourage Regional Committees to develop the work, and to establish personal contacts between groups and between members.

Domestic news could be circulated through Regional Newsletters, and the National Newsletter will include items of widespread interest and general reports from the region.

5. GOALS

The main spheres in which the Institute seeks to bring about Christian change are as follows: The Church, Economy and Labour, Education, Family Life and Health, Political Life and Youth.

D2.3 Attacks on the Christian Institute: Statement by the Executive Committee of the CI, 9 November 1963

Issued by the Director, Dr. C.F. Beyers Naude, on behalf of the Institute and published on 5 December 1963 in the second issue of Pro Veritate.

Since its inception, numerous attacks have been launched from several quarters against the Institute. The Executive Committee had felt all along that our aims and objects are so clear and above reproach that in fact no defence is necessary for attacks launched against the Institute. Therefore, we will certainly not reply to individual attacks or accusations by irresponsible people.

STATEMENT BY THE EXECUTIVE COMMITTEE

The Christian Institute considers it necessary to issue a statement in the light of the unfounded attacks which have been made against it from various quarters and the malicious rumours which have been spread. On the instructions of its Executive Committee, it makes the following declarations:

Accusations of Liberalism and Communism

The Christian Institute wishes to point out that the deliberately false equation of Liberalism with Communism is a subtle method, which will ultimately prove unsuccessful, of creating confusion in the minds of those ordinary members of the public who have not yet learnt to distinguish very clearly between these two concepts. The Christian Institute has not yet received from those who have attacked it a clear definition of what precisely they mean by Liberalism. If by Liberalism is meant the liberty to be free to depart from the Word of God and the binding nature of that Word, then the Institute wishes clearly to dissociate itself from that interpretation of Liberalism. Likewise, if Liberalism means collaboration with any organisation or ideology which may seek to misuse the Church of Christ in order to propagate its own political self-interest, then the Institute again dissociates itself completely from any such attempt.

As for Communism, the subtle reference to the Christian Institute as a conscious or unconscious instrument of Communism are patently false to anyone who has honestly and sincerely taken note of the basis, composition and aims of the Institute, and have an obvious parallel in the 'McCarthyism' at one time so common in the United State of America when people furthered their own ends by sowing suspicions and doubts concerning convinced Christians and respected Christian organisations by the technique of equating them with Communism. For all those whose minds are sincerely open to conviction, we therefore reaffirm that the Christian Institute is based on the Bible as the Word of God, on the belief in God the Father, in Jesus Christ the Son, Redeemer and Lord, and in the Holy Spirit; that the Institute wishes to serve the Church of Christ in all possible ways; and that it therefore rejects the aims and methods of the Communist ideology of which it is not, nor will be, an instrument. Indeed, one of the first study projects which the Institute will undertake, will in fact concern communism.

Christianity and Multi-racialism
Since the establishment of the Institute, it has clearly been in the interests of certain bodies to cite the so-called multi-racialism of the organisation as a convenient method of sowing suspicion and arousing hostility against it. The fact has been overlooked that the Christian Church in its inception did not distinguish between Christians of different groups or races and that Paul condemned any discrimination based on this sort of distinction.

Because the Christian Institute is based on the acceptance of the World of God, its racial composition is merely incidental; what is decisive is the fact that it is Christian and wishes to be Christian.

Unity and Diversity

The Christian Institute recognize and respect with gratitude the God-given diversity of the various races and cultures, nations and peoples of the world and is compelled to withstand the cries and demands for a unity which cannot stand against the test of the Scriptures. Precisely for this reason, the Institute wishes to aid its members to understand and to put into practice the true unity of all believers according to the Will of Christ within and for his Church. If this is to be condemned as a 'false striving to unity' ('valse eenheidstrewe'), then the Word of God is false.

Politics and Political Parties

Certain people and circles have alleged that the Christian Institute was born as the result of political motivation, and that it wishes to be (or could unwittingly become) the instrument of political interests. We categorically declare that these allegations are completely without foundation and that the Institute is not planning to align or associate itself with any political party or interests. At the same time it must be clearly understood that the Gospel of Jesus Christ is for the whole man, in the whole throughout the whole world. Therefore, where the Scriptures have a word to say on man living in community, that is on political questions, the Institute will not evade its responsibility in enunciating the principles which are involved in legislation.

Finance and Support

Malicious rumours have been spread concerning a number of allegedly dubious sources from which the Institute is supposed to have received support. For this reason the Institute declares:

1. Numbers of members of the various churches in South Africa (including the Afrikaans churches) have already made contributions and donations which have enabled work to be started.
2. The Executive Committee of the Institute decided some time ago that every donation would be considered on its merit and that no donation could be accepted which could in any way compromise or damage the carrying out of its aims. It is therefore self-evident that the Institute cannot possibly consider accepting money from leftist or other dubious sources. The conditions referred to above apply equally to donations offered by Christian or Christian organisations in other countries.
3. The income of the Institute has been augmented by membership subscriptions and by numerous small donations received daily which have enabled it to meet ordinary day-to-day administration and running costs.
4. For the information of those persons who are implying that the World Council of Churches is giving financial support to the Institute, we wish to make it clear that in terms of the Constitution of the World Council it is permitted to give support only to Churches and to councils affiliated on behalf of churches. The Christian Institute is neither a church nor is it competent or qualified to act as a church, and for these reasons it would be quite impossible for the World Council of Churches to lend it financial support.

Origins and Method of Attack on Institute

There is an obvious pattern of similarity in the methods that have been used by the various bodies which have attacked the Institute and in the content of the arguments and imputations which have been employed to substantiate these allegations. One is therefore faced with the irresistible conclusion that a centrally-directed campaign must have been organised somewhere behind the scenes.

The influence of the Christian Institute is feared, wholly unnecessarily, because no person ever needs to be afraid of an organisation which is seeking, quite openly and in the light of the Word of God, to try to bring about the greatest good for the welfare of all the inhabitants of South Africa. Every honest and sincere Christian will at least give the Christian Institute a reasonable opportunity to prove the validity of its aims before he makes up his mind.

The most extravagant methods which have been used to damage the integrity of the Christian Institute are those which employ cheap propaganda and false logic. The so-called logic employed in this technique 'reasons' generally as follows: 'Both the Christian Institute and Communism concern themselves with unity.' 'Therefore, the Christian Institute is Communist.' Those who reason in this way show a total and reckless disregard for the principles and claims of truth and justice.

In conclusion, the fear has been expressed that the Christian Institute could be misused for various purposes. Whilst not denying this possibility, the Christian Institute considers that it applies equally to the Church of Christ or to any other Christian organization. It is precisely for this reason that the Institute will watch and pray to test the spirits to see if they be of God.

On behalf of the Executive Committee
C.F.B Naude
Director

D2.4 Statement from the WCC Mindolo Consultation on Christians And Race Relations in Southern Africa. 4 June 1964

Christian Practice and Desirable Action Social Change and Race Relations In Southern Africa

A primary concern of our consultation has been to ask how we may recapture something of the autonomy, the dignity, and the integrity of the Church in the midst of the racially divided societies in Southern Africa. We have seen anew the need for courageous ministry, dedicated leadership, a loyal laity and youth prepared to represent the communion of God's people among the peoples of Southern Africa. In reaction to white prejudice, many non-whites are developing a revolutionary attitude born of the realization that the white group which sets the patterns of society is oblivious to the deepest human aspirations of its underprivileged partners. The present social stratification seems to the Africans to deprive them of any Christian, as well as civic, responsibility towards society at large.

In this situation of racial tension and sensitivity, the churches are particularly vulnerable if their leaders, indigenous and expatriate, clergy and laity, are not fully committed to the responsible autonomy, dignity and equality of all churches.

Urgency of the Situation

As the discussion proceeded, the urgency of the situation became increasingly clear to every member. The decision by African States taken individually and collectively, the training of 'freedom fighters' in different parts of Africa, the increased defence and military measures of the governments concerned, the strong determination of two opposing groups – one passionately determined to retain its present privileged position and the other just as passionately determined to alter it – all add up to a situation fraught with dangerous possibilities.

Although it is felt in some circles that the implementation of the Bantustan policy and the general economic development in South Africa has reduced tensions, there was a general agreement among us that the situation has increased in gravity to such an extent that it has almost reached a point of no return. In spite of this, the impression remains that large numbers of people in Southern Africa are still ignorant of the factual situation or the issues at stake, while others live in a false complacency that the military power and measures of their governments will ensure prolonged peace and prosperity and the maintenance of the status quo.

The Trend from Non-Violence to Violence
The urgency of the situation in South Africa is further increased by the conviction of leading Africans that, as all peaceful measures tried by African political organisations over a period of many years to bring about an ordered change have proved abortive, only one avenue remains open – that of violence. On the other hand, it is precisely this conviction and possible resultant action which consolidates the white electorate, hardens its general attitude, and leads to ever-increasing measures which eventually precipitate the danger they wish to avoid. For many Christians involved in the struggle for a just solution, the question of possible violence as the only remaining alternative has become an urgent and ever-pressing one. Reports indicate that many are convinced that war has already begun. Although there is still a slender chance for a negotiated settlement in Southern Rhodesia, already a similar polarization of social attitudes has taken place there. It is feared that any outbreak of racial violence on a large scale in any part of Southern Africa may seriously affect the situation in all other areas and adversely influence the possibility of peaceful negotiation and solution.

Many African leaders maintain that violence has never been desired or sought if any other mode of effective negotiation could be established or remained open. The consultation feared that if the urgency of the situation is not recognized, negotiations established, and further effective measures taken, violence will increase. Every inhabitant of Southern Africa bears a heavy responsibility to do everything in their power to prevent this.

Racial Pattern in Economic Life: The challenge to Christians
There can and should be no doubt of the Christian concern for the justice in the dual pattern of economic life in Southern Africa. Indeed, in view of the involvement of many lay Christians in the struggle for economic justice in countries of Southern Africa, the Church must ask whether it had done enough to support them. It must not cease to remind those in authority of the moral judgments upon the many features of the dual economic system which are repugnant to Christian conscience. These include:
a) The great inequalities of wealth and income between racial groups, and the social conflicts and sense of injustice which they engender.
b) The selfish possession by a minority racial group of great economic power over the majority racial group.
c) The frustration of the sense of Christian vocation which comes from the inability of Christians of a particular race to realize their abilities and capabilities as persons, due to arbitrary restrictions and restraints upon their economic activity. The fact that these restrictions are imposed by other Christians who are in authority, increases the moral responsibility of the Church.

The victims of these economic injustices are looking to the Church largely in vain to secure relief for their grievances. There is already much disillusionment with Christianity and many are looking elsewhere for relief. Churches have to prepare themselves to speak out against specific injustices in economic life; they must set an example in their own institutional life and their sacrificial witness and action for man in society; and they must support every movement to the improvement of economic conditions for the African.

The call to Churches and Christians
The Commission was convinced that we have no right to speak to anybody else unless we speak to ourselves and our fellow-Christians. The church of Christ and all its members must come to a sincere recognition and confession of their guilt in a situation for which they have long been responsible, a guilt which we must bear with, and on behalf of, the whole community. It includes the guilt of sinful silence when there was urgent need to speak both in prophecy and in reconciliation, of lack of identification with the suffering and the oppressed, of indifference and unwillingness to become involved, of lack of real fellowship among Christians, and of neglect of duty in the education of the laity through proclamation and instruction. There is no renewal possible without confession, supplication, intercession and identification. Once this is understood and accepted, many as yet unexploited avenues of witness, service and reconciliation will open to all Christians.

If unavoidable violence erupts, all Christians should use their full influence to limit it to the point at which there can be negotiation and settlement as early as possible. This is the time when Christian goodwill should lead to reconciliation, and thus lay the foundation of a new society.

D2.5 Press statement by iNkosi Albert Luthuli on the Rivonia Trial verdict, 12 June 1964

Sentence of life imprisonment have been pronounced on Nelson Mandela, Walter Sisulu, Ahmed Kathrada, Govan Mbeki, Denis Goldberg, Raymond Mhlaba, Elias Motsoaledi and Andrew Mlangeni in the 'Rivonia trial' in Pretoria.

Over the long years these leaders advocated a policy of racial co-operation, of goodwill, and of peaceful struggle that made the South African liberation movement one of the most ethical and responsible of our time. In the face of the most bitter racial persecution, they resolutely set themselves against racialism; in the face of continued provocation, they consistently chose the path of reason.

The African National Congress, with allied organisations representing all racial sections, sought every possible means of redress for intolerable conditions, and held consistently to a policy of using militant, non-violent means of struggle. Their common aim was to create a South Africa in which all South Africans would live and work together as fellow-citizens, enjoying equal rights without discrimination on grounds of race, colour or creed.
To this end, they used every accepted method: propaganda, public meetings and rallies, petitions, stay-at-home strikes, appeals, boycotts. So carefully did they educate the people that in the four-year-long Treason Trial, one police witness after another voluntarily testified to this emphasis on non-violent methods of struggle in all aspects of their activities.

But finally, all avenues of resistance were closed; the African National Congress and other organisations were made illegal; their leaders jailed, exiled or forced underground. The government sharpened its oppression of the people of South Africa, using its all-white parliament as the vehicle for making repression legal, and utilizing every weapon of this highly industrialised and modern state to enforce that 'legality.' The stage was even reached where a white spokesman for the disenfranchised Africans was regarded by the government as a traitor. In addition, sporadic acts of uncontrolled violence were increasing throughout the country. At first in one place, then in another, there were spontaneous eruptions against intolerable conditions; many of these acts increasingly assumed a racial character.

The African National Congress never abandoned its method of a militant, non-violent struggle, and of creating in the process a spirit of militancy in the people. However, in the face of the uncompromising white refusal to abandon a policy which denies the African and other oppressed South Africans their rightful heritage – freedom – no one can blame brave and just men for seeking justice by the use of violent methods; nor could they be blamed if they tried to create an organized force in order to ultimately establish peace and racial harmony.

For this, they are sentenced to be shut away for long years in the brutal and degrading prisons of South Africa. With them will be interred this country's hopes for racial co-operation. They will leave a vacuum in leadership that may only be filled by bitter hate and racial strife.

They represent the highest morality and ethics in South African political struggle; this morality and ethics has been sentenced to an imprisonment it may never survive. Their policies are in accordance with the deepest international principles of brotherhood and humanity; without their leadership, brotherhood and humanity may be blasted out of existence in South Africa for long decades to come. They believe profoundly in justice and reason; when they are locked away, justice and reason will have departed from the South African scene.

This is an appeal to save these men, not merely as individuals, but for what they stand for. In the name of justice, of hope, of truth and of peace, I appeal to South Africa's strongest allies, Britain and America. In the name of what we have come to believe Britain and America stand for, I appeal to those two powerful countries to take a decisive action for full-scale action for sanctions that would precipitate the end of the hateful system of apartheid.

I appeal to all governments throughout the world, to people everywhere, to organizations and institutions in every land and at every level, to act now to impose such sanctions on South Africa that will bring about the vital necessary change and avert what can become the greatest African tragedy of our times.

CHAPTER THREE

Triumphant Apartheid

The period from early 1963 onwards saw not just the recovery of the South African economy from the devastation in investor confidence which followed the Sharpeville massacre, it also marked a juncture of remarkable economic expansion. In the last quarter of 1962, for example, the amount of new foreign capital raised from industrial, mining and financial enterprises stood at £19 million. Just a year later, in the last quarter of 1963, the corresponding figure was £135 million.[53] How did the apartheid regime survive the grave and complex socio-political and moral crisis it faced following the Sharpeville killings?

In forming his first post-Republic cabinet, Hendrik Verwoerd was intensely aware that he had to organise a 'council of war' in view of the growing militancy of anti-apartheid forces and the fact that South Africa's adverse image was reducing the flow of foreign investment and skilled immigrants into the economy. As far as he was concerned, the world at large was unjustly hostile to Afrikanerdom, and the greatest problems facing South Africa were the 'liberalism' of the English press and 'communist infiltration'. South Africa in general, and the Afrikaner nation in particular, would have to defend themselves against these at all costs.

The entire state security apparatus was reviewed, the police and army reorganised, and legislation prepared to veil their activities and conduct from public scrutiny. The Defence budget rose from R44 million in 1960, to R129 million in 1962, R157 million in 1963/64, and R210 million in the 1964/5 fiscal year[54].

Verwoerd, in June 1961, appointed John Balthazar Vorster – a former general in the pro-Nazi Ossewabrandwag who had led a sabotage campaign against British interests in South Africa during the Second World War – his Minister of Justice and right-hand man. They embarked on a double-pronged strategy of propaganda abroad and merciless repression at home. Within a global climate of the Cold War, anticommunism was conveniently embraced as the philosophy that underpinned this strategy.

State propaganda machinery laboured to convince the Western world that, with the Cape of Good Hope sea route, South Africa was directly strategic to the Soviet Union, and that government's repression of its opponents (who were either communists or influenced by communists) should therefore receive the support of the capitalist West. From 1963 onwards, the West was pointedly reminded that 71 per cent of its gold production came from South Africa. The South African government repeatedly argued that this made the country so strategically important to the West that it should never be allowed to fall into the hands of a Black majority government which would be sympathetic to the Soviet Union's interests.

As evidence that all discontent and protest that led to the Sharpeville events had been the work of communists, in November 1962 Vorster issued a press release listing 129 Whites and 308 Blacks alleged to be communists.[55] This 'evidence' turned out to be a list of people who were in detention or under house arrest due to the Suppression of Communism Act. The apogee of this campaign was achieved by orchestrating the media coverage of the arrest of Abram Fischer, Q.C., on a charge of membership to the South African Communist Party on 9 July 1964.[56] Fischer was the eminent defence lawyer who had represented Nelson Mandela in the Rivonia Trial. The campaign successfully drummed up some sympathy for South Africa in the Western world, particularly in the Conservative government and business community in Britain, and in the United States of America.

As Minister of Justice, Vorster declared his intention to sweep away from South African life all anti-apartheid activists, whether African nationalists or White democrats associated with extra-parliamentary organisations. In August 1964, he told his Party conference:

It is our duty to defend this Republic, if necessary, against the whole world. Ultimately, the struggle in South Africa will be between those who want one man one vote, and those who are uncompromisingly opposed to that.[57]

Soon thereafter, in early 1965, Parliament passed two laws, the Suppression of Communism Amendment Act of 1965, and the Criminal

Laws Amendment Act. These fortified the powers of the Minister of Justice to ban or restrict any person or publication deemed a threat to any programme or policy of the government.

The clause, permitting 90 days detention without trial since the late 1950s, was replaced with a clause which permitted a renewable 180 days detention without trial. For the first time in South Africa's legal history, potential state witnesses in political trials could be held in custody until the state was satisfied that it could no longer use them. Refusal to act as a state witness was punishable by at least twelve months imprisonment (See **Document D3.3**). Additionally, it now became a criminal offence for one banned person to communicate with another, and for anyone to publish the utterance or writing of a banned person.

All known political activists of organisations that constituted the 1955 Congress Alliance which were still unbanned, particularly the South African Indian Congress and South African Congress of Trade Unions (SACTU), were either served with banning orders or detained without trial for extensive periods. The Congress of Democrats, the White constituent organisation of the Congress Alliance, had been outlawed in September 1962 and the Coloured Peoples Convention, a regrouping of the Coloured People's Organisation, was put under such pressure that it was virtually unable to operate and had to be formally dissolved in March 1966.

In a plethora of trials between October 1963 and October 1965 about 1 000 women and men were charged for belonging to outlawed organisations.[58] Political trials were often conducted in camera to avoid media coverage that could tarnish the image of South Africa which the regime sought to portray. Long punitive prison sentences were generally imposed at these trials. Mary Benson, in 1966, observed that:

Injustice is most apparent, though blessed by the law ... in the framing of the charges, for these have been broken down under multiple counts: membership of an unlawful organisation, furthering its aims, collecting funds for it, attending meetings, distributing leaflets; maximum sentence on each count being three years; with in some cases each leaflet treated as a separate count.[59]

While in Sweden on a propaganda mission in 1965, the Chief Commissioner of Prisons declared that there were 8 000 political prisoners in South Africa in the four-year period since 1961.[60] The Minister of Justice informed parliament that 2 436 people had been charged with subversive activities between February 1963 and December 1964. Against this background, Vorster and Verwoerd could announce that all was peaceful and quiet in South Africa.

Massive repression of political dissent occurred in tandem with an economic boom the likes of which the country had not experienced since the great gold rush-of the 1890s (in 2020 South Africa's total mine production of gold stood at 120 tons, in 1970 it was 1,040 tons)[61]. Calls for economic sanctions against the apartheid regime, initiated by iNkosi Luthuli's pleas to the international community in 1959, and repeated in his press statement following the Rivonia Trial, had fallen on deaf ears. Verwoerd and Vorster's mixture of strong-arm tactics at home and diplomatic-propaganda work abroad paid off, and further lulled the White section of society into rightness life of apartheid. On the other hand, despair at any prospects of change was being inculcated into the collective psyche of the Black oppressed and exploited.

At the end of 1963, the government began to strengthen the legislative apparatus which facilitated the squeezing of as much profit as possible from cheaper African labour. Early in 1964, the Bantu Laws Amendment Act was passed. Prior to the introduction of this amendment to the pass law, the only reason for conviction under the pass laws was a failure to be in personal possession of a passbook. From 1964, Black people were charged for possession of a passbook without the appropriate employment and residency status endorsement. It literally became a crime to be unemployed whilst in an urban area. An African adult had to secure employment within seventy-two hours or leave town. Only Africans needed by White industry would be allowed to reside in the urban areas, while the rest would face removal to the Bantustans ('the Native Reserves'). This provoked the rebuke from even the traditionally reticent Catholic Bishops Conference of South Africa (**Document D3.2**)

The Verwoerd-Vorster regime had envisioned that there should be no Black people with rights of residency in urban South Africa by 1978. The movement of Africans from the poor and arid outskirts of the country, to which they were banished, would be severely restricted – a process called 'Influx Control' in apartheid legalese. Only those who had been recruited and contracted for work would be allowed to move out of these 'Bantu reserves'.

The integrity of family units was not respected by the Act: only officially employed members of family units would be permitted to live in the urban areas in which they worked. Married men would have to leave their families at home, hundreds of miles away from their places of work. They would have to live in compounds for unmarried men in the mines and in special quarters outside the segregated Black 'locations'. No African was to be allowed to be in town or city as a work-seeker for more than 72 hours, nor, generally, be in town after 10pm without a 'night special' permit.

The creation of a vulnerable and controlled Black labour force – one with no trade union rights and forbidden by law to engage in any industrial protest action – was finalised during this apex of the affluence of the apartheid state. The Bantustans, Verwoerd's brainchild, were to be ruled by Black puppets, and to serve as reservoirs of cheap labour for White Capital.

In 1964, the first year of the implementation of the Bantu Laws Amendment Act, more than 350 000 African men and women with ages ranging from sixteen were convicted under the pass laws. The most revolting aspect of this was that these 'convicts' would, while serving sentences of up to six months imprisonment, be sold to White farmers under conditions closely resembling slavery.[62] In the course of the same year, 170 000 people were 'endorsed' out of the urban areas and forced to go 'home' to the barren Bantustans. They were those who were no longer fit to work, living rejects of the White economic machinery.

It was in this context that the Christian Council of South Africa (CCSA), a largely conservative council of European missionary institutions that had been active in the country for the preceding thirty years, was forced to shed its non-political stance, as they also found reason to object to some aspects of this new socio-economic regime. See (**Document D3.3**).

In practice, the Bantu Laws Amendment Act, meant that Black people could not spend a night in a White residential area without a permit from the authorities. This meant that whenever the churches held residential conferences, Black delegates needed government permission to attend, since purpose-built venues for such conferences were normally located in the affluent White suburbs.

Matters came to a head when the Roodepoort municipality issued a summary prohibition of all kinds of inter-racial gatherings in its territory. This was a reaction to the churches' frequent use of the Wilgespruit Fellowship Centre, which had been built with ecumenical funding to encourage inter-racial meetings. On 17 August 1965 the Roodepoort Municipality announced, after consultation with the government, that it would no longer grant permits for Africans to stay overnight at Wilgespruit.

After some deliberation and theological reflection, the CCSA drafted a Declaration of Christian Principles, and sent it to the Prime Minister, Hendrik Verwoerd, with a letter of protest. The document is reproduced in this collection as **Document D3.4** together with the Prime Minister's reply. The reply concludes with an ominous assertion that "... it may not be expected of the government to change its political convictions to suit the different political outlook of opponents, even if these are defended in terms of religion".

What immediately attracted the churches' attention and evoked their concern during the debates about the Bantu Laws Amendment Act was its anticipated effects on the family life of Africans. This concern is most clearly dominant in the statement issued CCSA **(Document D3.1)**. Like the statement of the Catholic bishops, it failed to note the systematic pauperization of Africans that were being affected by this legislation. An opportunity to confront the issue of justice in the apartheid economy and the distribution of South Africa's economic wealth had been missed. It may be the case that the use of explicitly economic language was avoided for fear that it would be used by the government as 'evidence' of communistic sympathies.

As the economic success of South Africa was being paraded to the outside world, the various churches and their agencies in the country faced the indirect consequence of these reports: foreign funding agencies began to refuse financial assistance to South African church projects on the grounds that they were no longer underdeveloped. This prompted the CCSA to issue a rather awkward communication **(Document 3.5)** on behalf of its member churches and missionary bodies in June 1965, asking for continued material resources, pointing out that the benefits of the economic boom in South Africa were not shared by Africans, and that the CCSA's constituency included 4 million African Christians and only 8 000 (eight- thousand) Whites.

In this plea for further ecumenical and international support and understanding, the CCSA declared that in view of the political situation in the country "the Church is the one remaining bastion against Apartheid". The erosion of human rights because of the regime's systematic clampdown on all voices of opposition, noted in **Document 3.3**, fostered the belief that the political outspokenness of the Church was the only remaining hope for South Africa. The years 1964 and 1965 witnessed the CCSA embarking on an unprecedented public foray, issuing press statements challenging and condemning every move of the Verwoerd–Vorster regime. At the end of 1965 it released a booklet with the title *The Last Bastion* – a collection of its public documents of 1964 and 1965. The ground-work done by the Christian Institute, and the participation of its members in the councils of the CCSA, had begun to bear fruit.

D3.1 Statement of the Christian Council of South Africa on the Bantu Laws Amendment Bill, February 1964

This statement was sent to the Prime Minister, the Minister of Bantu Administration and Development, the Leader of the Opposition and to the representative of the Progressive Federal Party in Parliament.

The Christian Council of South Africa, speaking in the name of its 27-member denominations and on behalf of a Christian constituency of nearly four million members, having carefully considered the revised edition of the Bantu Laws Amendment Bill at present before Parliament, reiterates its strong opposition to the basic content of the Bill and its grave concern about its numerous contentious clauses.

We believe this Bill to infringe certain basic Christian concepts concerning family life and the freedom and dignity of the individual. Despite denials to the contrary, we believe it perpetuates and extends the system of migrant labour, with all its concomitant problems in the individual moral and social life of the African people and its disruptive influence in African family relationships. We believe it to be discriminatory and restrictive in relation to one section of the population, and to place dangerously arbitrary powers in the hands of officers and officials of the State without obvious legal safeguards in the case of possible misapplication of the law or individual cases of injustice.

Despite widespread representations made to the Government, we find no basic modification in the present Bill and claim not only that it is substantially and in essence the same as that concerning which detailed criticisms were made last year, but that in many respects it is harsher and more rigid; and in as much as that is so, our objections to the Bill, on matters of principle, then made, are still valid.

D3.2 Bantu Laws Amendment Bill: A press statement of the Conference of the Catholic Bishops of South Africa, July 1964

The Conference of the Catholic Bishops of South Africa deeply regrets that the Government has judged it opportune to proceed with the Bantu Laws Amendment Bill, 1964. Although the Bill contains some provisions which are to the benefit of Africans, as for instance, the protection given to Africans against malpractices, and the permission for re-entry to prescribed area, the Bill, as a whole, is an invasion of primary human rights, and the minor concessions it contains are deprived of any real value by the dead-weight of restrictions under which they are buried.

The effect of the Bill would be to deprive seven million African citizens of a strict right to residence, movement and employment outside the Bantu areas; that is, in four-fifths of the entire Republic. It would strip the African of his basic freedom in the country of his birth, making him dependent upon the possession of a permit to explain his presence anywhere, and at any time, outside the 'Bantu Homelands'. This is not consonant with any concept of the dignity of the human person.

This conference fails to see how such a drastic curtailment of rights can be reconciled with natural justice and Christian charity. The Bill is a negation of social morality and Christian thinking, striking, as it does, at the basic Christian institution, the family, through its inflexible restriction of the individual. The Archbishops and Bishops of the Conference feel in conscience bound to join their voices with those of other Churches and Christian bodies in the Republic, in protest against the Bill.

D3.3 Statement on the End of Session Legislation, June 1964

The Christian Council of South Africa, while once again placing on record its strongest condemnation of sabotage and violence and its rejection of the ideology of communism, cannot but feel deeply concerned at the further inroads into individual freedom and the departure from the rule of law inherent in the proposed amendments to the Suppression of Communism Act and the Criminal Laws Amendment Bill.

While welcoming the abolition of compulsory whipping, we are disturbed that in this age when general trends are in the direction of dispensing with the death sentence in many countries, other crimes should have been added to the list of capital offences in South Africa.

We protest most vigorously at the reintroduction of the ninety-day clause under another guise, and at the comprehensive powers of arrest and detention placed in the hands of the attorney-general, including the right to hold for a period of six months without access to the courts someone who may be entirely innocent of a crime, but whose presence may be required by the State as a witness.

D3.4 Declaration of Church Principles as accepted by the Christian Council of South Africa, August 1965

This was appended to a letter sent to the Prime Minister, Dr H F Verwoerd, on 17 August 1965 to protest against the withdrawal of permission for Africans to stay overnight in Church-owned conference centres in 'white' areas.

The Church is a unity created by the grace of God through the redeeming work of Jesus Christ. It is a company of those who are reconciled to the Heavenly Father in Jesus Christ and to one another through baptism and a common faith, and through the worship and fellowship of the Church which is Christ's Body. The Church has moreover a vocation to continue God's work of reconciling love among all men. The Unity of the Church finds expression in common prayer and communion and in a fellowship, which is being sanctified by the Holy Spirit and used by God for the blessing and enrichment of all who share in it.

Affirmations

1. Believing that it is basic to membership of the Church that there is neither Jew nor Greek, bond nor free, male nor female, but all are one in Christ:
    (a) It is essential to the nature of the Church that its membership be representative of the variety of human communities in a single body.
    (b) It is essential to the nature of the Church that there be no barriers to its membership being representative of the variety of human communities in a single body at worship.
    (c) Consequent upon (a) and (b) the Church should take the initiative in expressing its unity by bringing together in

worship and Christian fellowship people who differ in race, culture or language.

2. The nature of the Christian Church requires that its members have the liberty to meet and live together for purposes of conference and study.

3. The Church must meet frequently for consultation and purposes of administration. Because of vast geographical distances it is necessary to provide residential facilities for persons attending such meetings.

   These are not, however, the only meetings convened by the Church and are not in fact sufficient to sustain its growth into unity. Meetings convened for discussion, study and spiritual growth promote the personal encounter at depth which is required. It is the growing experience of the Churches that this is fully possible only when persons live together for an extended period in residence and share a common table.

4. (i) Our unity in Jesus Christ which is experienced in Holy Communion, prayer and worship must find effective expression in our common life in society.
   (ii) Apart from worship together in Churches and meeting together for non-residential conferences, almost all other expressions of Christian fellowship are permissive only. The civil power clearly disapproves of normal social intercourse between Christians of different races.
   (iii) The Church has, however, not adequately expressed her vocation as God's means of reconciliation in many areas of the life of Society, and must humbly confess past failures. She should nevertheless seek now to make a more faithful witness.

(iv) In making her witness to the unity of believers in the Lord Jesus Christ the Church will be aware of the fact that she will be misunderstood and misinterpreted and that some will seek to make use of her for their own political purposes. Neither fear of consequence, however, nor fear of misrepresentation should deter the Church from being faithful to her creation.

Principles

1. That the Church of Jesus Christ is every bit as much as the church when it is in conference and study as when it is in worship.

2. That the Church and the Church alone has the right to regulate its own programme of study, worship and conference, and to decide who may participate and how the programme is to be organised.

In order to achieve and express effective fellowship in study and conference it is often both necessary and important that Christians of different races should be able to live under one roof and share a common board.

THE PRIME MINISTER'S REPLY

I wish to acknowledge the receipt of your letter dated August 17, 1965. The matter to which you more particularly refer falls within the administration of the Minister of Bantu Administration and Development, and your letter will therefore be forwarded to that Department to investigate whether reconsideration is possible or not.
The Government's general policy has been laid down after most careful study of all it involves and has received the approval of the

electorate. Your Churches should be able to fulfil their functions fully, as other protestant churches do, while observing the country's law and customs as they exist. It may not be expected of the Government to change its political convictions to suit different political outlook of opponents even if these are defended in terms of religion.

D3.5 Message to Overseas Partners, June 1965

There has been a growing concern among our Churches in South Africa at what seems to be an accelerating tendency on the part of Churches and Ecumenical Agencies overseas to clamp down on their grants to work in this country, either on the score of disapproval of our Government's policies or that South Africa is claimed to be no longer an undeveloped country.

We feel that it is necessary to draw attention of our Christian brethren in the outside world to four important factors in this situation.

1. The Church of Jesus Christ must continue to exercise her reconciling and pastoral ministry to the people of all races in this land, despite the policies of any temporal power. It is an incontestable fact that the Church is the one remaining bastion against apartheid, providing a fellowship in worship, study, conference and consultation, across all barriers. A recent conference of Church leaders which included the Roman Catholic Church affirmed anew the conviction that inter-racialism was of the essence of the Church and an important expression of her unity. Individual Churches belonging to our Council, and the Council itself have been courageous in their utterance and unequivocal in their stand against apartheid and its discriminating and divisive policies. It is therefore distressing to find Churches and Agencies outside the country talking in terms of withdrawing personnel and money at a time when our work and witness needs to be at its peak of efficiency, and when the outreach of the Church's mission in this land is to advance rather than to withdraw.

2. The Church has a special responsibility towards those in this country who accept either tacitly or openly the policy of apartheid and all it has come to signify. Our witness needs to be more certain, our ministry more certain, our ministry more far-reaching than has ever been the case before. Folk who have 'never had it so good', who support present policies because of personal or group advantages or material benefits, whether they were born in this country or have been attracted to it by the present economic boom, need the ministry and the message of the Church. Our ministry cannot cease and our responsibility cannot falter because there are many in the white group who are quite happy and content with the status quo. Any diminution of the Church's witness or its effectiveness would be sheer tragedy at the present time. Her message, her call to and emphasis upon togetherness in an apartheid society are crucial to the whole future of our land.

3. The Churches working together within our Council numbering 27-member denominations are primarily engaged in what must still be described as 'a missionary task'. Recent census figures indicate that in our overall constituency of four million Christians, only 800,000 belong to the white group. This means that we are ministering to a large extent to folk who are living at a bare subsistence level, and who are not benefiting in any considerable way from the present booming economy of the country. While it may be true that South Africa is enjoying an economic boom, the increase of money is not being shared with or experienced by the Churches to any marked extent. The division between the 'haves' and the 'have-nots' in South Africa has always been real and it needs to be appreciated overseas that four-fifths of the work done by our Churches in South Africa is among the 'have-nots'.

4. The Churches in South Africa are faced by a major financial challenge at the present time. This is caused by the implementation of the Group Areas Act all over the country, under which whole communities are being moved into separated areas for their own race group. Apart from the tremendous upheaval in home and family life which this involves, the financial costs to the individual family under such enforced removals are not inconsiderable. Compensation is never adequate, and family purse strings in a community almost always in the lower income brackets, are strained to the maximum, so that there is little margin left to cope with the enforced removal of their Churches. A recent survey among our Churches has indicated that at a conservative estimate R6,000,000 is needed to cope with Church rebuilding and replacement plans under this legislation. This naturally must be a top priority in the life and planning of our member Churches. The work and witness of the Church must go on. We must have buildings for schooling, for worship, for Church activity, and this is vital to the life of our Coloured and African people. The Church is often the social, as well as the educational and spiritual centre of their lives.

But this tremendous prior commitment means that money which might be available for other Christian work, expansion of literature programmes for example, or the development of new denominational or ecumenical projects, just cannot be found.

We feel that our brethren in the Churches of other countries need to know these facts. We would plead with you not to abandon us because of the policies of our Government, nor to be over critical of us in the difficulties of our witness in this land, where we are trying with many imperfections to be faithful to our Lord and Saviour Jesus Christ. We would plead that you would make the above factors known to your member Churches. We would plead for prayers for your sympathy and understanding. We would plead for your continued help in manpower and resources. We would plead for reassurance that, in our often difficult and uphill task, we are not alone but that our arms are being upheld by our brethren overseas.

CHAPTER FOUR
Liberalism and Race Relations

By the second half of the 1960s all forms of organised political protest in the Black community had been extinguished by the intense clampdown of 1961–1964. The only remaining legal political organisations operating in the country in critical opposition to the status quo were the White-led Black Sash, the National Union of South African Students (NUSAS), the South African Institute of Race Relations (SAIRR), and emblematically, the Christian Institute. The title of the Christian Council of South Africa's booklet, *The Last Bastion*, which reflected the events of 1964-65 and suggested that the church was 'the last bastion' remaining against apartheid rule after the banning of the PAC and the ANC, implied that the aforementioned organisations were not viewed to be challenging the apartheid state in a significant way.

Two features distinguished the Black Sash, NUSAS and SAIRR from those organisations which the state outlawed. All three organisations were founded and led by White English-speaking liberals and their support-bases were White. Additionally, with the possible exception of the Black Sash, they were historically established organisations whose *raison d'être* predated the specifically anti-apartheid developments of the period dating back to around 1955.

NUSAS was founded in 1924 and had exclusively been for English and Afrikaans students until the Fort Hare University College student body was admitted to its membership in 1945. By 1936, however, all the Afrikaans universities except for the University of Stellenbosch had disaffiliated from NUSAS. Towards the end of the 1960s and after a walk-out of Black students from the organisation in 1968, NUSAS became the opposition organisation that was most outspokenly radical.

The Black Sash, originally called 'The Woman's Defence of the Constitution League', was founded in 1955 by a group of English-speaking women to protest and mourn the removal of Coloured voters from the common voters roll. The name 'Black Sash' denoted the form of their protest vigils, in which black sashes were worn as a sign of mourning in demonstration against various governmental violations of human rights. By the mid-1960s, as it became clear that the National Party government would not be moved by such forms of protest, the Black Sash revised its objectives and embarked on an active programme of public political education aimed at making South Africans aware of the evils of apartheid, and offering advice to Africans on how to survive migrant labour, 'urban influx control' laws, and the hated pass laws.

During the period under review in this chapter, that is the years between 1965 and 1968, Black Sash, NUSAS and the CI bore the brunt of the apartheid regime's rage. At the initial stages of their dissent from the political *status quo*, instead of the swift and crude repression that Black political activists were accustomed to, the method used to attack these White people was a carefully orchestrated campaign of sociocultural ostracism. To the blunt accusation of being 'communists', with its implication that they were 'un-South African', was added the 'insult' that these White anti-apartheid activists were 'Kaffirboeties' (meaning roughly the same as the racist American derogatory term 'nigger-lover'). State propaganda conveyed the impression that they were misguided, unpatriotic and ungrateful social misfits.

It was in the same vein that the General Synod of the Nederduitse Gereformeerde Kerk declared in October 1966 that the CI was "an un-Christian organisation" and ordered all NGK members to withdraw their membership and support in its activities. The assertion that the philosophy and practice of apartheid is consonant with biblical faith continued to be vigorously defended by NGK and other Reformed Church tradition theologians and church leaders, who happened to be pastors to a racialised White community from which the governance, administrative and repressive machinery of the state was drawn. They used a distorted interpretation of Calvinism (John Calvin), that held that the 'separate development' of peoples was divinely predestined, to give moral legitimacy to apartheid. On the other hand, the CI, which was led by former NGK ministers, was declared to have not only fallen into political liberalism and Communism in its criticism of apartheid, but to have also betrayed orthodox Reformed biblical theology. Together with the World Council of Churches, they deemed were heretics who were maliciously importing liberalism into their interpretation of the Bible by seeking to uphold scriptural precepts as the guide of their critical analysis of political policy.

This religious conviction that the policies of the apartheid regime had some divine support and that critics of the state were agents of atheistic Communism gradually hardened and sharpened the attitude of the government towards White liberals. Starting around the early 1970s, the kind of repressive state brutality that had routinely been reserved for Blacks and 'communists', began to feature in the regime's attempts to silence White people who broke ranks on grounds of conscience with the privileged 'white laager'.

However, from an ideological front, it was the SAIRR that was to emerge as the most significant of those organisations opposed to official government policy that were to become prominent in South African politics once the ANC and PAC had been forced to operate clandestinely. The relative importance of the SAIRR lay in the fact that its existence and its work were premised on an ideologically specific analysis of South African society and politics. Two American educationists, visiting South Africa in 1922 under the sponsorship of the US Carnegie Corporation following a strike by African miners in 1920 and a massacre of Africans by the police at Bullhoek in 1922, proposed to local White liberals that inter-racial study and action commissions be established in a number of major cities as an "experiment in improving race relations". This was to be modelled upon the inter-racial commissions established in several towns in the American South during and after the First World War.[63] In 1929, this movement of 'European-Bantu Joint Councils' culminated in the formation of the SAIRR.

In the period prior to the formation of the SAIRR, 'many prominent liberal intellectuals supported 'fair' segregation policies which, in particular, would create sufficient opportunities for 'ambitious blacks' to better themselves in the reserves.'[64] They hoped, in effect, that 'capable' Africans, given economic opportunities, would form a Black middle class which could act as a buffer and as the most important link between Whites and Blacks in South Africa. They were soon to be disillusioned by a rapid succession of racist legislation which denied Africans the requisite economic opportunities to rise in social class. By the time the SAIRR was founded, liberals had come to fear that this thwarted upward social mobility would foster radical nationalism and opposition to capitalism among Africans. To ward against this potential danger, members of South Africa's economic elite (many of whom were English liberals on the fringes of mainline South African parliamentary politics) thought it strategic to "accommodate and seek alliance with a black middle class outside the reserves."[65]

This brand of liberalism, formulated in the 1930s, was to demonstrate its potency in the 1960s. After the rise to power of the National Party in 1948 the SAIRR lost the role of an informal independent advisor to the State on race relations which it enjoyed under the preceding United Party government. The Afrikaans Broederbond had established the South African Bureau of Racial Affairs (SABRA) in 1947 as pro-apartheid alternative to the SAIRR. Since then the SAIRR was abruptly ignored and left in the hands of middle-of-the road English-speaking opponents of the government as merely a civil society think-tank. Its extensive 'moderate' language research material, upon which organisations emerging from the White community were heavily dependent, made the SAIRR very influential in shaping the idiom and boundaries of a critical framework for the analysis of South African politics. It inseminated the conviction that the problems of South Africa were the product of defective 'race relations' arising from the sincere ignorance of the country's rulers, and the daunting magnitude of the nature of the complexity of the problem. It was believed that when reliable information about the ill effects of apartheid on the Black working class could be brought to the attention of governmental decision-makers, it would lead them to accept that the sharing of political and economic power with other 'races' within something like the prevailing constitutional framework that protects White privilege, would solve all the problems of the country. The Anglo-American mining conglomerate, through its Chairman's Fund, was historically the SAIRR's main funder.

This 'Race relations' focus emerged as the dominant ideological frame of action which would even inform and regulate the anti-apartheid theological language of the time. The formal foundations of this development were laid at the consultation between the SAIRR and WCC on 'Christians and Race Relations in South Africa' at Kitwe, Zambia in June 1964 (See **Document D2.4**). In 1967 the Christina Institute organised a series of provincial conferences on 'The Church and Race Relations in South Africa'. On the night of 31 October 1967, during one of the local initiatives arising from the conference in the Western Cape, a group of Anglicans, led by the priest in charge of the Woodstock parish, marched to St. George's Cathedral, the seat of the Anglican Archbishop, and nailed a document of 95 theses **(Document D4.2)** to the main door of the Cathedral.[66] Although the theses referred directly only to racism within the Anglican Church, the drama of this act symbolically challenged the entire Christian ecumenical movement in the country. It forced the Church to realise that while it was castigating the apartheid regime for its racist policies, it was itself an institution infested with racism. The participants in this act intended to symbolically re-enact the reformation initiated by Martin Luther when he nailed his 95 theses attacking the Roman Catholic Church to the main door of the Schlosskirche in Wittenberg on 31 October 1517.

The pervasive concern of the South African political theology of the mid-1960s with 'race relations' was to reach its fullest expression when the South African Council of Churches, immediately after it was founded in 1968, appointed a theological commission which released a "Message to the People of South Africa" on 20 September 1968 under a joint-endorsement with the Christian Institute. **(Document D4.5)**.

The message succinctly outlined the fundamental Christian ethos against race as the basis of personal identity, and stratification of human community. At the time of its release it was translated into at least four of the main languages spoken in the country. Individuals were invited to sign it as an expression of their commitment to the faith proclaimed in this pamphlet, which was formulated as a denunciation of the religious claims of apartheid.

On closer scrutiny, this message was a reaction against what was then observed as the entrenchment of a psychological tendency among White people to view apartheid, which Verwoerd's sophistry was presenting as a political theory of separation along racial lines without which the 'European race' would be swamped by majority 'non-European' races, as the sole hope for their ethnic survival. The proliferation of this view in the media and other public forums alerted the vigilant members of the CI (who were delegates at the SACC conferences) of the fears and interests of White people in relation to apartheid. Two historic events had sharply brought the philosophy of apartheid into public discussion and review and induced the production of the 'The Message': the assassination of the Prime Minister H.F. Verwoerd in September 1967, and the widely publicised conduct of the NGK and Hervormde Nederduitse Kerk (HNK) representatives at the Ecumenical Reformed Synod held in August 1968 in the Dutch town of Lunteren. The South African delegation attempted a vigorous theological defence of apartheid and failed (**Document D4.4**). This was widely published in the state-controlled South African media.

Unlike the WCC's Uppsala Assembly, which was held a month earlier, the Lunteren Reformed Ecumenical Synod (RES) enjoyed detailed coverage in the South African media. Although the WCC condemnation of the regime could be dismissed out of hand, this could not be done in the case of the RES, to which three main Afrikaans churches belonged. In 1968 the NGK was the largest member church of the RES, and the preceding RES in 1957 had been held in Potchefstroom, South Africa. The prestige of the RES and the prominent place occupied in it by the NGK lent unrivalled authority to its deliberations on the political situation in South Africa.

In 1968 there was general anxiety as to whether the theological support given to apartheid by the Afrikaans Dutch reformed churches would be able to stand up to the scrutiny of international reformed theological scholarship. The RES delivered a negative verdict upon the South African government and the NGK, its moral and political patron. The preaching of racial discrimination and racism as a means of national salvation was denounced as being without any foundation in scripture and in its Calvinistic tradition. The Reformed Churches were accordingly asked to denounce racism. The world Synod instructed, *inter alia*, that "In her pastoral ministry the church should strive to eradicate attitudes of racial superiority and racial prejudice by leading her members into full Christian maturity in race relations. This should be done urgently, persistently and patiently" (**Document D4.4**).

A similar judgement from the WCC would have been dismissed as liberalistic and communistic, but that could not be done with the RES. What occasioned more anxiety for the apartheid regime and the NGK was the fact that the resolutions of this Synod vindicated the Christian Institute, which had been declared heretical two years earlier by the NGK. The 1968 Lunteren Reformed Synod established that it was the Afrikaans Dutch Reformed Churches – upon which the ruling party had relied for political support, power, moral justification and majorities at polls since 1948 – that were heretics, both in terms of Calvinist theology and the general Christian social ethic.

At the same time, the death of Dr Verwoerd, who had distinguished himself as the leading philosophical defender of apartheid, and his succession by his radical minister of repression, John B. Vorster, caused a sombre reckoning on what apartheid means in practice. With the attention of South Africans so strongly focused upon the meaning of apartheid, and emboldened by the disarming of the National Party ideology by the resolutions of the Lunteren Synod the ecumenical movement responded with a comprehensive rejection of all theological justifications of the philosophy and practice of apartheid.[67] The message declared that "We believe that this doctrine of separation is false faith, a novel gospel; it inevitably is in conflict with the Gospel of Jesus Christ". Prime Minster Vorster reacted, and initiated a propaganda campaign against those "who under the cloak of religion want to disturb order in South Africa", and who "are bandying about the idea that that they should do the sort of thing here in South Africa which Martin Luther King did in America . . . Cut it out; cut it out immediately, because the cloth you are wearing will not protect you if you try to do this in South Africa, he warned[68].

In its crafting and adoption of a programme of struggle for the normalisation of race relations in South Africa, the Church could not see any connection between the defective race relations and economic factors, that is, apartheid as an inherently extractive racial oppression of Africans for the economic exploitation of their humanity. A clear call for the dismantling of the social status quo and its replacement by a non-racial, just and democratic one was lacking. Instead of this political route, as an obvious follow-up to criticism of the policy of the South African state, the SACC and the CI instituted a Study Programme on Christianity in Apartheid Society (SPRO-CAS), which was charged with the exploration of those alternatives to apartheid that were commensurate with Christian values. It is only in the reflections of the international ecumenical that we find some insight into the connection between racism and economic exploitation, as well as a grasp of the consequent need for a radical challenge to the social structures that bred on this kind of racism. The resolutions of the World Conference on Church and Society: 'Christians in the Technical and Social Revolutions of our Time' held in Geneva in 1966 **(Document D4.1)** and those of the WCC's fourth general assembly, held at Uppsala, Sweden, in July 1968 **(Document D4.3)**, - both which were available as background reading to the scribes of The Message - point to this awareness. Despite the clear shortcomings of their response to apartheid as a social system, the statements critical of apartheid issued by South African Christian organisations were deemed intolerable and subversive by the regime and its supporters. Throughout his premiership Vorster, treated the CI for the most part, as one of his greatest bugbears.

The growing awareness, expressed in the Woodstock Theses, that the organisation, forms and structures of all Christian denominations in South Africa were trapped in the ideological and social patterns of apartheid, was to stand out as the pivotal religious revolution of the 1960s in South Africa. The production of 'A Message to the people of South Africa' in the year after the promulgation of the Woodstock Theses and the establishment of SPRO-CAS in consequence of this theological declaration, marked a new sense of purpose which was to be strengthened by subsequent developments. Around the SPRO-CAS process and the University Christina Movement, would rise Black Theology and the Black Consciousness Movement that would mount a credible challenge to the race relations paradigm.

D4.1 World Conference on Church and Society – 'Christians In The Technical and Social Revolutions of our time', Geneva, July 1966

The following is an extract of relevant paragraphs from the report of the conference.

Section III: THEOLOGICAL ISSUES IN RACIAL AND ETHNIC RELATIONS

34. At this moment of history, the white race dominates the world economically and politically. This domination prevents the development of authentic human community both in nations and on an international level. Christians should be passionately concerned that this pattern of domination be broken down, in order that a more truly human society may be built. Christian theology has the responsibility to see this situation in historical perspective and to discern the need to destroy this idolatrous structure in order that God's purposes in history be advanced.

35. Reconciliation in this context cannot be mere sentimental harmonizing of conflicting groups. It demands sacrifice. It demands identification with the oppressed. It demands determination to break down the unjust patterns. It should restore the dignity of the oppressed. Changes in personal attitudes and reconciliation of individuals are of fundamental importance, but nothing less than structural change can create a pattern of justice in which the dignity and freedom of all will be assured.

36. It is not enough for churches and groups to condemn the sin of racial arrogance and oppression. The struggle for radical change in structure will inevitably bring suffering and will demand costly and bitter engagement. For Christians to stand aloof from this struggle is to be

disobedient to the call of God in history. The meaning of the cross for our time can be nothing less than this.

SECTION IV – MAN AND COMMUNITY IN CHANGING SOCIETIES

25. In dealing with racial and ethnic problems, Christian churches must be fully aware of the political and economic structures of society and see the problems in their contexts. That is to say, socialist countries, capitalist countries, and countries with mixed economies are bound to present different contexts within which to view the racial and ethnic problems. However, basic human rights as seen from a Christian perspective, must not be compromised under any circumstances in any manner. Otherwise Christian faith fails to provide that unity of mankind which transcends political and economic factors.

26. Since the people who control the social, economic and political structures are also members of the dominant racial group, and have so far failed to ensure equal opportunities for members of minority or subordinated racial groups, our society remains racially divided and even stratified, reinforcing and perpetuating modes of thinking and behaviour.

27. In national and local societies of multi-ethnic composition, similar tensions exist between dominant ethnic groups and minority or subordinate ethnic groups. Ethnocentrism, whether based on racial, ethnic or tribal distinction, remains a dangerous stumbling block in the development of human community on the national and supranational level.

28. There are many instances of ethnocentrism within the church preventing the wholesome growth of national churches and the unity of the Christian people. No continent, no nation, and few organised churches are without this problem.

SECTION V – CONCLUSION AND RECOMMENDATION

Race Relations
In the face of the explosive situations, described earlier, we urge Christians and churches everywhere:

85. to oppose openly and actively, the perpetuation of the myth of racial superiority as it finds expression in social conditions and human behaviour as well as in laws and social structures.
86. to engage in the common task of changing the structures of society through legislation, social planning, corporate action, and mobilise all its resources to ensure the full and equal participation of all racial and ethnic groups in the corporate life of a pluralistic society.
87. to recognize, support, and share the individual and collective interests of people who are disadvantaged by their race and ethnic origin, so they may gain the basic human, political, and economic rights enjoyed by the others in a pluralistic society.
88. to make organised efforts to eradicate from the Church and Christian community all forms of discrimination based on race, colour or ethnic origin in the selection of persons for church leadership, admission to the membership of congregations, and in adapting social and cultural values and traditions to the present.

D4.2 The Woodstock Theses, October 1967

Out of love and concern for the truth, and with the object of electing it, the following will be the subject of a declaration....

In the name of our Lord Jesus Christ.

Concerning the Doctrine of Man
1. The Gospel of Jesus Christ is the good news that in Christ God has broken down the wall of division between God and man, and man and man.
2. Because all men share in a measure of sin, all alike deserve God's judgement and punishment.
3. But, because by the grace of God all men share in a measure of hope through our Lord and Saviour Jesus Christ, all alike are called to share in the freedom and the glory of the children of God.
4. Because all men belong to the family which lives under God's command, God's rebuke and God's mercy, all men are equal in sight of God.
5. Because all men are equal in the sight of God, there can be no inequality between one man and another, or between one classification of people and another.
6. He who discriminates on the grounds of race or colour – let him beware of the judgement of God.
7. And let this be especially true of Christians who subscribe to the blasphemous assumption that God himself has made pigmentation to be a sign of subordination, inferiority and humiliation.
8. When our Lord and Master Jesus Christ said 'Repent' he called for the entire life of believers to be one of patience.
9. This life of patience must carry through a complete revolution of the basis of our lives, because there can be no compromise

between a life of security and preservation and the life which we are called to lose before we can find it.
10. It is only when our lives are discomforted and disrupted that the Word of God is experienced as judgement, and it is only when there is the possibility of judgement that the saying Word of God becomes a liberating reality in our lives.
11. If Christians, without let or hindrance, tolerate exploitation, injustice, direct and indirect alienation of man, especially when it is done under the blasphemous invocation of the Christian faith such as the slogan 'Western, National and Christian', they cut themselves off from the Word of judgement and the grace, and they shall answer to the Living God.
12. It is true that there are many areas in life in which man is alienated from his brother, yet it is not true to rationalise passivity by an assertion that the matter of race is but one instance which should not be emphasised out of proportion.
13. The crisis which faces Christians today is that of an inhuman doctrine of man, and there can be no challenge which compares with it.

Concerning the Anglican Church and Race
14. It is right that the Anglican Church has a record of opposition to the perverted doctrine of man.
15. It is true that Anglicans have been in the forefront in proclaiming the dignity of man and the value of the individual.
16. But if Anglicans imagine that their witness to the equality of all men is pleasing to their Lord and Master, they have not been grasped and confronted by the Word of God.
17. In Anglican churches there is segregated sitting.
18. In Anglican churches there are segregated Sunday Schools.
19. In Anglican churches there are segregated Sunday School parties for the children.
20. In Anglican churches there are segregated youth clubs and woman's groups.

21. There can be no quarrel with separate services based on language because this enables the faithful to hear the Word of God in the medium most intelligible to them.
22. But let Anglicans be quite certain that it is language and class or colour which is the basis of the distinction.
23. It is true that racial zoning makes it difficult for Anglicans to meet together, but let Anglicans be assured that they are too ready to scent danger where danger does not exist, that they are too ready to say that a meeting is impossible when in fact it has not been prohibited by law.
24. It is right we should obey the laws of the state for God has ordained the state to care for the welfare of his children.
25. But let the Anglicans know that a law of the state which is at variance with the will of God is not morally binding on Christians.
26. For no Christian can accept the authority of the state to determine who shall receive the sacraments of God, and in what manner the sacraments shall be received and administered.
27. But let Anglicans be warned that it is no light matter to decide whether a law of the State is at variance with the will of God.
28. And let Anglicans be warned that there is no person other than the individual concerned who can bear consequences of any decision made in this matter.
29. It is good that there should be exchanges of pulpits by ministers of different classifications, but let Anglicans be clear that this is no substitute for the meeting of the people themselves, and that this can be the means of salving an uneasy conscience.
30. It is right that the Anglicans should be taught to affirm the dignity of man and the value of the individual in their ordinary everyday life.

31. It is good that the Anglicans should seek to deepen and extend existing personal relationships and to encourage the fuller use of personal contact.
32. But let the Anglican Church know that a Church which allows its opposition to an inhuman doctrine of man to be met by the personal response of individual Christians and not corporate action of the Body of Christ is a Church which denies its nature and its calling.
33. It is right we should not undervalue the importance of the ordinary, regular churchgoer who is not yet alive to the issues of race conflict.
34. But the time is now long past that the Church can expect this blasphemous canker to be healed by the natural process of time.
35. For in the course of a single generation it has become increasingly difficult for members of the same church to meet without fear.
36. For this reason, it behoves the church deliberately to create the conditions in which such persons are able to meet and learn to know each other.
37. Correspondingly it behoves the church to create conditions in which all Anglicans are unavoidably faced with the issue race of relations within the Church.
38. Because the State by enactment is preventing the growth of sympathy, understanding and love between people of classification, the Church should encourage the development of these gifts of the Spirit.
39. To this end uniracial parishes in reasonable proximity should be paired so that congregations will not do separately what they can do together, and such parishes should form joint committees of persons of different classification to meet regularly.
40. The Church should set aside a full-time minister to serve as a liaison officer between the different classifications.

41. But let the Anglicans realize that ultimately there is no other person who can do what their Lord and Minister calls them personally to do.

Concerning Ecumenism
42. When our Lord and Master prayed that his disciples be one as he and his Father were one, he meant more than a spiritual oneness.
43. This unity is more than the coming together of all Christians, for God wills that the whole of creation comes under his kingly rule.
44. This unity is a unity of people and of nations, of races and classes, of the old and the young, of the poor and the rich.
45. Christians do wrong to think that God is well pleased when developed and industrialised nations bind themselves to each other in order to make themselves stronger.
46. Christians do wrong to think that God is well pleased by programmes of aid to underdeveloped countries when these are used by the donor country to include favourable trade agreements.
47. Christians do wrong to think God is well pleased by vast sums of money spent on armaments, defence and waging war, when two-thirds of the world is starving.
48. Christians do wrong to think God is well pleased when the ecumenical movement has as its goal a super-church and reconciliation of the whole of humanity.
49. Nevertheless, Christians are called to strive to make manifest the oneness of all who are in Christ, because thereby the oneness of all people is proclaimed.
50. It is good that the Anglican Church is involved in discussions with churches of other denominations.
51. But let Anglicans not think that a growing understanding between different denominations is a substitute for mutual acceptance of people within their own denomination.

Concerning Money

52. Christians should be taught that one who gives to the poor, or to the needy, does a better action than if he contributes to memorials, restoration funds, organs, stained-glass windows.
53. Christians are to be taught that he who shares what he has with any brother is actually sharing what he has with Christ.
54. And in giving less than is a real personal sacrifice the Christian falls short of the requirements of Christ.
55. Christians are to be taught that building up the Church is the same as building the Kingdom of God.
56. Stewardship campaigns which focus on church needs and not confront us with the mercies of God and the needs of people are not Christian.
57. Woe the Church which has a clean conscience about the use of its resources, for it feeds on false glory and it forgets grace.
58. For the treasure of the Church is not money or priority, because the ecclesiastical authorities allow few funds to trickle out, rather accumulating funds to the Church's economic base.
59. The treasure of the Church is not Christ himself, as though he were ours to contain within our buildings or Bible, for we are His and not He ours.
60. The true treasure of the Church is the Holy Gospel of glory and grace of God.

Concerning Authority and Prophecy

61. All Christians participate in the benefits of Christ, and this participation is granted to them by God who is not bound to any institution.
62. Yet the Church is not to be despised for it is the community of those who are called to bear witness that Jesus is Lord.
63. It is the whole Christian community which is the priesthood of believers, and there can be no greater priesthood than this.
64. Yet the ordained ministry is not to be despised for its mark of the priesthood of the faithful.

65. Neither is the ordained minister to lead the faithful nor are the faithful to lead the ordained minister, for all are to be led by God the Holy Spirit.
66. Nevertheless, those who are called to preach the faith of Christ crucified will have to answer for it they preach a sub-Christian doctrine of man, or if they fail to warn the faithful against a perverted doctrine of man.
67. Correspondingly the community of the faithful will have to answer for it if the ordained minister preaches a sub-Christian doctrine of man or fails to warn them against a perverted doctrine of man.
68. For within the community of the faithful God calls each believer to be responsible for himself and his neighbour.
69. It is right bishops should speak out boldly, and that synods pass resolutions.
70. Nevertheless, Anglicans are not to think that it is only bishops and synods who are called to make known the church's teaching.
71. And Christians are not to be silent when the house of God becomes the supermarket of the Lord where grace and piety are dispensed, where appearances must be kept up at all costs and ecclesiastical efficiency comes first.
72. The Church is victorious, not when outsiders admit that it is right but when it disappears among them.
73. And those who are called to serve the Church in a full-time capacity are called to be less secluded and more actively and knowledgeably concerned about their fellowman than anyone else.
74. Christians should be taught that they live only in community.
75. Where Christians do not need one another, where they are concerned to cultivate their private spiritual life, they may be avid consumers of sermons and Bible studies, but they fail the Body of Christ.

76. For Christians are concerned to be reconciled and reconciling community in a world in which man is alienated from his fellows, his work, and from God.
77. It makes a real difference whether, in a world torn apart by hate and bent on destroying itself, the Church is equally divided or whether it shows some signs that God's love makes all things new.
78. Nevertheless, there can be no harmony in a Church which refuses to acknowledge it shares a measure of sin with the world which is torn apart by hatred.
79. There can be no peace with the bishop, or a synod, who does not bear witness to the pure word of God.
80. There can be no peace with the synod which is shackled by the weight of establishment and respectability.
81. There can be no peace with the synod which allows representation only from members of one sex.
82. There can be no peace with the synod in which the lay representation does not take into account the numerical proportion of different congregations.
83. It is right that the church should be concerned with people and the effect an inhuman doctrine of man has on families and communities.
84. Nevertheless there can be no peace with the church which is not radically opposed to basic assumption of blasphemous ideology.
85. Away then with those prophets who say to Christ's people 'Peace, Peace' when there is no peace.
86. Hail to those prophets who say to Christ's people 'The Cross' where there is no cross.
87. For the agony of a suffering people is not eased by those who shut their ears and say, 'They do not complain'.

Concerning Christian Witness

88. It is right that all witness should confess their guilty complicity in the evil which blights the country.
89. But it is not right that we insist that we need complete answers before we can begin to act.
90. For Christians are to be more concerned with the rightness of their immediate action than with ultimate ends which lie within the knowledge of God alone.
91. It is equally not right that we should have allusion about the effectiveness that we are doing.
92. It is right that Christians should know that he who would freely encounter truth must pay for the price of being alone.
93. Yet it is clear that Christians are called to be willing to make the whole gospel of Jesus Christ a personal and institutional priority.
94. And let Christians be assured that their Lord and Master Jesus Christ is already ahead of them, waiting for him to answer his call to come where he already is.
95. We, the young people of St Mary's Church, Woodstock, call on all who are filled with the impatience of the gospel to take heart, and not to despair, for God is not mocked, he is faithful and just and his kingdom will come.

The grace of our Lord Jesus Christ, and the love of God, and the fellowship of the Holy Spirit, be with us all evermore.

D4.3 Statement from the Fourth Assembly of the World Council of Churches, Uppsala, 20 July 1968

REPORT OF SECTION IV – TOWARDS JUSTICE AND PEACE IN INTERNATIONAL AFFAIRS

[...]

Race Relations

28. Racism is a blatant denial of the Christian faith.
    1) It denies the effectiveness of the reconciling work of Jesus Christ through whose love human diversities lose their divisive significance;
    2) It denies our common humanity in creation of our belief that all men are made in God's image;
    3) It falsely asserts that we find our significance in terms of racial identity rather than in Jesus Christ.
        a) Racism is linked with economic, and political exploitation. The church must be actively concerned for the economic and political well-being of exploited groups so that the statements and action may be relevant ... They should also withdraw investments from institutions that perpetuate racism. They must also argue that similar assistance be given to both public and private sectors. Such economic help is an essential compensatory measure to counteract and overcome the present systematic exclusion of victims of racism from the main stream of economic life. The churches must also work for the change of those political processes which prevents the victims of racism from participating fully in the civic and the governmental structures of the countries.

b) Racism employs fallacious generalizations and distortion to sustain its existence, and these result in personal denigration, segregation and other forms of isolation. The churches must eradicate all forms of racism from their own life. That many have not done so, particularly where institutional racism assumes subtle forms, is a scandal. The churches must also fight to secure legislation to eliminate racism. This will involve new approaches in education and the mass media, so that false value-judgements can be eliminated and the true grounds of human dignity made to evident to all mankind.
c) Racism produces counter-racism as a defensive measure for human survival. It also perpetuates itself from generation to generation. The Church must break this vicious spiral. It must control individuals who hold racial prejudices with the truth about our common humanity and emphasize the personal worth of all men. It must demonstrate that the grace of God is sufficient to reconcile and unite all members of the human race.
d) The Secretariat of Race Relations of the World Council of Churches needs to be strengthened to help churches embark on a vigorous campaign against racism.

RECOMMENDATIONS FOR POST-ASSEMBLY PROGRAMME

The Elimination of Racism – Programme of Study and Action
7. The World Council of Churches in numerous ecumenical statements since 1948 has recognised the increasing urgency for the Christian Church to participate actively in the struggle for racial equality, dignity and self-respect and has noted that

this struggle is rapidly reaching a climax. The ominous events which occurred since New Delhi 1961, oblige us to promote new efforts to eliminate racism.

8. By racism we mean ethnocentric pride in one's own racial group and preference for the distinctive characteristics of that group; belief that these characteristics are fundamentally biological in nature and are thus transmitted to succeeding generations; strong negative feelings towards others who do not share these characteristics coupled with a thrust to discriminate against and exclude the outgroup from full participation in the life of the community.

9. By white racism we mean the conscious belief in the inherent superiority of persons of European ancestry (particularly those of Northern European origin), which entitles all white peoples to a position of dominance and privilege, coupled with the belief in the innate inferiority of all darker peoples, especially those of African ancestry, which justifies their subordination and exploitation. By focusing upon white racism, we are not aware of other forms of ethnocentrism which produce inter-tribal and inter-tribal tensions and conflicts throughout the world today.

10. We believe, however, that white racism has special historical significance because its roots lie in powerful, highly developed countries, the stability of which is crucial to any hope for international peace and development. The racial crisis in these countries is to be taken as seriously as the threat of nuclear war. The revolt against racism is one of the most inflammatory elements of the social revolution now sweeping the earth; it is fought at the level of mankind's deepest and most vulnerable emotions – the universal passion for human dignity. The threatened internal chaos of those countries in which racial conflict is most intense has immediate worldwide impact, for racism under attack tends to generate and spread counter-racism. We submit that this crisis will grow worse

unless we understand the historical phenomenon of white racism, what has distinguished it from other forms of inter group conflict, and what must be done to resolve the crisis on the basis of racial justice.

11. It is urged that the World Council of Churches undertake a crash programme to guide the Council and the member churches in the urgent matter of racism. This programme would involve:
    a. the development of comprehensive and up-to-date reports on the racial situation in various regions of the world. The prototype for this might well be the comprehensive PEP (Political and Economic Planning) report from the United Kingdom. Immediate studies are needed from Southern Africa, USA and Australia;
    b. Consultations on racism on a regional and international level;
    c. Creation of consultant service to make available the counsel of experts to various secular and church agencies;
    d. relating the view and experience of the church to various international agencies, especially the United Nations;
    e. research on the areas of potential crisis and alerting the churches and secular agencies in helping to prevent the growth of tension arising from racism.
    f. action-coalition projects, particularly for developing models for action (e.g., in some of the joint action for mission projects);
    g. mass educational material on racial issues;
    h. establishing within the General Secretariat a coordinated secretariat on the elimination of racism, and the appointment of an ecumenical commission to supervise this programme.

D4.4 The Reformed Ecumenical Synod, Lunteren, August 1968

Resolutions on Race Relations

1. God's commands to men that they display love and practise righteousness are not contradictory but harmonious norms, for man's personal and group attitudes and conduct and are guiding norms for race relations.

2. True love among men requires that we accept our neighbour regardless of his race or culture in the image of God, respect him in person as God's creature, and be willing to put ourselves in his place in order us to understand how we should behave toward him in personal and social relations.

3. Since men inherently seek their own interests rather than the welfare of their fellows, the church should stress on the duty of men individually and collectively, to practise self-sacrifice for the welfare of others. Self-sacrifice for the sake of Christ is the highest form of self-preservation, self-preservation is only the concomitant with obedience to the second great commandment when it is qualified and limited by the biblical demands of love and righteousness, so that it does not interfere with the inalienable rights of other people.

4. For a true understanding of the rights, equality, and dignity of man, we should see all men not only as creatures of God, made in his image, but also as those who have sinned, and need redemption. Therefore in our relation to fellow believers we should recognize the new unity which all Christians, regardless of race, have by virtue of their being redeemed by Christ.

5. Christians should be urged to acknowledge their common involvement in guilt with a world torn by sinful divisions and attitudes. They should be called upon to repent of their own sin in this respect and to make restitution by following Christ in the way of love.

6. In the proclamation of the Word, the church, to whom has been entrusted the message of Christ's Kingdom, should speak courageously and relevantly on the issues of the day, both for the identification and correction of her members and, where necessary, in criticism of the activities and policies of governments and organisations.

7. Believers should be equipped by the church through teaching and discipline to serve God, in all spheres of society, individually, and where possible, corporately. Believers must also proclaim the commandment of love in race relations and make it applicable to the affairs of civil government and the structures of society.

8. Christians in general and the church in particular bear a responsibility towards members of all races who suffer from poverty, under-development, and political oppression. Believers should be willing to lend every effort to alleviate the suffering of such peoples.

9. In her pastoral ministry the church should strive to eradicate attitudes of racial superiority and racial prejudice by leading her members into full Christian maturity in race relations. This should be done urgently, persistently and patiently.

10. In obedience to the mission mandate of Christ, the Church must bring the Gospel to all nations regardless of race. The

principle of love for the neighbour requires that the mission respect the character and culture of the recipients of the Gospel so that new churches may come to self-expression in harmony with Scripture.

11. The unity of the Body of Christ should come to expression in common worship, including Holy Communion, among Christians regardless of race. It may happen that linguistic or cultural differences make the formation of separate congregations, often with their own type of preaching and worship, advisable, in these cases it is wise not to force an outward and therefore artificial form of unity but to recognise the differentiation within the circle of God's people. However, the worshipping together of people of different races, is a sign of the deepest unity of the church and can be an example for the life of society as a whole.

12. Holy Scripture does not give a judgement about racially mixed marriages; contracting a marriage is primarily a personal and family concern. Church and state should refrain from prohibiting racially mixed marriages, because they have no right to limit the free choice of a marriage partner.

13. Each racial group should have the right to prefer a measure of distinct development, but never at the expense of a racially distinct group in the same country. While the manner of such development may vary from place to place, it is a requirement of the Christian ethic that love, and justice be exercised, and that all groups avoid isolation and promote a relation of mutual helpfulness.

14. With a view to the great tensions in the sphere of race relations in the world today, Synod strongly urges the member-churches to test conditions in their churches and

countries by the norms set forth in these resolutions, and to report back to the next Synod.

15. Recognizing that the real problem of race relations in member-churches of the RES lies not so much in the area of acceptance but in that of the application of the above principles, Synod urges its member-churches
    a. To put forth renewed efforts to live wholly in accord with biblical norms;
    b. To reject every form of racial discrimination and racism;
    c. To reject every attempt to maintain racial supremacy by military, economic, or any other means;
    d. To reject subtle forms of racial discrimination found in many countries today with respect to housing, employment, education, law enforcement, etc.;
    e. To pray for themselves and for one another that God may give wisdom and faithfulness in every circumstance.

D4.5 Message to the People of South Africa, 20 September 1968

THE AUTHORISED SUMMARY

In the name of Jesus Christ

We are under an obligation to confess anew our commitment to the universal faith of Christians, the eternal Gospel of salvation and security in Christ Jesus alone.

The Gospel of Jesus Christ is the good news that in Christ God has broken down the walls of division between God and man, and between man and man.

The Gospel of Jesus Christ declares that Christ is the truth who sets men free from all false hopes of freedom and security.

The Gospel of Jesus Christ declares that God has shown himself as the conqueror of all the forces that threaten to separate and isolate and destroy us.

The Gospel of Jesus Christ declares that God is reconciling us to himself and to each other; and that therefore such barriers as race and nationality have no rightful place in the inclusive brotherhood of Christian disciples.

The Gospel of Jesus Christ declares that God is the master of this world, and that it is to him alone that we owe our primary commitment.

The Gospel of Jesus Christ declares that the Kingdom of God is already present in Christ, demanding our obedience and our faith now.

The Gospel of Jesus Christ offers hope and security for the whole life of man, not just in man's spiritual and ecclesiastic relationships, but for human existence in its entirety. Consequently, we are called to witness to the meaning of the Gospel in the particular circumstances of time and place in which we find ourselves. In South Africa, at this time, we find ourselves in a situation where a policy of racial separation is being deliberately affected with increasing rigidity. The doctrine of racial separation is being seen by many not merely as a temporary political policy but as a necessary and permanent expression of the Will of God, and as the genuine form of Christian obedience for this country. It is holding out to men a security built not on Christ but on the theory of separation and the preservation of our race groups as the way for the people of South Africa to save themselves. And this claim is being made to us in the name of Christianity.

We believe that this doctrine of separation is a false faith. A novel gospel; it inevitably is in conflict with the Gospel of Jesus Christ, which offers salvation, both individual and social, through faith in Christ alone. It is keeping people away from the real knowledge of Christ; therefore it is the Church's duty to enable our people to distinguish between the demands of the South African state and the demands of the Christian discipleship.

The Christian Gospel requires us to assert the truth proclaimed by the first Christians, who discovered that God was creating a new community in which differences of race, language, nation, culture, and tradition no longer had power to separate man from man. The most important features of a man are not the details of his racial group, but the nature which he has in common with all men and also the gifts and abilities which are given to him as a unique individual by the grace of God; to insist that racial characteristics are more important than these is to reject what is most significant about our own humanity and that of others.

But, in South Africa, everyone is expected to believe that a man's racial identity is the most important thing about him: only when it is clearly settled can any significant decisions be made about him. Those whose racial classification is in doubt are tragically insecure and helpless. Without racial identity, it seems, we can do nothing; he who has it, has life; he who has no racial identity has not life. This belief in the supreme importance of racial identity amounts to a denial of the central statements of the Christian Gospel. In practice, it severely restricts the ability of Christian brothers to serve and know each other, and even to give each other simple hospitality; it limits the ability of a person to obey Christ's command to love his neighbour as himself. For, according to the Christian Gospel, our brothers are not merely the members of our own race group. Our brother is the person whom God gives to us. To dissociate from our brother on the grounds of natural distinction is to despise God's gift and to reject Christ.

Where different groups of people are hostile to each other, this is due to human sin, not to the plan of the Creator. The Scriptures do not require such groups to be kept separate from each other; on the contrary, the Gospel requires us to believe in and to act on the reconciliation made for us in Christ. A policy of separation is a demonstration of unbelief in the power of the Gospel; any demonstration of the reality of reconciliation would endanger this policy. Therefore, the advocates of this policy inevitably find themselves opposed to the Church if it seeks to live according to the Gospel and to show that God's grace has overcome hostilities. A thorough policy of racial separation must ultimately require that the Church should cease to be a Church.

The Gospel of Jesus Christ declares that God is love; separation is the opposite force of love. The Christian Gospel declares that separation is the supreme threat and danger, but that in Christ it has been overcome; it is in association with Christ and with each other that we find our true identity in dissociation and distinction from each other; it rejects as undesirable the reconciliation which God is giving to us by his Son; it reinforces distinctions which the Holy Spirit is calling the people of God to overcome; it calls good evil. This policy is, therefore, a form of resistance to the Holy Spirit.

The Gospel of Jesus Christ declares that Christ is our master, and that to him all authority is given. Christians betray their calling if they give the highest loyalty, which is due to Christ alone, to one group of tradition, especially where that group is demanding self-expression at the expense of other groups. God judges us, not by our loyalty to a sectional group but by our willingness to be made new in the community of Christ. Christ is inevitably a threat to much that is called 'the South African way of life'; many features of our social order will have to pass away if the lordship of Christ is to be truly acknowledged and if the peace of Christ is to be revealed as the destroyer of our fear.

And Christ is the master of the Church also. If the Church fails to witness to the true Gospel of Jesus Christ it will find itself witnessing to a false gospel. If we seek to reconcile Christianity with the so-called 'South African way of life' we shall find that we have allowed an idol to take the place of Christ. Where the Church abandons its obedience to Jesus Christ, it ceases to be the Church; it breaks the links between itself and the Kingdom of God. The task of the Church is to enable people to see the power of God at work, changing hostility into love of the brethren, and to express God's reconciliation here and now. For we are not required to wait for a distant 'heaven' where all problems will have been solved. What Christ has done, he has done already. We can accept his work or reject it; we can hide from it or seek to live by it. But we cannot postpone it, for it is already achieved; and we cannot destroy it, for it is the work of the eternal God.

We believe that Christ is Lord, and that South Africa is part of his world. We believe that his Kingdom and its righteousness have power to cast out all that opposes and keeps men in darkness. We believe that the word of God is not bound, and that it will move with power in these days, whether men hear or whether they refuse to hear. And so, we wish to put every Christian person in the country the question which we ourselves face each day; to whom, or to what, are you giving your first loyalty, your primary commitment? Is it to a subsection of mankind, an ethnic group, a human tradition, a political idea: or to Christ?

May God enable us to be faithful to the Gospel of Jesus Christ, and to be committed to Christ alone!

CHAPTER FIVE

Black Consciousness and Black Theology

In December 1968 a group of Black student leaders associated with the University Christian Movement (UCM) led a walkout from the multiracial National Union of South African Students. They founded the South African Students Organisation (SASO) under the leadership of Bantu Stephen Biko on the ideological platform of what came to be articulated as Black Consciousness.

With its Black Students Manifesto proclaiming: "We ... commit ourselves to the intellectual and physical development of our community and to the realization of liberation for Black People of South Africa"[69], the foundation of SASO inaugurated a Black political self-assertion not heard in South Africa since the banning of the national liberation movements in 1960. After a long and debilitating political silence under the intense repression of the Verwoerd regime, a Black organisation with an overt political imagery and a declared program for the 'liberation for black people' was founded.

Given the fact that they were founded under circumstances radically different from those of the 1950s and early 1960s and which gave rise to a different set of motivations, SASO and the organisations that budded from it in the early 1970s sprouted out of a new critical sense of radical awareness. On the basis of a profound perception of the way in which years of apartheid oppression had cowed Black people into self-denigration, a slave mentality and a dependency syndrome, this fresh wave of the South African liberation movement set out to construct a philosophy of revolutionary Black self-awareness and positive Black identity aimed at repairing the damage done to Black selfhood, while simultaneously serving as a means of political mobilization.[70] SASO's policy manifesto described Black Consciousness as an 'attitude of mind', a way of life, which leads a Black person to reject all value systems that seek to make him/her a foreigner in the country of his birth, while inculcating in him an awareness of the economic and political power which Black people as a group possess in South Africa.[71]

Following a series of debates around the controversy generated by the movement's denunciation of multiracial alliances in anti-apartheid initiatives , and its rejection of the hegemonic political paradigm of the 'normalisation of race relations', Black Consciousness began to take shape as a social force by 1971. The significance of this Black Renaissance within shroud of Apartheid South Africa was emblematically detected and articulated by Beyers Naude, Executive Director of the Christian Institute, in a public lecture entitled 'Black Anger and White Power in An Unreal Society', delivered in May 1971 at the invitation of the University of Natal's Student's Representative Council (**Document D5.1**).

At a time when many White liberals were alarmed by the radical Black self-assertion of the Black Consciousness movement, Naude launched into a rigorous and passionate account of the reasons for Black Consciousness and the implications it might have on the future of South Africa. When, during his trial in November 1973, he was cross-examined for refusing to give evidence to the Schlebusch Commission about the extent of the Christian Institute's attachment to the Black Consciousness movement, Naude referred to this lecture as his considered view on Black Consciousness.[72]

Although Naude perceived Black Consciousness as a manifestation of Black anger, advocates of the movement held that this Black anger was no more than an initial stage. They argued that Black people had moved beyond anger at the system of White minority rule by 1971 and had entered a period of self-understanding and creative self-expression of their political aspirations. They had moved from Black anger to purposeful political liberation.[73]

This shift into the second stage of Black Consciousness was accompanied by agitated efforts to extend the articulation of its praxis from the student elite which had dominated it to 'grassroots' Black communities in order to maximise its impact. In December 1972 the Black Peoples Convention (BPC) was launched as the national umbrella body of a variety of African, Coloured and Indian organisations. At the time of its banning in

1977, the BPC had grown into a convention of seventy affiliates which ranged from local civic organisations and cultural bodies to national political organisations and trade unions. The third phase of the Black Consciousness movement, the founding of the Black Community Programmes, signified the resolve to end dependence on 'white charity' and political patronage, emphasising practical steps directed at cultivating a culture of self-reliance among Black people.

One way in which the theory of Black Consciousness was elaborated and enriched was through its vigorous criticism of the Study Project on Christianity in Apartheid Society (SPRO-CAS). SPRO-CAS had been launched by the SACC and the CI in 1969 as an attempt to translate the proclamation of the 'Message to the People of South Africa' into some form of positive action. The leadership of SASO and the BPC pointed to the interim reports of SPRO-CAS as evidence of the paternalism of White liberals attempting to analyse South Africa and to propose solutions to its problems without any meaningful consultation with Black people. This criticism was articulated by Steve Biko in his editorial introduction to a SPRO-CAS publication, *Black Viewpoint,* where he wrote: "So many things are said so often to us and for us but very seldom by us".[74]

The ensuing dialogue between the CI leadership and the BPC led to the relaunching of the entire programme in 1972. The reconstructed project was called 'Special Programme on Christianity in Apartheid Society' and had separated and partially independent wings of Black Community Programmes (BCP) and White Community Programmes. The latter soon fizzled out, while the former grew into a very successful black community development educational and relief organization.[75]

The Black Consciousness movement's description and radical analysis of the psychological damage inflicted upon Black people by apartheid racism of apartheid, as well as its call for blacks to assert themselves in all spheres of South African life, induced a theological tradition of South African Black Theology[76]. Having made the informed judgment that colonial Christianity served as one of the most powerful means of inculcating a negative self-perception and political passivity in Black people, the Black Theology movement sought to construct a framework for the interpretation of the Christian faith in a manner that would counteract religious colonialism and serve as a liberation theory for black people.[77] With its emphasis on the divine origin of the dignity of Black people, and resonance with the enthusiastically Christian Black communities, it served as the most significant response to the state Black life was in, as unveiled by Black Consciousness. The seeds for the sprouting of this theological movement in the South African situation were availed by publications in the USA such as James H. Cone's seminal *Black Theology and Black Power* (1969).[78]

The formulation of Black Theology as a tool of liberation in South Africa formally took shape when Sabelo Stan Ntwasa was appointed the Traveling Secretary to the UCM in 1971, with the promotion of Black Theology as his specific task.[79] In the same year "The Black Theology Project" was founded and a national theological conference of Black clergy and theological students was held at Wilgespruit near Johannesburg. The widely publicized statement[80] from this conference is **Document D5.2**.

After the UCM was dissolved in 1972 the BCP took over the task and formed the Black Theology Agency.[81] Despite a banning order served on Ntwasa in 1973, the Black Theology Agency continued its work, operating largely throughout the Interdenominational African Ministries Association of South Africa (IDAMASA) and the African Independent Churches Association of Southern Africa (AICA).

In an indication of an eagerness to transform Black Theology from being an abstract theology, to a socially impactful movement, in early 1972 a conference of Church leaders was convened to "bring together black church leaders working in the so-called multiracial churches with a view to examining their roles within these churches and ways and means of increasing the effectiveness of their leadership of black people in black communities."[82] During early 1976 Black Catholic clergy in the Johannesburg area, led by Fr Lebamang Sebidi, formed the Black Priests Solidarity Group (BPSG) with the stated aim of studying and reflecting together on Black Theology and its implications for the solidarity the church is to demonstrate for the "discarded people" (**Document D5.3**).

During this time the organisation expanded into a multi-denominational body and its character mutated into being a network of priests, minsters and pastors who were ever ready to intervene against government actions on behalf of the communities they served. In 1983 it was named MUCCOR (Ministers United for Christian Co-responsibility). Rev John Lamola was its last serving Secretary in1986-1988.

The immediate visible achievement of Black Theology was the abundant manifestation of Black self-expression in the churches which had hitherto been exclusively led theologically and administratively by White people. From around 1971 Black Christians started making demands that the leadership of the church reflect its racial composition. It was pointed out that it was scandalous that the membership of almost every church in South Africa was about 80 per cent Black, whilst more than 80 per cent of the power of these churches was vested in White hands.

SACC aligned churches began to respond positively to these criticisms. Around this period the language of the Church and its demographic image began to change as Black delegates in Church conferences and synods began to put forth their view that fundamental political transformation of the status quo was the only acceptable aim of the Church's prophetic criticism of the South African state.

This trend reached its climax and found its symbol with the appointment of Desmond Tutu as the Dean of the Johannesburg Diocese of the Anglican Church in 1975. He was the first Black person to hold such a critical office in the history of the Anglican Church in South Africa. It was by now generally agreed that the terms of the articulation of opposition to apartheid had passed from White to Black hands. With a historically charged sense of national prophetic responsibility (whose only precedent was the involvement of African Church leaders in the early history of the ANC) Black church leaders – Sam Buti, Manas Buthelezi, Ernst Baartman, Allan Boesak, and Desmond Tutu – valiantly moved to the forefront of the challenge to apartheid. A major indicator of this new spirit was the ominous open letter that Tutu wrote to Prime Minister J.B. Vorster in May 1976 (**Document D5.4**). Tutu pleaded:

> I am writing to you Sir, because I have a growing nightmarish fear that unless something drastic is done very soon then bloodshed and violence are going to happen in South Africa almost inevitably. A people can only take so much and no more.

On June 16, 1976, six weeks after the publication of Tutu's letter, Soweto erupted, sparking off a nationwide uprising.

The June 1976 uprisings – which in many ways were the result of the political work of SASO, South African Students Movement (SASM) and the BPC –ushered in a new era in the history of South African protest. The apartheid regime reacted to the crisis in its customary manner, unleashing a wave of indiscriminate repression. The targets this time were a host of Black political and cultural organisations which had come into being since 1968, including the two Black newspapers: the *World* and the *Weekend World*. The banning of all these organisations on 10 October 1977, a month after the murder in detention of Steve Biko, and the detention of the leaders of this broad movement, effectively closed a chapter on one of the most creative periods of Black history.

On the religious front, the Black Consciousness movement continued to exercise an influence in and through Black Theology's academic, ecclesiastical and social networks. Black Theology persisted as an intellectual and spiritual force that sustained the strength required for maintaining the momentum of the struggle for freedom against very harsh torture in widespread police detention, and killings that would be punctuated by mass funerals led by Black theologically conscious priests.

At a "Consultation on Racism" convened by the SACC at Hammanskraal in February 1980, by way of preparation for an international WCC conference on the same theme in the Netherlands, Black delegates went into a protest caucus to formulate a historic statement that was incorporated into the official report of the consultation. They threatened to initiate a campaign for the withdrawal of Black people from the 'multiracial churches' and to form a Black Confessing Church unless there was a joint-commitment to "uproot racism within the churches and to work towards its total elimination within wider society" **(Document D5.5).**

The main reason for this statement was the discussion of the WCC's Programme to Combat Racism, which had given financial aid to the ANC and the PAC since 1970. Certain sectors of the churches voiced an opinion that this was unwarranted and an immoral expression of support for violence by the World Council of Churches. Black delegates saw the issue entirely differently. They viewed the equivocation of their White colleagues as the symptom of an innate tendency to seek to preserve the apartheid status quo, vitiating the sentiments expressed in their public pronouncements (see **Document D6.2 and Document D6.5**).

One significant legacy of the Black Consciousness philosophy of the early 1970s was its awakening effect on the Black members of the NGK 'daughter' churches. Allan Boesak, a minister in the Coloured daughter church who earned his doctoral degree at the university of Amsterdam in 1977 with a dissertation entitled "A Socio-ethical Study of Black Theology and Black Power"[83], was the leading figure in this renaissance. Under his leadership, Black Christians (in the sense 'Blackness' had been redefined by the Black Consciousness Movement) of the Reformed tradition began, for the first time in their history, to collectively and systematically interrogate the contradictions involved in being Black and oppressed under apartheid yet in communion with a church and tradition that had been used as a theological catalyst of that oppression and humiliation. On 26 October 1981, Boesak and his associates gathered at Hammanskraal and founded the Alliance of Black Reformed Christians in South Africa (ABRESCA) based on a charter which unequivocally stated that their Blackness demanded a fundamental critique of their denominational affiliation, and a redefinition of their relationship with the White NGK **(Document D5.4)**.

D5.1 "Black Anger and White Power in an Unreal Society" Dr CF Beyers Naude

The Annual Edgar Brookes Academic Freedom Lecture, University of Natal, Pietermaritzburg, 19 May 1971.

The most adequate description I could give to the social system, which we have created, is to define it as an unreal society maintained by White power and now threatened by Black anger.

Why do I describe it as an unreal society? And in what sense could it be termed such?

1. Morally it is an unreal society because the basic religious and moral suppositions upon which it is being built are immoral and therefore indefensible ...
2. Politically it is unreal ... an oligarchy by a small white minority with the deliberate and intentional exclusion in political participation of four-fifths of the population.
3. Economically it is unreal because ... South Africa is probably the only example in the world of an already industrialised society with a high economic growth rate which practices an economic policy which legally restricts the field of skilled employment to one fifth of the population in the misguided belief that in some unique way the economic laws would operate differently for South African whites that they would for any other society in the world ...
4. Educationally it is an unreal society ... despite the fact that it has been repeatedly proved beyond any doubt that the system of Bantu Education is educationally unsound, economically wasteful, culturally harmful, and politically distasteful the white minority continues to support and implement it. What an unreal society!
5. Socially it is an unreal society ... a small white minority tries to create and maintain a structure of the largest political measure of social separation of people of different races of

which the greater part is living and working together in regular and close proximity in the same geographical area.

A number of white leaders in the past have described our situation as unique, thereby implying, usually with a measure of pride, that because of its uniqueness it should not be judged on the same level and with the same criteria as other societies. I would rather in the face of the factors mentioned above operative in our society, describe our society as unique in the sense of its unreality – an unreality created and maintained on the basis of certain racial concepts which although they were initially subscribed to and practiced in some other communities, are not in keeping with the ethical values, cultural norms and economic demands of the world to-day.

Human nature being what it is, it was inevitable at that stage that some of the millions of people subjected to these many forms of discrimination and humiliation would rise in protest, rejection, and rebellion against such an unreal and unjust society ...

At the outset, there was the sincere hope that the white man would understand and accept the demand for sharing the political future of the country with blacks. As time went on and in the view of the fearful reaction of Whites, it became clear that a long struggle would ensue before any political power would be accorded to the Blacks.

The ruthless suppression of strong political movements and organisations with the declared aim to secure political rights by peaceful means, such as the ANC, led to the growing disillusionment in the Black man. The peaceful protest marches of Sharpeville and Langa stimulating the irrational fears of many whites led not only to a severe increase in racial tension but also to more repressive legislation on the part of Government against the different non-white racial groups. This in turn created from 1961 onwards a deep sense of despondency amongst Africans, Coloureds, and Indians, a spiritual and mental lethargy born out of any hope that any meaningful change would be affected in the foreseeable future. It also expressed itself in an attitude of lack of interest in matters political and this was aggravated by the widespread police system of harassment, interrogation, and intimidation which created a society where suspicion, distrust and fear became part and parcel of the life of the whole community, both Black and White.

In the meantime, the Government slowly began to realize that with the winds of change blowing all over South Africa the granting of basic political rights to the black community could not be withheld indeterminately, started to create limited channels of government within the framework of separate developments through the establishment of the territorial authorities of the homeland, the creation of a Transkei Parliament or Urban Bantu Councils and eventually of the Coloured Representative Council ... It also caused a deep division within the different black communities as some regarded any support of and participation in these 'separate development structures' as a betrayal of the idea of equal rights and opportunities for all in a common society, whilst others saw this as possible though very limited and unsatisfactory ways of gaining some political foothold in a long and precarious climb to the top of the mountain.

In the meantime, however, slow but significant changes were taking place, which were destined to bring about a totally new situation. First and foremost, of these was the completion of the process of de-colonization throughout the whole of Africa except the southern politically White controlled part and the establishment of a number of sovereign African states, which were able to establish responsible and reasonably stable forms of Government.

A second factor which deeply influenced the development in South Africa was the increased awareness and concern throughout the world during the last ten years of the dangers which racialism in any from constitute to sound human relations and world peace. The racism proclaimed and practiced by Hitler in Nazi Germany engendered a new consciousness of the evil inherent in any form of racism. The serious form of racial friction and continued outburst of racial violence in the USA from 1964 onwards deepened this concern and naturally focused attention and interest of the world on a country like South Africa, where a system of racial discrimination unprecedented in the history of the world was being enforced with a measure of political sophistication and determination unparalleled in the history of the same world. And here in South Africa the blacks became increasingly conscious of the fact that world opinion and sympathy was on their side. As a leading African said to me in the early sixties 'We can afford to wait a little longer because we have three unconquerable forces on our side: truth, world opinion, and numbers.'

A third factor which led to significant change in mood and attitude in the ranks of the blacks of South Africa was the discovery of the crucial role the Black labour force was playing in the South African economy and the fact that large and ever-growing lack of white skilled labour necessitated the relaxation of job reservation laws and the training of many blacks for new skills. This in turn led to the increased wages for a substantial number of workers and the placing of many blacks on a higher economic and social level much nearer to the whites than ever before. Economic need was bringing in its wake a gradual social revolution in many Blacks for the first time discovered and began to assert their human dignity.

A fourth factor which has emerged during the last five years is the discovery and growing acknowledgement of the world of the existence of the Third World and the serious and ever enlarging gap between the affluence and economic development of the First (Western White) World and the poverty and economic backlog of the Third (Non-Western Non-White) World. This awareness accentuated the role in which Marxist and communist philosophy was playing to highlight a growing disparity between these two worlds. This has a special significance for South Africa where in more than one sense these two worlds meet and exist alongside each other thereby creating a potential situation of collision and violence. The emergence of both Russia and China on the African Continent and the fear which this has brought in the hearts of many Whites in South Africa has led to a new awareness that serious attention had to be given to legitimate grievances and aspirations of the black masses if the whites wanted to prevent a turning of their hearts and hopes to Communism as the liberator of the oppressed.

A fifth factor which has only recently emerged but which already has begun to exert a deep influence on the attitude and thinking of South African Blacks is the emergence of a Black Power consciousness , and a new call for Black Power and Black Identity which was first heard in the United States but which has now been taken up by many in our country , especially our younger generation. The rapidly deteriorating race relations and the inability of the government to recognize the real reason for this has created an excellent opportunity for the just and rapid development of Black Anger opposing the racialism of a white society.

If we analyse the development of the last few years, we become increasingly aware of new forces at work, many of which are growing expressions of Black Power and black bitterness. From every quarter of our country many voices are heard which prove how rapidly (almost overnight) and how widespread this concept has grown. This became clear in the last few months. Think of SASO, the black counterpart of NUSAS, already operating over a wide field. Think of ASSECA (The Association for Educational, and Cultural Advancement) ... an action which has significantly strengthened the confidence and self-esteem of the blacks. Think of the new mood amongst African clergy as reflected in the call for Black Clergy to stay together, to reject the concept of a White Christ and to insist that Black theologians should take over from Whites in Black seminaries

But the new trend of Black awareness and black anger was nowhere revealed more clearly than in two recent developments. First of these latest calls of Chief Kaiser Matanzima, with his pro-apartheid parliamentarians and Chief Mangosuthu Buthelezi of Zululand for more rights and more opportunities for their people. The fact that neither Matanzima nor his followers could be silenced by the reprimand of an angry Minister M.C. Botha shows very clearly that a long-suffering patience of more than seven years has now been exhausted and a new feeling of controlled anger, understandable impatience with overtones of racial hostility is taking over.

The second clear indication of a new outlook and attitude is the new aggressiveness so clearly noticeable amongst the Coloured people – especially amongst the more educated groups. Gone is the old attitude of subservience and submissiveness; gone is the apathy and lethargy regarding political and civic matters; gone are the days when whites could dictate and Coloureds had to obey. A deep bitterness has entered the soul of Coloured people and anger long suppressed, has come to the surface in the recent eruptions of violence at Gelvandale (Port Elizabeth) and Dysselsdorp (Outsdhoorn). More and more Coloureds are rejecting the Afrikaans language as the language of the oppressor; more and more Coloureds are calling for closer links to be forged with the African and Indian communities in the solidarity of a common Black front against the white. In both these two groups (African and

Coloured) the major thrust is made with the acceptance of the concept of separate development as interpreted by Blacks for Blacks – which in many respects is fundamentally different in interpretation or in motivation from the concept as created and developed by the whites. The circle is now being completed: White power has created its counterpart of Black Power; insistence on white identity has now led to an emphasis on Black identity and white separate rights have now developed an even impetus for Black separate rights. The Frankenstein creation is now slowly turning against its creator.

In such a situation, it is inevitable that white power, privilege and prestige must assert itself in order to curb any dangerous growth and to contain the possible development of bitterness and anger which could so easily lead to violence. The tremendous political, economic and military power held by the whites has strengthened their belief in the inherent and disputed supremacy of their own kind; it has created a sense of security in their position and has developed an attitude of indifference to the suffering of the Blacks. This in turn has increased the frustration, bitterness and anger in the hearts of many Blacks which must eventually steer towards a collision course. Black anger as a reaction against white supremacy is like a rumbling volcano which could erupt at the most unpredictable moment in the most unpredictable way.

The question arises: What could one reasonably expect to happen under these circumstances? It seems to me that in such a situation of uncertainty and of so many new factors at work only a prophet could dare to predict what the future will bring but I will be bold and suggest that one could reasonably expect the following:

1. The political awareness of all the black communities in South Africa is going to gather increased momentum thereby creating increasing embarrassment and serious problems not

only for the government but for every white person in South Africa. It will take the form of a growing militant Black Power consciousness accompanied by an increased psychological withdrawal from the White man and a deliberate estrangement of himself as a black man from everyone and everything white.

2. Existing Black organisations will be gaining more support and new all-black movements will emerge. Everywhere voices will arise to Africanize ('or should we say Blackanize'?) all bodies and institutions operating amongst and serving the African, Coloured and Indian communities. I would not be surprised if in the near future the demand would increasingly be made that whites should withdraw or be excluded from academic institutions, business concerns, Government departments, sporting bodies, student societies, theological colleges and welfare organisations catering for the needs of the Black communities. Increasingly efforts are going to be made to establish business, banking and other economic concerns which would normally operate in predominant African and Coloured townships with Black initiative and Black capital. It should create no surprise if a number of ventures are going to flounder and fail but where previously this would have effectively curbed similar future efforts this would no longer be the case. A new determination to grow economically at all costs and against all odds has been born in the heart of the Black man – and it will no longer be quenched by adversity, opposition or failure

3. Increasingly there will be an organizational and/or psychological link up with Black organizations in other parts of the world. Publications dealing with the emergence and growth, the struggles and victories of Black Power movements outside South Africa will be read, studied and debated on

much larger scale than up till now. Even if a number of such publications be banned the natural strength of the idea inherent in the concept of Black power as strengthened by decades of discrimination and humiliation will impel it forward in to the heart of millions of Blacks and force it to expression. The outward policy of our Government, the increased dialogue with African States, the inevitable exchange and interflow of ideas emanating from such dialogue, the increased interest and contact with black politicians, journalists, sportsmen, academic and religious leaders – all these will strengthen the position and increase the demands of the South African Blacks

4. If the pace of change towards full political economic and social participation on the basis of justice is not substantially increased in the near future for all Black groups, it is inevitable that the existing bitterness and emerging anger will lead to the eruption of violence. More and more such flashpoints which could lead to uncontrolled outbursts are building up and on the basis of the trend of events in other countries it does not need a prophet to predict what could happen. This black backlash of anger and hatred will in turn lead to a strong white reaction of initially effectively suppressing any uprising of violence thereby increasing the estrangement, and bitterness in the hearts of the blacks. This fact alone should cause the white population of our country to consider now while there is still time, which steps should be taken to prevent or to minimize any occurrence of violence. I do not notice however that there is at present an awareness sufficiently strong to comprehend the serious danger potentially present in our situation. And without such awareness no significant changes will be agreed to by those in power – the whites

5. The architects and protagonists of the concept of separate development will very soon discover (if they have not already done so) that the hope of the voluntary full acceptance of apartheid by the blacks as envisioned and idealized by the whites, is turning into disillusionment ...

6. The position of organizations usually described in the terms of 'White liberal' or 'white controlled' will increasingly become unenviable. Organizations such as the South African Institute of Race Relations, the Black Sash, the Civil Rights League and NUSAS (and on the religious side the 'liberal' churches and ecumenical bodies like the Christian Institute) will find that as pressures build up from the black side there will be a measure of increase of support coming in from Whites who formerly refused to face the realities as presented to the country by these organizations. On the Black side however there will be an inevitable withdrawal of active participation and support not because of disagreement with the ideals and goals which these organizations have stood for but because firstly there were too many whites in these institutions who with the best intentions never fathomed the depth of humiliation and rejection which the blacks experienced for so long at the hands of a supremacist White society and secondly because many Blacks in the growing consciousness of their own dignity and identity would rather go it alone with the possibility of failure that do it together in the White Man's way. It seems to me that therefore that there will be a certain period of temporary rejection and estrangement from such organizations until the black community feels it is strong enough to move back as equals or unless these organizations are willing to change their understanding and methodology in order to meet the legitimate demands and to deal wisely and sympathetically with the unreasonable demands which a racial relationship such as South Africa's inevitably calls forth...

To meet Black anger with duplicity or delay is dangerous. To try and meet it with brute white force is fatal. To talk about good will and tolerance without a concerted action is futile.

There is still time to avoid the tragic and dangerous consequences of an open conflict between Black and White power. I personally do not believe that we are going to avoid a confrontation of violence of some kind. But I do believe that the whites are still in a position of power to diminish the harmful and unpredictable results of such a conflict. There is still time – but time is running out. More than 20 years ago, one of South Africa's great sons and writers with rare and prophetic insight, made a gentle Black man in his *Cry the Beloved Country* say:

'I have one great fear in my heart that one day when they turn to loving, they will find we are turned to hating.'

D5.2 Statement of the Black Theology Conference, Wilgespruit, 1971

1. The white man is not the norm or yardstick to humanness;
2. The Church has helped the Blacks to realize their sense of humanity. Of itself, Christian tradition teaches respect of human dignity, but:
3. it was white controlled Church institutions that refuted the equality of humans before God.
4. Black Consciousness means blacks being aware of all that stood in the way of freedom.
5. Black Consciousness is not necessarily a whip-back against Whites although whites had to realize the harm they had meted out against blacks.
6. There could be no talk of Black Consciousness in any form without it being a reference to white racism.
7. Blacks are rejecting white ethical values and learning to do things for themselves instead of waiting for white handouts.
8. Blacks have come into a new relationship with whites – one based on love and mutual respect; but
9. that mutual respect could only come when Blacks have taken the power to demand their rights and then move from a strong position.
10. Blacks are waking up and working towards a solidarity that would support and sustain them; therefore, whites have to take suggestions from Blacks not vice versa.

D5.3 Black Priests Solidarity Group: Principles And Aims

1. To foster a lively sense of brotherhood and supportive fraternity among the Black Clergy and Laity by periodic and organized get-togethers and study groups
2. To commit ourselves as a black clerical brotherhood to play our meaningful role in the struggle as part of the oppressed Black people in South Africa and to full acceptance of the phenomenon of Black Consciousness
3. To find ways and means of making decrees of the Vatican II a living reality in our South African church; and to develop an authentic liturgical ethos that answers – not to yesterday's Black Christian – but to the deepest yearnings of today's worshiping Black man and woman; to awaken in ourselves the awareness that AFRICANISATION of the church in South Africa is the Black Clergy's task; to initiate a systematic study of some of our South African customs – ancestor cult, circumcision, funeral rites, sacrifices, etc.
4. To find ways and means as clerical brotherhood of activating and fostering a prophetic urge in our Black parishioners to liberate themselves from all forms of oppression: economic, political and social to encourage a healthy sense of self-reliance – at all levels of their lives
5. To instill in our black clergy a strong sense of mission, selfless service and a mature commitment to the ideals of Gospel of Jesus our liberator
6. To elicit from the black clergy an unwavering commitment to preaching the gospel of liberation and justice fearlessly without let or hindrance following the great tradition of Paul of Tarsus – in season and out of season

7. To awaken pastoral interest in concern and concern for the specially afflicted and oppressed classes: prisoners, detainees, slum dwellers – in short, the discarded people
8. To inculcate in the minds of the black clergy a steady love of learning and study with a view to building up an authentic indigenous theology and the written word of God
9. To take up Black Theology as our special realm of study and research and give it a firm philosophic theological basis
10. To form in the black clergy a strong collective voice that articulates and spells out the feelings, hopes and aspirations of Black Christians in the South African Catholic Church
11. To run a news bulletin as vehicle for sharing of life experiences in our respective areas of work

D5.4 Desmond Tutu's Open Letter to John Vorster, 6 May 1976

The Honorable Prime Minister Mr. John Vorster
House of Assembly
Cape Town
8000

Dear Mr. Prime Minister

This will be my second letter to you. In 1972 after I had been refused a passport to take up a post as associate Director of the Theological Education Fund, I appealed to you to intervene on my behalf with the appropriate authorities. Your intervention was successful because soon thereafter the then Minister of Interior changed his mind and granted me and my family passports. I am writing therefore optimistically in the hope that this letter will have similar happy results for all of us

I am writing to you, Sir in all deep humility and courtesy in my capacity as Anglican dean of Johannesburg. I am writing to you as one who has come to be accepted by some Blacks (Africans, Indians and Coloured) as one of their spokespersons articulating their deepest aspirations as one who shares with them equal steadfastness. I am writing to you, Sir because I know you to be a loving and caring father and husband and doting grandfather who has experienced joys and anguish of family life, its laughter and gaiety, its sorrows and pangs. I am writing to you, Sir as one who is passionately devoted to a happy and stable family life as the indispensable foundation of a sound and healthy society. You have flung your arms open to embrace and hug your children and your grandchildren, to smother them with your kisses. You have loved, you have wept, you have watched by the bed of a sick one whom you loved, you have watched the deathbed of a beloved relative, you have been a proud father at the wedding of your children, you have shed tears by the graveside of one for whom your heart has been broken. In short I am writing to you as one human person to another human gloriously created in the image of the selfsame son of God who for all our sakes died on the cross and rose triumphant from the dead and reigns in glory now at the right hand of his father' sanctified by the selfsame holy spirit who works inwardly in all of us to change our hearts of stone into hearts of flesh. I am therefore writing to you, Sir as one Christian to another, for through our common Baptism we have become members of and are united in the body of our dear Lord and Saviour Jesus Christ. This Jesus Christ whatever we may have said or done has broken down all that separates us irrelevantly – such as race, sex, culture, status, etc. In this Jesus Christ we are forever bound together as one redeemed humanity Black and white together.

I'm writing to you, Sir as one who is a member of a race that has known what it has meant in frustrations and hurts in agony and humiliation to be a subject people. The history of your own race speaks eloquently of how utterly impossible it is when once the desire for freedom and self-determination is awakened in a people for it to be quenched or to be satisfied with anything less than freedom and self-determination. Your people against tremendous odds braved the unknown and faced up to daunting challenges and countless dangers rather than be held down as subjugated people. And in the end, they emerged as victorious. Your people more than any other section in the white community must surely know in the very core of their beings, if they are unaware of the lessons of history both ancient and modern, that absolutely nothing will stop a people from attaining their freedom to be a people who can hold their heads high, whose dignity to be human persons is respected, who can assume responsibility and obligations that are necessary concomitants of the freedom they yearn for with all their being. For most blacks this can never be in the homelands because they believe that they have contributed substantially to the prosperity of an undivided South Africa. Blacks find it hard to understand why the whites are said to form one nation when they are made up of Greeks, Italian, Portuguese, Afrikaners, French, German, English etc; and then by some tour de force blacks are said to form several nations – Xhosas Zulus Tswanas etc. The Xhosa and the Zulu are for example much closer to each other ethnically than say the Italians, Germans and the white community. We all, black and white together all belong to South Africa against a visiting Argentina side. The South African team won hands down and perhaps the first time in our sporting history South Africans of all races found themselves supporting vociferously the same side against a common adversary. The heavens did not fall down. It is fanciful to see this as a parable of what will happen when all South Africans together are given a stake in this country so that they will be ready to defend it against a common foe and struggle for its prosperity vigorously and enthusiastically.

I write to you, Sir because our Ambassador to the United Nations, Mr. Botha declared that South Africa was moving away from discrimination based on race. This declaration exited not only us, but also the world at large. I am afraid that very little of this has been in evidence so far. It is not to move substantially from discrimination when some signs are removed from park benches. These are only superficial changes which do not fundamentally affect the lives of Blacks. Husbands and fathers are still separated from their loved ones as a result of the pernicious system of migratory labour which a DRC {NGK} Synod once castigated as a cancer in South Africa society, one which had deleterious consequences on Black family life, thus undermining the stability of society which I referred to earlier. We don't see this much longed for movement when we look at the overcrowded schools in the Black townships, at the inadequate housing and woefully inadequate crowded system of transport, etc.

I write to you, Sir to give you all the credit for your efforts at promoting détente and dialogue. In these efforts many of us here wanted to support you eagerly, but we feel we cannot in honesty do this when external détente is not paralleled by equally vigorous efforts at internal détente. Blacks are grateful for all that has been done for them, but now they claim an inalienable right to do things for themselves in cooperation with their fellow South Africans of all races.

I write to you because like you I am deeply committed to a real reconciliation with justice for all and to peaceful change to a more just and open South African society in which the wonderful riches and wealth of our country will be shared more equitably. I write to you Sir to say with all eloquence I can command that the security of our country ultimately depends not on military strength and a Security police being given more and more draconian power to do virtually as they please without being accountable to the courts of our land which have a splendid reputation throughout the world for fairness and justice. That is why we have called and continue to call for the release of all detainees or that they be brought before the courts where they should be punished if they have been found guilty of indictable offences. There is much disquiet in our land that people can be held for such long periods in detention and then often either released without being charged, or when charged, usually acquitted but this does not free them from police harassment. Though often declared innocent by the courts they are often punished by being banned or placed under house arrest or immediately detained. How long can people, do you think, bear such blatant injustice and suffering? Much of the white community by and large, with all its prosperity, its privilege, its beautiful homes, its servants, its leisure is hard riddened by fear and a sense of insecurity. And this will continue to be the case until South Africans of all races are free. Freedom, Sir, is indivisible. The whites in this land will not be free until all sections of our community are genuinely free. Then we will have a security that does not require such astronomical sums to maintain it, huge funds which could have been used for more creative and profitable ways for the good of our community, which would take its rightful place as a leader in Africa and elsewhere, demonstrating as it will that people of different races can live amicably together. We need one another, and Blacks have tried to assure Whites they do not want to drive them into the sea. How long can they go on giving assurances and have them thrown back in their faces with contempt?

I am writing to you Sir because I have a growing nightmarish fear that unless something drastic is done very soon, bloodshed and violence is going to happen in South Africa almost inevitably. A people can only take so much and no more. The history of your own people which I referred to earlier demonstrated this. Vietnam has shown this, the struggle against Portugal has shown this. I wish to God that I am wrong and that I have misread history and the situation in my beloved homeland, my mother country South Africa. A people made desperate by despair, injustice and oppression will use desperate means. I am frightened , dreadfully frightened that we may soon reach a point of no return, when events will generate a momentum of their own, when nothing will stop reaching a bloody denouncement which is 'too ghastly to contemplate' to quote your words Sir.
I am frightened because I have some experience of the awfulness of violence. My wife and I with our two youngest children stayed for two months in Jerusalem in 1996 and we saw the escalating violence and the mounting tension between the Jew and Arab which proceeded the six-day war. I was in Addis Ababa when there was rioting in the street, a prelude to overthrow the dynasty of Haile Selassie. I was in Uganda just before the expulsion of the Asians from that country and have returned there since and experienced the fear and the evil of things there. I have visited the

Sudan admittedly after the end of seventeen years of civil strife, but I could see what this internecine war had done to the people and their property. I have visited Nigeria and the former Biafra and have seen the awful ravages of that ghastly civil war on property and the souls of the defeated Biafrans. Last year I was privileged to address the General Assembly of the Presbyterian Church in Ireland in Belfast – and what I saw shook me to the core of my being. We saw daily on television in Britain horrific pictures of the pillage and destruction being perpetrated in Vietnam: children screaming from the excruciating agony of burns caused by napalm bombing, a people rushing helter skelter looking so forlorn and bewildered that one wanted to cry out 'but is there no God who cares in heaven. No, I know violence and bloodshed and I and many of our people don't want that at all.

But we blacks are exceedingly patient and peace loving. We are aware that politics is the art of the possible. We cannot expect you to move so far in advance of your voters that you alienate their support. We are ready to accept some meaningful signs, which would demonstrate that you, your government, and all whites really mean business when you say you want peaceful change. First, accept the urban black as a permanent inhabitant of what is wrongly called White South Africa, with consequent freehold property rights. He will have a stake in the land and would not easily join those who wish to destroy his country. Indeed, he would be willing to die to defend his mother country and his birthright. Secondly, and also as a matter of urgency, repeal the pass laws which demonstrate to Blacks more clearly than anything else that they are third rate citizens in their own country. Thirdly it is imperative, Sir that you call a national convention made up of the genuine leaders (leaders recognized as such by their section of the community) to try and work out an orderly evolution of South Africa into a nonracial open and just society. I firmly believe that your leadership is quite unassailable, that the white electorate has given you virtually a blank cheque, and that you have little fear from the so-called right-wing backlash. For if the things which I suggest are not done soon and a rapidly deteriorating situation arrested, then there will be no right wing to fear – there will be nothing.

I am writing this letter to you, Sir, during a three-day clergy retreat in Johannesburg when in the atmosphere of deep silence, worship, and adoration and daily services of the Lord's supper we seek to draw closer to our Lord and to try and discover the will of God for us and what are the promptings and inspirations of God's holy spirit. It is during this time that God seemed to move me to write this letter.

I hope to hear from you, Sir, as soon as you can conveniently respond because I want to make this correspondence available to the press, preferably with your concurrence, so that all our people both black and white will know from our side that we have done all that is humanly possible to do, to appeal not only to the rank and file of whites, but to the highest political figure in the land and to have issued a grave warning contained in my letter. This flows from a deep love and anguish for my country. I shall soon become Bishop of Lesotho, where I must reside in my new diocese. But I am quite clear in my own mind and my wife supports me in this resolve that we should retain our South African citizenship, no matter how long we have to remain in Lesotho.

Please may God inspire you to hear us before it is too late and may he bless your government now and always.

Should you think it might serve any purpose, I am more than willing to meet with you to discuss the issues I raise here as you say in Afrikaans *onder vier oë*.

Since coming to this cathedral last year, we have had a regular service praying for justice and reconciliation in this country every Friday. And at all services in the cathedral we pray:

God bless Africa
Guard his children
Guide her rulers
Give her peace
For Jesus Christ's sake

And

O Lord make us instruments of thy peace: where there is hatred let us sow love; where there is injury, pardon; where there is despair, hope; where there is darkness, light; where there is sadness, joy.
O divine master grant that we may not so much seek to be consoled as to console, to be understood as to understand, to be loved as to love: For it is in giving that we receive, it is in pardoning that we are pardoned, it is in dying that we are born to eternal life.
Amen

And we mean it
Yours Respectfully
Desmond Tutu

D5.5 Resolution on the Black Confessing Church, SACC Consultation on Racism, Hammanskraal, 11–15 February 1980

Preliminary note: the black delegates at the conference drew up a statement concerning the Black confessing church in order to underline the seriousness and urgency of a need of a joint commitment (i.e. by both black and white Christians) to uproot racism within the churches and to work towards its total elimination within the wider society. The reluctance on the part of white Christians to translate this commitment into visible action is likely to lead to further divisions within the church. The statement reads thus:

We the black representatives in this consultation wish to place on record the painful realization that the churches to which we belong have conformed to patterns of racist society. The persistent cries of the black people that the church is not consistent with the demands of the gospel of Jesus Christ have fallen on deaf ears.

We acknowledge our participation in the sin of the church. We are aware that God has been calling and continues to call his church to be a community that transcends all barriers of denominations and race.
We realize that the racial situation in this county has reached a critical stage and that God is calling the church as a liberating and reconciling community to identify itself with the oppressed and the poor in the struggle for in their struggle for the dignity which is theirs as human persons in the image of the Triune God.

We call upon Black Christians prayerfully to seek the guidance of God in our desire to understand what obedience means in this situation.

We further call upon all white Christians to demonstrate their willingness to purge the church of racism.

If after a period of twelve months there is no evidence of repentance shown in concrete action, the Black Christians will have no alternative but to witness to the gospel of Jesus Christ by becoming a Confessing Church.

CHAPTER SIX
Church Support for Armed Resistance?

The concern of the international Christian community about structural and institutionalised racism which had been given significant expression since the WCC assembly at Evanston in 1954, reached a decisive point at its fourth assembly, held at Uppsala in 1968. This Assembly followed the highly successful and important 1966 Geneva World Conference on Church and Society that met under the theme 'Christians in the Technical and Social Revolutions of our Time' (see **Document D4.1**).

Uppsala deliberations and resolutions became both a historical watershed and a canon on Christian response against the injustice of racist regimes in southern Africa.[84] It set out the rationale and process of supporting active resistance against these regimes. This moment of action sparked widespread agony, debate and dissension on the one hand, and celebration on the other.

A commission of the Uppsala Assembly that was devoted to race relations, in which Beyers Naude (representing the Christian Institute) had been invited to participate as an 'extraordinary observer', concluded that the time had come for the WCC to translate its condemnation of racism into concrete action. A theological perspective on racism was developed. It was argued that racism is not merely a 'personal sin', but a structurally based, ideological programme of some sections of humanity seeking to dominate and exploit others, which must actively be combated as such (see**, Document D4.3)**. The assembly adopted a resolution that the WCC would set up a "coordinated secretariat on the elimination of racism" within its General Secretariat.

Immediately thereafter, a Consultation on Racism was held at Notting Hill in London from 19 to 24 May 1969, at which the Programme to Combat Racism (a WCC departmental unit, PCR) was to be established. The Notting Hill consultation resolved that "the World Council of Churches should serve as coordinating centre for the implementation of multiple strategies for the struggle against racism in Southern Africa by the

Churches", and that "all else failing . . . churches should support resistance movements, including revolutions, which are aimed at the elimination of the political and economic tyranny which makes racism possible'.[85]

These recommendations were formally adopted by the WCC's Central Committee when it met in Canterbury in August 1969. These included the establishment of a Special Fund ('Special Fund of the PCR') to be used to sponsor endeavours aimed at combating racism. The latter resolution was not welcomed by everyone. It occasioned considerable disquiet, particularly in some European and North American churches.[86]

The Uppsala perspective, particularly its analysis of 'white racism', with logic surprisingly similar to that of the then nascent Black Consciousness movement, provoked self-critical questioning of South Africa's liberal 'race relations' thesis in the White-led South African ecumenical movement. The primacy of the 'normalisation of race relations' praxis in South African church circles was finally shattered by the effect of the programmatic affirmation of the WCC's Central Committee meeting in Canterbury on the imperative for the liquidation of institutionalised White racism. The meeting had stated: "Racism is not an unalterable feature of human life. Like slavery and social manifestations of man's sin, it can be eliminated."[87]

On September 6th, 1970, both the Johannesburg national daily newspaper, *Rand Daily Mail*, and the National Party's daily, *Die Vaderland*, carried reports that the WCC's Special Fund of the PCR had donated thousands of USA Dollars to the ANC and the PAC, Namibia's SWAPO, Mozambique's FRELIMO, as well as to the Zimbabwean liberation movements, ZAPU and ZANU. An unanticipated storm of political controversy, theological debate and threats from the South African government erupted. Many white Christians who had tacitly supported the CI, the SACC and their 'politico-theological' programme, were shocked at what they considered to be a politically unwarranted and theologically unethical support of violence by the world Christian body.

To make matters worse, the SACC, the symbolic representative of the WCC in South Africa, found itself in a position where it could neither explain nor defend this action by the WCC. Although the SACC leadership was aware of developments connected with the Special Fund, the newspaper reports were the first news received of the grants to the ANC and PAC.[88] The regime government's propaganda machinery saw the news as a golden opportunity to malign the WCC. State radio and press painted the WCC as an uncritical supporter of 'terrorism', and the Prime Minister, John Vorster, issued an order banning all WCC officials from ever setting foot in South Africa. He also made an unheeded call to all South African churches belonging to the WCC to withdraw their membership from this body.

The SACC 'diplomatically' distanced itself from the WCC's action on the technicality that it was not consulted on the question of funding armed liberation organisations as it was not a direct member of the WCC, but merely a consultative council of churches who were members of the WCC[89]. In the meantime, conservative Christian groups and some WCC member churches in parts of Europe had already mounted a well-orchestrated outrage against the PCR's Special Fund. This reaction forced the WCC Executive Committee to immediately elucidate the objectives of the Special Fund and the criteria for the disbursement of grants. This was done while sticking to the principle that 'these grants are made without control of the manner in which they are spent' (**Documents D6.1**).

In addition, pressure on the apartheid regime was not relaxed in this enforced clarification, since it was decided to recognise the situation in southern Africa as a priority in all future grants. Notwithstanding, the debate around this raged for years, stoked and influenced in part by fears of government retribution and the conflicting opinions from both sides of the still racially segregated pews of WCC members churches in South Africa (See **Document D6.4**: recording the Methodist Church in Southern Africa's objections in 1979, as representative of the reaction of white-led churches).

As the storm raised by the announcement of the PCR grants began to subside, a theological and ethical debate on the moral value and place of 'revolutionary violence' against a regime such as National Party rule ensued. It soon became apparent that a debate about violence and non-violence was subordinate to differences over competing social analyses.

Views depended on differing life-experiences of apartheid, as well as contrasting characterisations of the apartheid system. The debate degenerated into a contestation between a 'black view' that was coagulating around rising Black Consciousness which was deeply appreciative and implicitly supportive of armed struggle, and a 'white view' which felt a direct and real personal threat in any attempt to use force in order to change the government in South Africa.

Black Christians vehemently pointed out the hypocrisy of the church that seconded military chaplains to the South African army, thus giving support and legitimacy to the violence of the apartheid state, while condemning the armies of Black national liberation and their actions out of hand as reprehensible and terroristic.[90]

At the 1974 National Conference of the SACC, Beyers Naude and Douglas Bax (a Presbyterian minister) captured this argument by drafting a resolution which was adopted after long and illuminating discussion. The resolution urged the churches to support and encourage White people to conscientiously object to the then legally compulsory service in the South African defence force (**Document D6.2).**

In addition to the social factors and conflicting political views that determined the line-up of forces in the debate on violence, the momentum of debate was spurred by events in the country. The more the Vorster regime became entrenched in its tyrannical posture, the more people came to doubt the possibility of dismantling apartheid non-violently.

In this context, the 1976 Soweto uprising, and the brutal repression with which the regime responded, became a major catalyst in transforming the initially abstract debate into an agonised search for the means to end with minimal loss of life what was now clearly an armed conflict between the forces of freedom and those of oppression.

In the aftermath of the Soweto uprising the South African government once again silenced all forms of Black non-violent opposition, including the Christian Institute. When on 19 October 1977, three weeks after the funeral of Steve Biko, the entire institutional system of the Black Consciousness movement was outlawed, and Beyers Naude, amongst others, was placed under 5-year house arrest, the PCR prepared an elaborate background paper on South Africa entitled "South Africa's Hope: What Price Now?" (**Document D6.3**). The paper was distributed in December 1977 to all WCC member churches and individuals in the leadership of other influential international bodies.

The original includes a covering introductory letter by the then director of the PCR, Baldwin Sjollema, background information on the unjust nature of the apartheid system and steps taken against it in the past by international organisations such as the United Nations organsiation, a table showing the extent of the dependence of South Africa on foreign investments, and a list and description of the nineteen organizations banned by the South Africa government on 19 October 1977. The gist of the paper considered the long intellectual debate in Europe on the subject of Christian theology, violence and the WCC's programme in South Africa. It concluded by proposing a 'Just Revolution' paradigm as applicable to the South African situation and reaffirmed the commitment of the churches of the world to campaign for the economic isolation of South Africa.

From 1977 onwards the general position of the SACC, then the foremost representative of the opinion of the churches which made their position against the apartheid system clear, was nuanced. It expressed sympathetic understanding of the liberation movement's reasons for engagement in armed struggle on the one hand, and on the other hand it took extreme care not to play into the hands of the government by conspicuously supporting the violent overthrow of the state **(Document D6.5)**. For example, families of combatants of the liberation movements that were captured and sentenced to Robben Island received humanitarian and legal aid from the SACC's Dependents Conference. Yet, the SACC's tactical position was vulnerable to abuse by some church leaders who, while criticising the violence of the state, directed a disproportionate amount of criticism at what they considered the violence of the oppressed in resisting the state (for example **Document D6.4**).

This equivocation was sharply brought to the fore by the events that started in September 1984 when the state moved with unprecedented brutality against ordinary Black civilians opposing a new constitution aimed at entrenching apartheid. This precipitated a deeply critical assessment of the church's commitment to the struggle for liberation by theologians who were influenced by the rising presence of the ANC's underground structures that were run by activists who emerged out of the June 1976 experience, and were part of a non-ecclesiastical movement of Christian leaders who saw themselves as driven by their consciences, lived-experiences, and consideration of the illegitimacy of the apartheid state.

The result was the production in September 1985 of the "Kairos Document: Challenge to the Church", as a statement of 'Peoples Theology' as opposed to 'Church Theology' with its most controverted pronouncements being its scathing declarations against the official church's views on violence and non-violence **(Document D6.6)**. The Kairos Document's call for a categorical distinction between justified force used by the oppressed as a means of resistance, and the violence of what was adjudged a tyrannous state, marked a watershed in the evaluation of the nature and ethical complexities of the violent conflict, which by then, was inexorably escalating in South Africa.

D6.1 Statement of the WCC Executive Committee, Arnoldshain, West Germany, September 1970

RECOMMENDATIONS FOR THE PROGRAMME TO COMBAT RACISM REGARDING SPECIAL FUND

The International Advisory Committee recommends that the Special Fund shall be allocated in accordance with the following criteria:

1. The proceeds of the Fund shall be used to support organizations that combat racism, rather than welfare organizations that alleviate the effects of racism, which would normally be eligible for support from other units of the World Council of Churches.

2. (a) The focus of the grant should be on raising the level of awareness and strengthening the organizational capability of racially oppressed people.
   (b) In addition, we recognize the need to support organizations that align themselves with the victims of racial injustice and pursue the same objectives.

While these grants are made without control of the manner in which they are spent, they are at the same time a commitment of the Programme to Combat Racism to the causes the organizations themselves are fighting for.

3. (a) The situation in Southern Africa is recognized as a priority due to the overt and intensive nature of white racism and the increased awareness on the part of the struggle for liberation.

(b) In the selection of other areas, we have taken account of those places where the struggle is most intensive and where a grant might make substantial contribution to the process of liberation particularly where racial groups are in imminent danger of being physically or culturally exterminated.

(c) In considering applications from organizations in countries of white and affluent majorities we have taken note only of those cases where political involvement precludes help from other sources.

4. Grants should be made with due regard to where they can have the maximum effect; token grants should not be made unless there is a possibility of their eliciting a substantial response from other organizations.

D6.2 SACC Resolution on Conscientious Objection to Compulsory Military Conscription to the South African Military Forces, National Conference, August 1974

The National Conference of the SACC acknowledge the one and only God who mightily delivered the people of Israel from their bondage in Egypt and who in Jesus Christ still proclaims that He will 'set at liberty those who are oppressed' (Luke 4:18). He alone is supreme Lord and Saviour and to Him alone we owe ultimate obedience. Therefore 'we must obey God rather than men' in those areas where the Government fails to fulfil its calling to be 'God's servant for good' rather than for evil and for oppression (Acts 5:29; Romans 13:4).

In the Light of this, the Conference:

1. Maintains that Christians are called to strive for justice and the true peace which can be found only on justice;
2. does not accept that it is automatically the duty of those who follow Christ, the Prince of Peace to engage in violence and war, or to prepare to engage in violence and war, whenever the State demands it;
3. reminds its member-churches that both Catholic and Reformation theology has regarded the taking up of arms as justifiable, if at all, only in order to fight a 'just war';
4. points out that theological definition of a 'just war' excludes war in defence of a basically unjust and discriminatory society;
5. points out that the Republic of South Africa is at present a fundamentally unjust and discriminatory society and that this injustice and discrimination constitutes the primary, institutionalized violence which has provoked the counter-violence of the terrorists [sic] or freedom fighters;

6. points out that military forces of our country are being prepared to defend this unjust and discriminatory society and that the threat of military force is in fact already used to defend the status quo against moves for radical change from outside the white electorate;
7. maintains that it is hypocritical to deplore the violence of terrorists or freedom fighters while we ourselves prepare to defend our society with its primary, institutionalized violence by means of yet more violence;
8. points out further that the injustice and oppression under which the black people of South Africa labour is far worse than that against which Afrikaners waged their First and Second Wars of Independence and that if we have justified the Afrikaners' resort to violence (or the violence of the imperialism of the English) or claimed that God was on their side, it is hypocritical to deny that the same applies to the black people in their struggle today;
9. questions the basis upon which chaplains are seconded to the military forces lest their presence indicate moral support for the defence of our unjust and discriminatory society.

The Conference Therefore:
1. Deplores violence as a means to solve problems;
2. calls on its member Churches to challenge all their members to consider in view of the above whether Christ's call to take up the cross and follow Him in identifying with the oppressed does not, in our situation, involve becoming conscientious objectors;
3. calls on those of its member Churches who have Chaplains in the military forces to consider the basis on which they are appointed and to investigate the state of pastoral care available to the communicants at present in exile or under arms beyond our borders and to seek ways and means of ensuring that such pastoral care may be properly exercised;

4. commends the courage and witness of those who have been willing to go to jail in protest against unjust laws and policies in our land, and who challenge all of us by their example;
5. request the SACC's task force on Violence and Non-violence to study methods of non-violent action for change which can be recommended to its member Churches;
6. prays for the Government and people of our land and urgently calls on them to make rapid strides towards radical and peaceful change in our society so that the violence and war to which our social, economic and political policies are leading us may be avoided.

Proposed: D. Bax
Seconded: C.F.B. Naude

D6.3 South Africa: What Hope Now? December 1977

[*An except*]

Those outside South Africa who abhor apartheid and the violence and exploitation which are integral to it are called into action. Now more than ever, they are needed for the contribution they can make to the ending of injustice.

In their concern to help a just society to birth in South Africa there are three areas where outsiders need to develop a clear understanding of reality.

A Just Struggle
The first area concerns the nature of the struggle against apartheid which is going ahead within South Africa itself. It is now all too clear that the Government will not countenance a negotiated and peaceful dismantling of apartheid but is adamant that it will be maintained with however much violence is necessary. This means that opposition to apartheid is increasingly likely to be not only illegal but violent as well. If this proves true, the Government will be answerable for provoking that violence on a larger scale than ever before. Those outside South Africa who wish to see the structures of apartheid abolished peacefully will now understand that this Government has rendered that possibility ever more remote by its new restrictions. For whatever hope was left of the development of the African tradition of non-violent change has now been officially snuffed out.

How then do we respond as Christians to this threat of violence? Perhaps the most relevant recent statement by the WCC on this issue was the resolution adopted – without dissent – by its Central Committee in Addis Ababa in 1971:

The Churches must always stand for the liberation of the oppressed and of victims of violent measures which deny basic human rights. It (the Central Committee) calls attention to the fact that violence is in many cases inherent in the status quo.

Nevertheless, the WCC does not and cannot identify itself completely with any political movement, nor does it pass judgement on those victims of racism who are driven to violence as the only way left to them to redress grievances and so open the way for a new and more just order.

It is worth remembering also the distinction that Christians have sometimes made between their person and their office in connection with violence. According to this distinction, there may be a significant difference between violence used for one's self-preservation and violence used in protection of another.

This refusal to pass judgement on those who believe they have no option but to answer repressive violence with the violence of rebellion is reflected by the WCC's Programme to Combat Racism, which has made and continues to make grants from its Special Fund to a number of liberation movements in Southern Africa, including the African National Congress and the Pan-Africanist Congress (both of them black people's political movements banned by the South African Government in 1960).

But can we claim to stand in solidarity with those who rebel for a just cause if we simply refuse to pass judgement on them? The new situation in South Africa demands from us far more precision in saying what we mean by a just rebellion ... some definition of a just rebellion still awaits formulation by the churches – most of which found no difficulty in supporting the concept of a just war. The continuing lack of such a definition can be no excuse for failure to support the struggle of black South Africa now.

Those who are certain about the legitimacy of the unfolding struggle to end apartheid may find it helpful to recall that it is the struggle of a historically non-violent majority against a determinedly violent minority. To compare, as the Vorster Government does, the black revolution in South Africa with current terrorism in Europe is simply fraudulent, as the terrorists are a minority using violence against Government which still allow avenues of peaceful opposition ...

In debates about violence such distinctions are constantly drawn. A report commended in 1973 by the WCC Central Committee stated: 'There are some forms of violence in which Christians may not participate and which the churches must condemn. There are violent causes – the conquest of one people by another or the deliberate oppression of one class or race by another – which offend divine justice. There are violent means of struggle – torture in all forms, the holding of innocent hostages and the deliberate or indiscriminate killing of innocent non-combatants, for example – which destroy the soul of the perpetrator as surely as the life and health of the victim'.

We do not define the resistance fighters of Occupied Europe, who used violence against their Nazi oppressors, as terrorist, because we accept that their cause was just, and their methods disciplined. Christians who refuse to condemn the use of violence in the attempt to end injustice must constantly make such distinctions. They recognize that we have no right to condemn the use of violence by others in pursuit of justice if we are prepared to use it ourselves for the same end. They also acknowledge that down the ages there have been Christians to whom violence is an attempt to end a still greater evil. One of the best-known recent examples is Dietrich Bonhoeffer's participation in the plot to kill Hitler.

It is on the grounds of exactly such arguments that South Africa's black people today claim our struggle as a just rebellion ...

The words of a black South African who lived through June 1976 in Soweto speaks to us today: "I was in Soweto when police came in. I saw them shoot an eight-year-old child dead in the street. And you ask me to be non-violent?"

D6.4 A Critique of the WCC Programme to Combat Racism: A statement adopted by the Conference of the Methodist Church of Southern Africa, Cape Town, 1979

The Methodist Church of Southern Africa [MCSA] is a foundation member of the World Council of Churches and values its continued membership highly. The basis of the Council and most of its activities raise no questions among us. Our Church appreciates especially the grants for development, educational institutions, scholarship, families of detainees, and legal defence which are being made to projects and people in Southern Africa. The MCSA joins the WCC in condemning all forms of racism, and in recognizing that the history of white expansionism has made white racism particularly potent in social, political, legal and economic affairs. The MCSA is sadly aware of racism within its own membership and is endeavouring to counter it by positive programmes of action. We have many times expressed our objection to racist policies in the State and have called for a National Convention representing all sections of the population to plan the political future of South Africa.

The following criticisms are not in the form of a theological critique of the WCC. The Methodist Annual Conference of 1978 received, considered, and added its own resolutions to a doctrinal study of the WCC in relation to Methodism. It has also published a brochure of its own members. The present document will merely highlight the main criticisms of the PCR which, in view of the MCSA, justify serious objection to it. The MCSA believes that certain aspects of policy and practice relating to the Special Fund to Combat Racism are mistaken and indeed endanger the positive work of the WCC in general and PCR in particular.

1. Our primary criticism is concerned with the use of the Special Fund to make uncontrolled grants to organizations which are involved in armed conflict anywhere in the world. We question whether Aim 4 of the Fund can be held to apply without qualification in such circumstances. The Aim states:
   > The grants are made without control of the manner in which they are spent and are intended as an expression of commitment by the PCR to the cause of economic, social and political justice which these organizations promote.

   The General Secretary of the WCC in a letter to the Netherlands Reformed Church (2 November 1978) has further stated:
   > The Special Fund to Combat Racism has always been a combination of a political judgment and support for humanitarian programmes of particular group or movement.

   He goes on to say:
   > When we make grants, these are not meant, either explicitly or implicitly, as criticism against a movement about its use of counter-violence, nor are we attempting to show another, better way of achieving liberation. Rather the grants are intended as an expression of our commitment to the cause of economic, social and political justice which the organization concerned promote, as the criteria of the Fund states.

2. The policy of armed opposition to established government in South Africa can be defended by the argument that there is no other available means of making changes sufficient to create a more just regime. Opponents of these governments point to physical and psychological violence against individuals, and to

the institutional violence involved in such policies as Group Areas, Influx Control, Migratory Labour, and the Security Legislation. To respond by revolutionary violence is both a natural and human reaction and an attractive means of gaining revenge and overturning the power-structure. It may well be argued that it is only violence and the threat of violence which made the whites of Zimbabwe and Namibia contemplate a genuine sharing of power with blacks. Many African members of the MCSA endorse this line of thinking. At the opposite extreme, many white members approve of harsh measures to ensure security.

We would make two observations at this point. First, if there is any validity in the democratic rule of law, a revolutionary movement can claim legitimacy if it can show that it represents the will of the majority of the inhabitants of the area involved (hence the UN demand for supervised elections). Second, we doubt whether a body representing the Christian Churches throughout the world may legitimately link itself to an organization which is committed to violence and which rejects the ballot box even under UN supervision. Only where there is no way of ascertaining the majority will, and only until such a way has been made possible, can the appalling destructiveness of armed conflict be regarded as politically justified.

3. In the early seventies the struggle in Southern Africa could be regarded as a struggle of black against white. In Zimbabwe and Namibia this is no longer the case. Blacks are co-operating with whites, not merely here and there but in larger numbers. Some would claim that a majority desires this co-operation, others would deny this. But it is certain that the process of change has begun and that it cannot be reversed. The conflicts in those countries now involve many

complications such as tribal and personal rivalries, differing ideologies, and the sheer desire for power. Grants to particular movements such as the Patriotic Front and the external wing of SWAPO manifest support for political parties and ideologies rather than for justice.

Making such grants has serious implications for the integrity of the WCC and for its prophetic role. Surely a Christian body should devote its efforts to persuading all parties to negotiate, recognize that any peaceful political solution will be a compromise which, although it will provide justice to the greatest degree, will never be perfect. The PCR should take more seriously its duty to understand, interpret and criticize all points of view. At present its documents concentrate upon the undeniable wrong-doings of white-supported governments and fail to balance this by an equally critical view of the military liberation movements. There is a tendency to accept them at their own valuation and to study only their view of situation.

We submit that in the present situation in Zimbabwe and Namibia uncontrolled grants to particular political movements are not justifiable. Rehabilitative and reconciling work which would be commendable will be mentioned later.

4. Events in Southern African during the seventies have forced all the major Churches in that area to grapple with the ethical problem of violence. This is an instance of the well-known fact that God frequently has to use extreme historical events to drive the Church to repentance and new understanding. We are aware, far more than were our fathers, of the nature and consequences of violence, both individual and institutional, of the escalation of its horror with the use of modern weapons, and of the urgent need to find alternatives. We acknowledge

that we are members of a violent society and cannot dissociate ourselves from it, but we are committed to the task of creating something different and better and we do not believe that the Church ought to bless violent policies and acts now as it has done in past. Verbal declarations of fine intentions do not justify the use of evil other than stated as intention of the users. We criticize and deplore the methods used by the South African Government in implementing its policy of separate development. We submit that the world Church should similarly criticize the violence of liberation movements and should not legitimize such violence by linking itself to them.

5. In the WCC report, 'Violence, non-violence and the struggle for racial justice', it is stated that:

> There are some forms of violence in which Christians may not participate and which the churches must condemn. There are violent causes – the conquest of one people by another or the deliberate oppression of one class or race by another – which offend divine justice. There are violent means of struggle – torture in all forms, the holding of innocent hostages and deliberate indiscriminate killing of innocent non-combatants, for example – which destroy the soul of the perpetrator as surely as the life and health of the victim. (Quoted in Background Paper on Southern Africa, Document No. 17, WCC Central Committee 1979, p.11).

We concur with this judgement but would point out that it involves the condemnation of both sides in the struggle in Southern Africa. In Zimbabwe and Namibia many innocent non-combatants have been killed and horribly injured, some by government forces and others by liberation troops. These have not all been accidental victims of actions aimed; they have been accidental victims of actions at the enemy; they have been intended victims of planned actions, and the vast majority have been black. Whatever the philosophy of the leaders may have been, the actions are pure terrorism, aimed at creating and maintaining a state of tension and fear, and loss of morale, by means of indiscriminate killing, the seizing of hostages and torture. This is precisely what the WCC report condemns.

It is disingenuous to condemn government forces and condone liberation movements when they do the same things. Such actions are evil, whoever commits them, and the Christian Church cannot rightly support those who are guilty of them. It may be argued that the grants from the Special Fund are intended for humanitarian purposes. It is, however, equally true that they are allocated so as to express political and to show general support for the receiving organization. Other grants from the WCC are strictly controlled and reports and audited accounts are required. Nobody objects to this – it is normal practice. The failure to follow the practice in respect to grants to selected liberation movements suggests paternalism and arouses suspicion.

We believe that the WCC should apply the condemnation implicit in the paragraph quoted at the beginning of this section. Not to do so involves the WCC in moral responsibility for the dreadful suffering of many innocent people. To make a stand would entail suspending grants from the Special Fund to any organization in any part of the world which adopts the killing of innocent persons as a means of gaining power. At the same time each Christian Church in its own country must oppose by every means in its power the use of indiscriminate violence by government agencies and all non-judicial penalization of individuals.

6. Our desire is that the WCC should become deeply involved in Southern Africa in some of the following ways:
   (a) Christians should together work for a just society in which members of all racial groups can live together in fellowship. We endorse the following statement from WCC documents.
   ... the faithful action of the Christian community must manifest itself in ministries of peace based on justice, equality and human dignity. The over-riding concern must be to aim at peaceful and peace-producing resolutions of conflict and to assist in the creating of social and political structure which sustain just and participatory relationship. (Background paper on Southern Africa, p.9).
   and
   What is needed now is no longer only a unanimity in realizing and fighting against matters that must be rejected. Now it is time to unfold a version of how to attain and secure a peaceful way for races and classes to live together in the days to come. (South Africa's Hope – What Price Now? (Documents 12e, WCC Central Committee, 1979, p.4).

   The second quotation in particular summarises admirably the transition from an Old Testament to a New Testament way of dealing with a plural community. Christ came not to set the Romans over the Jews or Jews over the Romans, but to break down the walls of separation, and to that end he called his followers to be ministers of reconciliation, makers of peace.
   b) Such a future for Southern Africa will involve, inter alia:
   (i) A thorough and realistic assessment of the many factors hindering peaceful change – the injustice suffered by blacks and their tribal divisions and

rivalries – the guilt of whites and their fears concerning the future – and so on – which will entail both criticism of and sympathy with all parties;

(ii) A recognition that there is no single black point of view or white point of view;

(iii) An insistence that only genuine power-sharing will provide a way forward, and that the method of sharing must be decided by consultation amongst the parties involved, through democratically elected and not officially appointed representatives;

(iv) Recognition that defined minorities in a culturally plural society must be assured of justice and of reasonable security and cannot be expected to rely on utterances of general goodwill;

(v) Insistence that all parties must be prepared to accept and loyally abide by a compromise which is politically and economically workable.

c) Scripture makes it transparently clear that the People of God are required to help the weak against the strong, the poor against the rich, and the oppressed against the oppressor. But it is equally clear that this is not to be done by reversing the roles of the parties; to do that would be to usurp God's position as judge. We are repeatedly commanded by God to establish justice, and to create a community which is a 'koinonia' – a sharing fellowship. We believe that the WCC both could and should direct its energies toward constructive steps leading to such a community. Only thus can its explicit aims of economic, social and political justice be achieved.

This will call for actions which create negotiation and promote understanding between conflicting parties in Southern Africa. However difficult such projects might be, they would be vastly preferable to a further escalation of the process of mutual slaughter.

d) The WCC should continue and intensify humanitarian aid to people on both sides of the conflict, but this should be done under the direction of the Commission on Inter-Church Aid, Refugee and World Service and through independent agencies, such as Churches, Christian Council, Red Cross, and the like. We consider it inappropriate for financial assistance to be given directly to any of the parties involved in the conflict. We also believe that all grants should be strictly controlled and that reports, and audited accounts should be required in these as in other financial outlays by the WCC.

The Christian Church should not leave entirely to the local Churches the task of ministering to the spiritual needs of those involved in the conflict. Local Churches are too deeply entangled in the emotions and politics of the situation. For example, we would value assistance from the WCC in our own attempt to provide pastoral care to members of the MCSA serving with the liberation movements, as resolved by our conference in 1978.

7. It is our belief that the traditional attitude of the Churches towards armed conflict as a means of settling disputes needs radical revision today. We are not here concerned with the question whether it ever was true to the Gospel of Christ; we are not judging our fathers. Nor are we judging 'the world', which inevitably uses the methods of the world with its principalities and powers. We are concerned with the attitudes and actions of the Christian community as an organized body,

as, in other words, the representative and active organ of Christ in the world.

It seems to us to be beyond question that the WCC as the agent of the world Christianity should never align itself with one among a group of conflicting parties. By doing so it makes itself a servant of the world instead of a servant of God. On the contrary, it should follow the way of Christ and his apostles, breaking down barriers, bridging gulfs, and reconciling enemies.

D6.5 SACC NATIONAL CONSULTATION ON RACISM, HAMMANSKRAAL, FEBRUARY 1980

The conference notes that events this year (e.g. the Silverton siege, attacks on Police Stations, etc.) had already set a pattern of violence which cannot be ignored and therefore recommends that material be prepared that specifically deals with violence. Research topics can include the following:
a. Alternatives to violence.
b. How to minimize violence.
c. The education of society on the nature and extent of violence.
d. How to care for the victims of violence and their families.
e. What should be the immediate response by local churches to incidents of violence?

[...]

6. The Programme to Combat Racism (with special reference to South Africa)

Grants from the Special Fund:

6.1. The conference recognizes that young men beyond the border [ed: freedom fighters] have been forced into this situation by their experience of racism and violence in this country. The church must care for them as people and recognize their political viewpoint. This can be done without necessarily approving the political policies or methods.

　　6.1.1. Some feel that the grants from the Special Fund identify the WCC with the policy and methods of the movements in spite of assurances to the contrary. Some members feel that the grants are basically in order but should be accompanied by open criticism of the movements where necessary. They are therefore disturbed by the deliberate refusal to criticize. Other members feel that grants which endeavoured to combine political judgement and humanitarian aims should not be made to political movements of this nature, that humanitarian aims should not be directed through third parties. It was also noted that some of the grants from the Special Fund conflicted with the criteria laid down by the WCC.

6.2. Resolutions and documents relating to the PCR passed by the Provincial Synod of the CPSA [ed: Anglican], the Methodist Conference and the Assembly of the UCCSA (United Congregational Church of Southern Africa) were submitted to the consultation.

    6.2.1. It was recommended that these documents from member churches of the WCC should be forwarded to the Council as part of the documentation.

6.3. It was recommended that the consultation adopt the following statement of the UCCSA (Report of the Task Force, paragraph 6b, noting that the Methodist Conference adopted a stance on sub-paragraph (v):

> 6(b)(iv)
> The Church cannot reduce its commitment to combat racism and to bring about a more just society, but it will fail in its healing and reconciling role unless it advocates change by concrete non-violent means. Not to do so is to leave the field open to military methods.

The United Congregational Church of Southern Africa urges the WCC to consider again the statement made by its former General Secretary, Dr. Carson Blake, in a letter addressed to the German Churches at the time of the inauguration of the Programme to Combat Racism. He wrote:

Violence and the counter-violence it produces are not the best way to obtain real peace and true justice; non-violent methods are at all times to be exalted as the more excellent means to obtain these goods and that even when violence is being used the first task of the Christian Church is to encourage people at the first opportunity to leave the battle field and seek the conference table:

> 6(b)(v)
> Without prescribing how its grants should be used, we would urge the WCC in making further grants to Liberation Movements to ensure that intensive dialogue takes place. The Church should have something to say about the more excellent way, even when violence is already being used.

In proposing the above suggestions for the consideration of the WCC, the Task Force would point out to the Assembly that much bitterness amongst black Christians who are the victims of institutionalized violence has been caused by the ineffectiveness of repeated calls to bring about change by non-violent means. A call to non-violent action by the Church will only be heeded if it is accompanied by effective action to combat racism and injustice. In Southern Africa today, the Church is called to live more excellently than the way it preaches; nothing less will make it in an Alternative Society. Unless this happens, the Church will lose its credibility amongst the black young people, many whom have already left the Church disillusioned.

6.4. While recognizing that certain aspects of the Special Fund are open to criticism, the conference affirms its support for and appreciation of the general aims of the Programme to Combat Racism.

D6.6 The Kairos Document, 13 September 1985

The following are extracts from the first edition of The Kairos Document, pages 14-16 and 20-23.

Non-Violence
The stance of 'Church Theology' on non-violence, expressed as a blanket condemnation of all that is called violence, has not only been unable to curb the violence of our situation, it has actually, although unwittingly, been a major contributing factor in the recent escalation of State violence. Here again non-violence has been made into an absolute principle that applies to anything anyone calls violence without regard for who is using it, which side they are on or what purpose they may have in mind. In our situation, this is simply counter-productive.

The problem for the Church here is the way the word violence is being used in the propaganda of the State. The State and the media have chosen to call violence what some people do in townships as the struggle for their liberation i.e. throwing stones, burning cars and buildings and sometimes killing collaborators. But this excludes the structural, institutional and unrepentant violence of the State and especially the oppressive and naked violence of the police and the army.
These things are not counted as violence. And even when they are acknowledged to be 'excessive', they are called 'misconduct' or even 'atrocities' but never violence. Thus, the phrase 'violence in the townships' comes to mean what the young people are doing and not what the police are doing or what apartheid in general is doing to people. If one calls for non-violence in such circumstances one appears to be criticizing the resistance of young people while justifying or at least overlooking the violence of the police and the State. That is how it is understood not only by the State and its

supporters but also by the people who are struggling for their freedom. Violence, especially in our circumstances, is a loaded word.

It is true that Church statements and pronouncements do also condemn all violence. But is it legitimate, especially in our circumstances, to use the same word 'violence' in a blanket condemnation to cover the people to defend themselves? Do such abstractions and generalizations not confuse the issue? How can acts of oppression, injustice and domination be equated with acts of resistance and self-defence? Would it be legitimate to describe both the physical force used by a rapist and the physical force used by a woman trying to resist the rapist as violence?

Moreover, there is nothing in the Bible or in our Christian tradition that would permit us to make such generalizations. Throughout the Bible the word violence is used to describe everything that is done by a wicked oppressor (e.g. Ps 72: 12-14; Is 59: 1-8; Jer 22: 13-17; Amos 3: 9-10; 6: 3; Mic 2: 2; 3: 1-3; 6: 12). It is never used to describe the activities of Israel's armies in attempting to liberate themselves or to resist aggression. When Jesus says that we should turn the other cheek he is telling us that we must not take revenge; he is not saying that we should never defend ourselves or others. There is a long and consistent Christian tradition about the use of physical force to defend oneself against aggressors and tyrants. In other words there are circumstances when physical force may be used. They are very restrictive circumstances, only as the very last resort and only as the lesser of two evils, or, as Bonhoeffer put it, 'the lesser of two guilts'. But it is simply not true that every possible use of physical force is violence and that no matter what the circumstances may be it is never permissible.

This is not to say that any use of force at any time by people who are oppressed is permissible simply because they are struggling for their liberation. There have been cases of killing and maiming that no Christian would want to approve of. But then our disapproval is based upon a concern for genuine liberation and conviction that such acts are unnecessary, counter-productive and unjustifiable and not because they fall under a blanket condemnation of any use of physical force in any circumstances.

And finally, what makes the professed non-violence of 'Church Theology' extremely suspect in the eyes of very many people, including ourselves, is the tacit support that many Church leaders give to the growing militarization of the South African State. How can one condemn all violence and then appoint chaplains to a very violent and oppressed army? How can one condemn all violence and then allow young white males to accept their conscription into the armed forces? Is it because the activities of the armed forces and the police are counted as defensive? That raises very serious questions about whose side such Church leaders might be on. Why are the activities of young blacks in the townships not regarded as defensive?

In practice what one calls 'violence' and what one calls 'self-defence' seems to depend upon which side one is on. To call all physical force 'violence' is to try to be neutral and to refuse to make a judgement about who is right and who is wrong. The attempt to remain neutral in this kind of conflict is futile. Neutrality enables the status quo of oppression (and therefore violence) to continue. It is a way of giving tacit support to the oppressor.

Tyranny in the Christian Tradition
There is a long Christian tradition relating to oppression, but the word that has been used most frequently to describe this particular form of sinfulness is the word 'tyranny'. According to this once it is established beyond doubt that a particular ruler is a tyrant or that a particular regime is tyrannical, it forfeits the moral right to govern

and the people acquire the right to resist and to find the means to protect their own interest against injustice and oppression. In other words, a tyrannical regime has no moral legitimacy. It may be de facto government and it may even be recognized by other governments and therefore be the de iure or legal government. But if it is a tyrannical regime, it is, from a moral and a theological point of view, illegitimate. There are indeed some differences of opinion in the Christian tradition about the means that might be used to replace a tyrant but there has not been any doubt about our Christian duty to refuse to co-operate with tyranny and to do whatever we can to remove it.

Of course, everything hinges on the definition of a tyrant. At what point does a government become a tyrannical regime?
The traditional Latin definition of a tyrant is *hostis boni communis* – an enemy of the common good. The purpose of all government is the promotion of what is called the common good of the people governed. To promote the common good is to govern in the interest of, and for the benefit of, all the people. Many governments fail to do this at times. There might be this or that injustice done to some of the people. And such lapses would indeed have been criticized. But occasional acts of injustice would not make a government into an enemy of the people, a tyrant.

To be an enemy of the people a government would have to be hostile to the common good in principle. Such a government would be acting against the interests of the people as a whole and permanently. This would be clearest in cases where the very policy of a government is hostile towards the common good and where the government has a mandate to rule in the interests of some people rather than in the interest of all the people. Such a government would be in principle irreformable. Any reform that it might try to introduce would not be calculated to serve in the common good but to serve the interests of the minority from whom it received its mandate.

A tyrannical regime cannot continue to rule for very long without becoming more and more violent. As the majority of the people begin to demand their rights and to put pressure on the tyrant, so will the tyrant resort more and more to desperate, cruel, gross and ruthless forms of tyranny and repression. The reign of a tyrant always ends up as a reign of terror. It is inevitable because from the start the tyrant is an enemy of the common good.

This account of what we mean by a tyrant or a tyrannical regime can best be summed up in the words of a well-known moral theologian: 'a regime which is openly the enemy of the people and which violates the common good permanently and in the grossest manner' (B. Haring, *The Law of Christ*, Vo13, p, 150).

That leaves us with the question of whether the present government of South Africa is tyrannical or not? There can be no doubt what the majority of the people of South Africa think. For them the apartheid regime is indeed the enemy of the people and that is precisely what they call it: the enemy. In the present crisis, more than ever before, the regime has lost any legitimacy that it might have had in the eyes of the people. Are the people right or wrong?

Apartheid is a system whereby a minority regime elected by one small section of the population is given an explicit mandate to govern in the interests of, and for the benefit of, the white community. Such a mandate or policy is by definition hostile to the common good of all the people. In fact, because it tries to rule in the exclusive interests of whites and not in the interests of all, it ends up ruling in a way that is not even in the interests of those same whites. It becomes an enemy of all the people. A tyrant. A totalitarian regime. A reign of terror.

This also means that the apartheid minority regime is irreformable. We cannot expect the apartheid regime to experience a conversion or change of heart and totally abandon the policy of apartheid. It has no mandate from its electorate to do so. Any reforms or adjustments it might make would have to be done in the interests of those who elected it. Individual members of the government could experience a real conversion and repent but, if they did, they would simply have to follow this through by leaving a regime that was elected and put into power precisely because of its policy of apartheid.

And that is why we have reached the present impasse. As the oppressed majority becomes more insistent and puts more pressure on the tyrant by means of boycotts, strikes, uprising, and even armed struggle, the more tyrannical will this regime become. On the one hand it will use repressive measures: detentions, trials, killing, tortures, banning, propaganda, states of emergency and other desperate and tyrannical methods. And on the other hand, it will introduce reforms that will always be unacceptable to the majority because all its reforms must ensure that the white minority remains on top.

A regime that is in principle an enemy of the people cannot suddenly begin to rule in the interests of all the people. It can only be replaced by another government – one that has been elected by the majority of the people with an explicit mandate to govern in the interests of all the people.

A regime that has made itself the enemy of the people has thereby also made itself the enemy of God. People are made in the image and likeness of God and whatever we do to the least of them we do to God (Mt 25: 49, 45).

To say that the regime is the enemy of God is not to say that all those who support the system are aware of this. Many people have been blinded by the regime's propaganda. They are frequently quite ignorant of the consequences of their stance. However, such blindness does not make the State any less tyrannical or any less of an enemy of the people and an enemy of God.

On the other hand, the fact that the State is tyrannical, and an enemy of God is no excuse for hatred. As Christians we are called upon to love our enemies (Mt 5:44). It is not said that we should not or will have enemies or that we should not identify tyrannical regimes as indeed our enemies. But once we have identified our enemies, we must endeavour to love them. That is not always easy. But then we must also remember that the most loving thing we can do for both the oppressed and for our enemies who are to eliminate the oppression, is to remove the tyrants from power and establish a just government for the common good of all the people.

CHAPTER SEVEN

The State Versus the Christian Institute: Schlebush Commission

The turmoil following the debates around the rationale for the 1971 grants of the Special Fund of the World Council of Churches' Programme to Combat Racism to armed liberation movements fighting colonial and racist White minority regimes in southern Africa, and particularly the rise of a new crop of articulate Black community leaders emerging from the Black Consciousness Movement (BC) with whom the Christian Institute found some common cause with, left the latter a radically different organisation from what it was in its founding year. By 1974 the CI was working in close co-operation with the Black Community Programmes, and leading BC proponents were active participants in the SPROP-CAS project.

The change in the programme and in the political quality of the work of the CI was also, in part, provoked by the dramatic self-mutation of the already authoritarian apartheid state into an overt police state in the early 1970s under the leadership of Prime Minister J.B. Vorster. This sharpened the insight of many of the CI members into the illegitimate nature of the South African government, and strengthened their resolve to demonstrate their opposition to it.

A pertinent example of this radicalisation was the organisation of a Pilgrimage of Confession in 1972 by a group of 26 White CI members, later joined by Beyers Naude and the Anglican Archbishop, David Russell, who walked 900 kilometres from the Bible Monument in Grahamstown to the House of Parliament in Cape Town. The pilgrimage began on 16 December, a date celebrated by Afrikaners as the Day of the Vow, as a protest against the migratory labour system and as a confession of guilt for being associated with it as White people who benefit from the economic privileges derived from the unjust exploitation of Black labour **(Document D7.1)**.[91]

On 4 February, in his opening speech of the 1972 parliamentary session, Vorster had announced the establishment of a Parliamentary

Select Committee that would investigate the affairs, funding and activities of several organisations that the State claimed to have a *prima facie* case of subversion against. Upon establishment the committee was chaired by the Member of Parliament for Kroonstad, Jimmy Kruger and consisted of ten members, four of whom were from the United Party, the 'liberal' official opposition.

The organisations that were listed for investigation were: National Union of South African Students, the South African Institute of Race Relations, the University Christian Movement – which had by then ceased to exist – and the Christian Institute. The Wilgespruit Fellowship Centre, a multi-denominational conferencing and training venue, was added to the list during the investigations.

In his first interim report, Kruger successfully recommended that the Select Committee be turned into a Commission of Inquiry, a move which would give it extra-parliamentary judicial powers. When during the course of the commission's operation Kruger was appointed the Deputy Minister, and soon later Minister of Justice and Police, the Commission was chaired by Louis Le Grange for a short while, after which the chairmanship devolved upon Alwyn Schlebusch MP. It came to be known as 'the Schlebusch Commission'. The above-mentioned Pilgrimage of Confession took place amidst the forays of the establishment of this Schlebusch Commission.

The Commission was given extensive judicial authority even though its members were elected politicians and not judicial officers. It had power to subpoena witnesses and to interrogate them. Such witnesses were allowed no legal representation, they had no right to cross-examine state witnesses who testified against them, all proceedings of the commission were held in camera, and witnesses were not allowed to give the press any information about the proceedings. None of the interim findings of the commission could be published or challenged in a court of law even though they would serve as the basis of government action. In addition, the members of the commission were given powers to enter and search the premises of the organisations under investigation. Refusal to cooperate with the commission was an offence punishable by a jail sentence of at least 30 days under the Commissions Act.

Besides the fact that the very establishment of the commission would not have been an unexpected reaction from the repressive apartheid regime, the draconian terms under which the commission was to operate presented the leadership of the targeted organisation with an agonising dilemma of whether to cooperate under these conditions or face jail terms. The SAIRR decided that it would cooperate to refute the government's insinuations against it. NUSAS decided that its subpoenaed leadership would give evidence 'under protest'. An immediate decision on the part of the CI was delayed by a protracted consultation with its entire leadership and by the need to construct a theological response to what the CI perceived immediately as an unwarranted intrusion by the state into the church's legitimate mandate.

On 11 February 1973 the Commission released an interim report on NUSAS. It recommended that urgent action be taken against eight individuals connected with NUSAS. They were placed under house arrest in terms of the Suppression of Communism Act of 1950. Two days later, another set of eight student leaders, this time the SASO leadership who were targeted via the Commission's foray into the affairs of the UCM, were served with banning orders. These included Steve Biko and Barney Pityana, the then President of SASO, restricting them to their home towns of King Williams Town and Port Elizabeth respectively.

A few months later another interim report was issued, this time on the Wilgespruit Fellowship Centre. It was accompanied by a highly publicised government campaign, led by Vorster himself, to impugn the moral character of the events and training programmes held at Wilgespruit. As a result, Mr O'Leary, an Irish national who ran the Centre's Personal Responsibility and Organisation Development (PROD) programme, was deported after 13 years of residence in South Africa.

The O'Leary affair was the *causa bellum* for the CI and its SPRO-CAS staff, who were already subpoenaed by the commission. When their turn finally came in June 1973 Dr. Beyers Naude, Executive Director; Ms Jane Phakathi, the director of the CI's welfare programmes; Rev Brian

Brown, the CI's Administrative Director; Rev Roelf Meyer, the editor of *Pro Veritate*; Rev Theo Kotze, the Director of the Cape Town CI; Mr Peter Randall, the Director of SPRO-CAS and Ravan Press publisher; Rev Danie van Zyl, the Communications Directors of SPRO-CAS; and Mr Horst Kleinschmidt, the White Programmes Organiser of SPRO-CAS, issued a declaration stating their refusal to testify before the commission. On 24 September 1973 Naude went to the Raadsaal in Pretoria, the venue of the commission, entered the witness box and, upon being asked to take an oath, uttered not a word but produced a statement signed by him and four of his colleagues stating their objections to the commission. The statement had been issued earlier as a booklet under the title *Divine or Civil Obedience* **(Document D7.2)**.

On 28 September 1973 the Special Branch of the Police swooped into the offices of the CI and the SPRO-CAS nationally, confiscating financial documents on the orders of the Schlebusch Commission. Immediately hereafter, all the passports of all officers of the CI were seized. On 15 October 1973 Bennie Khoapa, the Director of the CI-sponsored Black Community Projects, was banned for five years, and on 6 December Dr Manas Buthelezi, the CI's Natal Regional Director, was also banned for five years. On 16 November 1973 Beyers Naude was found guilty under the Commission Act for refusing to testify before the Schlebusch Commission and was sentenced to 30 days imprisonment which was suspended for three years.[92]

On 28 November 1973, Naude, together with Peter Randall and Danie van Zyl were charged under the Suppression of Communism Act in their capacities as founders and Directors of Ravan Press for allowing the publication of utterances by a banned person, Paul Pretorius, one of the eight NUSAS leaders banned on 11 February 1973. The publication in question, a NUSAS dossier on unlawful police operations on university campuses, had already been in print and in the hands of the distributors days before Paul Pretorius was banned. The final report of SPRO-CAS, published in the same year as a book edited by Randall titled *A Taste of Power*[93] was peremptorily declared prohibited literature.

Throughout early 1974 the staff members of CI appeared in a series of trials for refusing to co-operate with the Schlebusch Commission. The trials were so rampant and appeared so routine that in the end they were routinely receiving sentences of about 25 days' imprisonment with an option of a fine of R25.00, and further sentences which were suspended. Against the background of these highly publicised trials, Parliament debated legislation which would incorporate commissions such as that chaired by Schlebusch into the normal legislative and judicial process which would ensure that refusal to testify before them would lead to stiffer penalties.[94]

In March 1974 the Affected Organisations Act (No 31 of 1974) was passed. The Act empowered the Minister of Justice and Police, the newly promoted Jimmy Kruger, to appoint an investigatory official, with powers of entry into any premises, search and interrogation, to examine the activities of any suspected organisation. Anyone obstructing the investigatory official or a commission headed by such an official would face a sentence of 12 months imprisonment. Based on the report of the investigatory official or his committee, the Minister could declare that the organisation would not be able to solicit or receive any monies from abroad, and a registrar would be appointed to 'keep an eye' on such organisations.[95] On the recommendation of the Schlebusch Commission's fourth interim, NUSAS was declared 'an affected organisation' on 13th September 1974.

The CI board of management hosted its half-yearly meeting in February 1974, considered the looming effect of this legislation as well as the concomitant amendment then made to the Riotous Assemblies Act to the effect that the police, having made radio announcements by way of warning, may use 'necessary force' to disperse an 'illegal gathering'. They ended the meeting with a press statement which declared that this "legislation now removes all doubt that South Africa is a police state" **(Document D7.3)**.

Raising an objection against the Affected Organisations Act, they pointedly underscoring that, "the curb on organisations receiving financial assistance from anywhere is a denial of the universality of the Christian Church. We are all members of the same body and no secular authority should have the right to prevent one member from assisting another where there is need".[96]

At the end of May 1975, the final Report of the Schlebusch Commission was released with a promptly implemented recommendation: that the CI be declared an Affected Organisation. **Document D7.4** which was originally publicised through the SACC's *Ecunews*[97] is the council of churches' expression of solidarity with the CI leadership. **Document D7.5** is a record of the concluding chapter of the Commission's report bearing all sorts of allegations that were subsequently refuted by the CI.

Following a flood of chronicle-defying repressive acts of the regime around this period – a spate of banning orders, murderous torture and detentions without trial, the imprisonment of the SASO-BPC leadership after the Frelimo Freedom celebrations of 1974, the June 1976 Soweto Uprising, the murder of Steve Biko in detention – when on 19th October 1977, 'Black Thursday', the regime clamped down with finality on this post ANC-PAC political re-awakening, banning all Black Consciousness institutions, the Christian Institute was on the list of the outlawed 19 organisations. Its publication, *Pro Veritate*, was banned together with Percy Qoboza's *The World* and *Weekend World*, and Beyers Naude was slapped with a five-year house arrest order, which was to be renewed for a further five years in October 1982.

D7.1 A Pilgrimage of Confession

A Religious Crisis – the Tearing apart of Families
...We feel moved to set out on this Pilgrimage of Confession because we are deeply disturbed by the situation in our country. We believe that we are in the midst of a most serious social and moral crisis. This society for which we are responsible is tearing husband and wife apart through the system of migratory labour. The lives of thousands of voteless citizens are being daily undermined by this set-up which flouts the command of our Lord: 'What God had joined together, let no man put asunder'.

Something must be done
For a long time, various groups have been drawing attention to the appalling consequences of the system of migratory labour. Violence is being done daily to families in this land – to God's people. It is imperative that something be done to stem the present disastrous trends.

It is not possible for us to 'wash our hands' of responsibility. If we try to opt out we automatically become accomplices – we commit the sin of omission. We betray our Christian calling.

As white Christians we must face the fact that we are identified with the White Power which is responsible for dividing Black families in this land. Moreover, this white power openly acts in the name of the Christian faith. It is therefore all the more urgent that we witness in word and deed to the Gospel of truth.

Resolutions and words though necessary are not enough. If they are not accompanied by effective and sacrificial action, they only testify to a hollow hypocrisy. The very integrity of the Christian Church is on trial in South Africa. The very integrity of each one of us is compromised as long as we condone through our lack of action, the blatant 'putting asunder' of families in our land.

Migratory labour therefore is not only a cancer in the life of our nation; it is a burden on our conscience. Something must be done.

Purpose of the Pilgrimage

We undertake this pilgrimage to communicate afresh the facts about migratory labour to move people to a new awareness of what is happening.

It is not our intention to accuse anyone or to demonstrate against any group; rather we set out on this pilgrimage to confess that we ourselves share the guilt and responsibility for what is being done and to invite fellow white South Africans to confess with us their share in our common guilt.

It is our purpose to encourage people to commit themselves to changing this situation which affronts the law of Christ.

This pilgrimage is symbolic of the personal and spiritual journey which white South African Christians need to make as we risk giving up those privileges and practices which do harm to others. Through this pilgrimage we wish to call others to aim for these goals in faith, with a new determination.

Finally we undertake this pilgrimage to witness to our hope in Christ as the Lord of our history, that in Him we need have no fear of change; that through obedience to Him we will find the way to heal the lives of people which are being undermined by the system of migratory labour; that through following Him we will be given the courage not to rest until His will is done.

Why did the Pilgrimage start in Grahamstown?

In 1837, when the Voortrekker leader Jacobus Uys camped with his party at Grahamstown, Thomas Phillips was delegated to present a Bible and an address of sympathy to the emigrant Boers.

A panel depicting this scene appears in the Voortrekker Monument and also on the Bible monument erected on the actual site at Grahamstown.

Phillips's gift of a Bible to Uys is symbolic of the claim that South Africa is a nation which has resolved to apply the Biblical message about God and man to our personal, political and economic affairs. By beginning our pilgrimage in Grahamstown, we are confessing our faith in God's revelation of himself through the Bible and pledging ourselves to take seriously his demands for justice and fairness; for mercy and concern for others.

Why did the Pilgrimage begin on the Day of the Covenant?

The God who reveals himself through the Bible is a God who involves himself, not only in the personal concerns of individuals, but in the political and economic affairs of a nation. And he does so by making a covenant with his people.

Why are we walking to Cape Town?

White involvement in politics and economy of South Africa began in Cape Town. This is the place where both our sin and the Gospel of Christ began to influence the live of black South Africans. By walking to Cape Town, we will have time to reflect on both these facts of our history. This will give us time to become more aware of the extent of our guilt and to accept both the forgiveness and the demands of Christ.

Cape Town is also the seat of government, of political authority and power, in South Africa. Only Parliament has the authority and the power to change the migratory labour system. By walking to Cape Town, we are requesting Parliament to do what we cannot do; namely, to make it legal for every South African husband and wife wish to do so to live together with their children in a family home.

D7.2 Divine or Civil Obedience: Statement Declaring Refusal to Testify Before the Schlebusch Commission by the Staff of the Christian Institute, 22 June 1973

A witness in the name of Jesus Christ to the commission of inquiry into certain organisations concerning the refusal to co-operate because of obedience to god as the highest authority.

As believers in Jesus Christ we wish to give account before our fatherland, before the Commission and above all before God, of why we cannot co-operate with the Commission and why we regard our refusal to testify as a Christian deed (1 Peter 3:15). The reasons for our viewpoint are set out here.

1. *The Commission's Method of Operation*

1.1 The mandate of the Commission requires that its work be done in secret

> Jesus said: 'For everyone who does evil hates the light and does not come to the light lest his deeds should be exposed. He who does what is true comes to the light that it may be clearly seen that his deeds have been wrought in God' (John 3:20-1).
> Do the following implications of the Gospel of Christ not apply to the Christian Institute, the Government and also to the Commission?
>
> The Church lives from the disclosure of the true God and his revelation, from him as the Light that has been lit in Jesus Christ to destroy the works of darkness. It lives in the dawning of the day of the Lord and its task in relation to the world is to

rouse it and tell it that this day has dawned. The inevitable political corollary of this is that the Church is the sworn enemy of all secret policies and secret diplomacy. It is just as true of the political sphere as of any other that only evil could want to be kept secret. The distinguished mark of good is that it presses forward to the light of day. Where freedom and responsibility in the service of the State are one, whatever is said and done must be said and done before ears and eyes of all, and the legislator, the ruler and the judge can and must be ready to answer openly for all their actions.

'The Statecraft that wraps itself up in darkness is the craft of a State which, because it is anarchic or tyrannical, is forced to hide the bad conscience of its citizens or officials. The church will not on any account lend its support to that kind of State' (*Karl Barth Christengemeinde und Burgergemeinde*). This means that the right and righteousness must not only be done but must also be seen by everybody to be done.

Because the investigation takes place in secret, there is abundant scope for false evidence and damage to the good name of Christians. The ninth commandment says: 'You shall not give false witness against your neighbour'. According to the Nederduits Gereformeerde this means 'that I do not judge, or join in condemning, any man rashly or unheard ... and that, as far as I am able, I defend and promote honour and reputation of my neighbour' (*Catechism*, answer 112).

1.2 Is the freedom of the people who give evidence not curtailed because they are sworn in secrecy? Does it not clash in a similar way with the following implication of the Gospel of Christ?

'The Church sees itself established and nourished by the free Word of God – the Word which proves its freedom in the Holy Scriptures at all times. And the Church believes that the human word is capable of being the free vehicle and the mouthpiece of this free Word of God. It will do all it can to see to it that there are opportunities for mutual discussion in the civil community as the basis of common endeavours. And it will try to see that such a discussion takes place openly. With all its strength it will be on the side of those who refuse to have anything to do with the regimentation, controlling and censoring of public opinion. It knows of no pretext which would make that a good thing and no situation in which it could be necessary.' *(op cit, Karl Bath)*

1.3 Does the Commission not deviate from the normal, acknowledged legal procedures of democracy and is it not true that in so doing it diverges from the rule of law?

Normally this means that the three usual functions, namely the legislative, the judicial and the executive power are attached to three different groups. Here the powers entrusted to the Commission include not only the legislative but also judicial aspects.

Since the Church is aware of the variety of the gifts and tasks of the one Holy Spirit in its own sphere, it will be alert and open in the political sphere to the need to separate the different functions and 'powers' – the legislative, executive and the judiciary - inasmuch as those who carry out any one of these functions should not carry out the other simultaneously. No human is a god able to unite on its own person the functions of the legislator and the ruler, the ruler and the judge, without endangering the sovereignty of the law. R. Wessler confirms the truth: 'The democratic State has definite indispensable characteristic features. To this belongs the division of power of state in (a) legislation, (b) government, (c) justice, which should be separate as far as possible' (*Social Ethics*, p. 142).

So long as the modus operandi of the commission does not adhere to the usual rule of the law of a democracy, neither the individual nor the Christian Institute organization is protected by the accepted legal procedures. The question must be asked whether this does not expose those who appear before the Commission to possible errors of judgement by this authority.

Are not certain indispensable elements inherent in the rule of law, elements which the Commission must of necessity ignore? '... that every person whose interest will be affected by a judicial or administrative decision has the right to a meaningful day "day in court"; that deciding officers shall be independent in the full sense, free from external direction by political and administrative superiors in the disposition of individual cases and inwardly free from the influences of personal gain and partisan or popular bias' (A.W. Jones as quoted by A.S. Mathews, *Law, Order and Liberty in S.A.*, p.15). And further: 'The inevitability of human error ... requires that the law, and the assumptions which underlie it, should be interpreted by a judiciary which is as far as possible independent of the Executive and the Legislature' (Report of the Fourth Committee, *The Rule of Law in a Free Society*, p.279, quoted by A.S. Mathews, op cit. p.45)

The normal legal process protects the basic rights of the individual and limits the power of the governing body in order that it will not become arbitrary power. Is it not clear therefore, that because it by-passes the rule of law and the usual democratic legal procedures, the Commission is in a position to violate justice, basically? If this happens, its power will not be the 'potestas' which adheres to the law and serves it but will become 'potentia' (power for the sake of power), which forestalls justice and subjects it, bends it, and breaks it. This type of authority in itself of necessity becomes evil: 'Notwithstanding their arbitrariness, power and justice are mutually adjoined sides of the God-maintained and ordained existence of man'. *(Macht und Recht,* H. Dombois and E. Wilkins, p.200**).**

The warning must be heard: 'He who takes up the sword shall perish by the sword'. He who employs absolute power shall be destroyed thereby. (Power corrupts, and absolute power corrupts absolutely).

1.4 The Commission's investigation resulted in the NUSAS leaders being punished by the Government, arbitrarily and harshly, by way of banning without trial

As opposed to this the Gospel of Jesus Christ must be stated: 'Jesus answered him: If I have spoken wrongly, bear witness to the wrong; but if I have spoken rightly, why do you strike me?' (John 18:23). This means that if there has been wrong doing according to God's will, then it must be proved openly, and punishment can be meted out. Whosoever does this, does it to Christ himself. '...none of our brothers may be hurt, despised, rejected, misused or offended in any manner by us, without at the same time hurting, despising and misusing Christ through the wrong things we do ... we should care for the bodies of our brothers as for our own' (J. Calvin, *Institution IV*, p.8).

2. The Right and Duty to Resist Unchristian Governmental Authority in the Name of Christ

The believer in Christ not only has the right, but the responsibility to hearken to the Word of God and his righteousness rather than to the Government, should the Government deviate from God's will. Does not the responsibility lie with the Christian not to co-operate with the Government in any matter which is in conflict with the Gospel? By doing so is he not witnessing to Christ and his righteousness?

Civil disobedience is an act of protest by the Christians on the grounds of Christian conscience. It is only permissible when authority expects of him an unchristian deed and pleas for a return to observance of the Gospel have not availed. 'The right of passive resistance can only be applied if it becomes apparent that no other method can overcome the emergency situation and restore righteousness' (H.G. Stoker, *Die Stryd om die Ordes*, p. 243). The State and its Commissions do have authority over the citizens, but in a moral sense the individual has a personal right towards the State for inasmuch as the citizen is part of the structure of the State, he is subject to the authority of the State; as a person before God even within the structures of the State he is, however, totally subject to God. 'In the last instance the Christian is not bound by the State's authority because it is not the final dominion of God and therefore belongs to the being of the historical world which passes (A. Rich, *Glaube in Politischen Entscheidung*, p. 161). Man never belongs totally to the State. He cannot be degraded into being a pawn of the State; the State exists for the benefit of man, not man for the benefit of the State.

Is it possible that the powers granted to this Commission by the Government and the result flowing from it reveal a totalitarian tendency? A totalitarian State usually wants complete control over its subjects. 'It's conflict with the Church is therefore not a coincidence but is inevitable for as long as the Church remains a Church which knows the absolute necessity of its inner independence. Such a State can tolerate the inner independence of the Church even less than its outward independence, because it wants to control the soul of man. Is it the soul that it wishes to control and shape after its own image?' (E. Brunner, *Gerechtigheit*, p.216)

It must be remembered that the most important matter for the citizens of a democratic state is not blind obedience and servile submissiveness to the Government, but joint responsibility for the concerns of State in the sight of God. 'Democracy strives to curtail the freedom of the individual as little as possible, but that freedom must result in maintaining the joint responsibility'. (Wessler, *op cit*. p.142). See also Wolfgang Trillhaas: 'Accordingly, obedience is no longer the predominant problem of the citizen. Much more is it the responsibility (or the joint responsibility) for the success of the State in the political life'. (Wolfgang Trillhaas, Ethik, p.373) It must also be remembered what Reinhold Niebuhr said about the Christian motivation of democracy, namely, that human striving towards justice makes democracy possible, but the human inclination towards injustice makes democracy essential.

It may be that this type of action on the part of the Government reveals tendencies towards fascism, and such a Government then no longer serves but dominates. In such a situation the tendency is to govern by means of arbitrary power and to control by force. Government becomes primarily a power structure. If such a Government continues in this headlong way, the logical outcome is that it becomes idolatrous because everything has to flow out of, through and towards the National State (cf. Revelation 13). The Government's task is not to create arbitrary law. Its task is to reduce to writing in the form of legislation the substantive will of God as revealed in the Gospel. A Government with fascist leanings, however, creates its own justice which it enforces by way of penal sanctions. Anything opposed to the will or policy of such a Government is then regarded as subversive or as dangerous to the State. Freedom is regarded as a concession from the Government and not the normal way of life. In this the Government as well as the Commission will have to answer to God in regard to the bannings and also in regard to punishment which may possibly follow for those who refuse on grounds of conscience to testify before the Commission.

The power of a State such as this is not only territorial and military but also moral. As a result, everything has to be subjected to the authoritarian, co-operative State – nothing is outside its power and authority and it determines the norms, even in relation to conscience. As a result, a person may be led to violate his conscience, make it comfortable and sacrifice it to the State. 'The more sensitive such a conscience is and the more receptive to the will of God, the more dangerous it is to offer it in sacrifice. He who is more obedient to man than to God against his better judgement and his conscience, destroys the integrity of his being, his unity within himself, and sooner or later he falls victim to schizophrenia' (T. Ellwyn, *Freitheit und Bindung des Christen in der Politik*, p.27).

In this kind of State, the real issue at stake is not whether the Government is right or wrong, good or bad, but whether the order, the policy and the will of the State, fails or succeeds.

If the present Government, as shown incidentally by the appointment of this Commission, reveals the above-mentioned traits, should it not be called back to the Gospel of Christ? If we too are guilty, the same applies to us. If such a call is ineffectual '... it becomes a matter of a clash between religious belief and Government, a clash in which man should be obedient to God rather than to the person in authority ...' (H.G. Stoker, op cit. p. 213). The believer can, however, only act outside the law and refuse to co-operate if he acts according to God's will which is being violated by authority. 'Without justification nobody should claim the "right" to offer resistance against the authorities. This justification should in my opinion, include the responsibility of resistance and must be included with the "Higher Authority" in whose name you are acting' (Wolfgang Trillhaas, *Ethik*, p.373).

When reading Romans 13:1, 'Let every person be subjected to governing authorities ...', it must be remembered that the Government does not have authority and power just because it is the Government as such, but because it is 'God's servant' (verse 4). 'The problem about the right to resist ... is in fact contained in Romans 13. We ought to consider whether the term "God's servant" does not include the right to resist when the authorities exceed their God-given mandate and turn away from the clearly articulated commandments of God' (W. Schulze, quoted in W. Künneth, *Politik zwischen Dämon und*

Gott, p. 301). Authority is only legitimate when it does not act contrary to God's will.

The same thought was expressed in the 1973 Studies of the Christian Institute as follows: '... the concept of the Government of a country as a creation and a system of God in itself, is false and a Government is always subject to the righteousness of the Gospel. "It is exegetically no longer possible to base obedience to Government on some peculiar character in them"' (H.W. Bartsch).

'Peter 2: 13, "Be submitted to every human ordinance because of the Lord", must be correctly translated as "Be subject to everyone (every human creature) for the Lord's sake"' (H.W. Bartsch).

'The words in Romans 13; "The Government is ordained by God" and "they are servants (ministers) of God" do not refer to a peculiar commission or dignity of the Government but to what it in fact is, whether it accepts Romans 13 or not. God did not give special commission to the Government as such. The trend therefore, is to debunk the false concept of Governments' (Roelf Meyer, *Poverty in Abundance or Abundance in Poverty?*, p.13).

Where such deviation from the Gospel occurs, it is therefore not only the right of the Christian to resist authority, but his duty to offer passive resistance in obedience to the Gospel, even if in so doing he has to disobey the Government. If a Government violates the Gospel, it loses its authority to be obeyed in its office as ruler. 'The Government loses its essential office because of its contradictory attitude towards God' (W. Kunneth, op cit. p. 294). And: 'As an extension of these thoughts the right, even the duty can be imposed on the subject to resist the tyrant who commits an act of violence against a private person by the misuse of his office' (W. Kunneth, op cit. p.295).

Therefore, one can only speak of Government and its authority '... as long as it is said that it possesses the intention and the capability to accept responsibility for justice and righteousness. If this governmental function is distorted, however, then that Government has dissolved itself, its authority is no longer from God, and it is plainly in conflict with God. As a result of this, according to Romans 13, the Christian is no longer required to be obedient to the guilty (Government), but to a much greater extent obliged to resist such a Government which has degenerated' (W. Kunneth, op cit., p.301).

The Calvinist John Knox also advocates the same idea. In his '... conversations with Queen Mary he had declared not only the right of the nobility to resist in defence of the people but the right of the subject to disobey where the ruler contravenes the law of God' (*Calvinism and the Political Order*, G.L. Hunt, p.14). Calvin championed this same truth in vigorous language: 'Because earthly princes forfeit all their power when they revolt against God... We should resist them rather than obey...' (Lecture XIII).

The authority of the Government and State as such is not rejected in general by these ideas but maintained, because it is still de facto the Government, even if it deviates in essential points from the Gospel and then it has to be resisted. 'Even a distorted governmental system still retains the remnants and elements of the stable order of God' (W. Kunneth, op cit, p. 302).

A step such as this disobeying the Government, must be taken on grounds of Christian conscience. The Christian's conscience is that God-given ability to distinguish between right and wrong according to the criterion of the Gospel, which inwardly compels him to follow the right course. '... Conscience also has the remarkable result that it can suddenly initiate resistance against the Government; an inner distress can also make itself felt when he allows the Government to force him to commit acts which he knows to be wrong'. Paul experiences a similar distress in Romans 9:1,2 (H. Schippers, *Christelijke Enzyclopedie, Deel III*, p.218). Conscience is the inner will that urges one to respond to the conscious norms, and the Christian conscience to resist it. Even if this results in breaking the law, it has to be done because God's will must be maintained above the law of man (Acts 4). The Government is God's servant, and this means that it cannot arbitrarily place itself above the rule of law without impinging on the highest authority. If it does, it becomes the evil doer, (Romans 13) which must be resisted in obedience to God.

3. *Christians May in Prayerful Anticipation Hope*

Christians may in prayerful anticipation hope that a Government which does not conform to the Gospel with regard to a particular matter may be brought to 'rethink' its attitude. They hope for even more; namely, that God's righteousness may become the criterion in every facet of their lives, and particularly in their political life in South Africa. For this they work and pray.

If, however, the Government persecutes a Christian who finds it impossible to co-operate when departure from the Gospel occurs, the pertinent question must be asked: What is the crime against Christ for which he has to be punished? For this the Government would have to supply an answer to God and to South Africa. The Government already persecuting and punishing people in an un-Christian manner, must remember that when Saul persecuted some believers, Christ asked him: 'Saul, Saul, why do you persecute Me?' (Acts 9: 4). Is it not the duty of a Christian in such a situation constantly and in deep humility to call his fellow men to the same obedience in the light of the Gospel? And should a Christian not appeal to the Government in terms of the Gospel to turn away from its wrong course? 'Repent ... even now the axe is laid to the root of the trees; every tree therefore that does not bear good fruit is cut down and thrown into the fire' (Matthew 3).

In conclusion we wish to repeat that we have nothing to hide and that, if an inquiry is necessary (which we do not believe), we are willing to give evidence before a public, impartial, judicial tribunal and to co-operate. We do not wish to make our-selves heroes or martyrs as the Afrikaans press has implied; to us it is not a matter of martyrdom or heroism but a matter of obedience to Christ, the highest authority.

Through the Grace of God, we only want to remain obedient to Christ, the Word of God, because:
Verbum Dei manet in aeternum.

Signed: Theo Kotze, Roelf Meyer, Beyers Naude, J E Phakathi.

D7.3 Statement by The Christian Institute on the 'Police State'

This statement was issued by the CI's Board of Management at its semi-annual meeting at the Wilgespruit Fellowship Centre on 16 February 1974.

1. The curb on organisations receiving financial assistance from anywhere is a denial of the universality of the Christian Church. We are all members of the same body and no secular authority should have the right to prevent one member from assisting another where there is need.
2. While we cannot regard the CI as a 'suspect political organisation' it would be naïve in the extreme not to see this legislation as inextricably connected with the Schlebusch Commission, which has been investigating the CI. Among others.
3. The CI has never made a secret of its commitment to fundamental Social Change in South Africa in line with the principles of the Gospel. The CI is committed to peaceful change. The Government itself, endangers peaceful change, which becomes increasingly impossible when the State takes ever more power to suppress, to intimidate and to control the lives and activities of those individuals and groups committed to change.
4. This proposed legislation now removes all doubt that South Africa is a police state. It is further step in the process of totalitarianism illustrated by the Suppression of Communism Act, the Terrorism Act, the Sabotage Act, the new bill on censorship, and the systematic use by successive Ministers of Justice of powers arbitrarily to ban, to restrict, and to confine those whom he regards as political opponents.

5. We note that the original recommendation of the Parliamentary Select Committee (later the Schlebusch Commission) to set up a permanent tribunal of enquiry composed of members of Parliament has here been amended in the sense that the Committee of Enquiry will be composed of Magistrates. The quasi-judicial appearance of such a committee must not blind us to the fact that real effectiveness lies with the Minister and the quaintly-named officials he will appoint. They are given wide and totally unacceptable powers. This is in fact yet another manifestation of authoritarian, administrative control which helps to clarify the motivations of those who refuse to co-operate with the Schlebusch Commission.
6. We view with abhorrence the yet further invasions of the citizen's privacy and of his rights of association envisaged in the proposed amendment to the Riotous Assemblies Act. The removal of customary and traditional safeguards against abuse of police violence bodes ill for our society.
7. Through this proposed legislation the clash between church and state, between the Christian conscience and the misuse of secular authority becomes yet more apparent and clearly defined. There can be no doubt that the State would not hesitate to use its proposed new powers to interfere in and obstruct the perfectly legitimate activities of Christian individuals and groups seeking to work out the implications of their faith in the socio-political sphere.
8. In view of the serious implication for Christian witness in South Africa, the CI calls urgently on all church leaders in the country to express their forthright condemnation of the proposed legislation and to announce unequivocal resistance to any further attempt by the State to encroach on and restrict the activities of the followers of Christ. It calls on individual Christians to prepare themselves for the pain and suffering which may be the consequence of their resistance to the

unacceptable demand of Caesar. We further call on the opposition parties to resist the passing of the proposal of the proposed legislation with every force at their command.

9. Despite this proposed legislation, the CI reaffirms its calm faith in the wisdom and the providence of God, and its sure knowledge that the efforts of rulers to thwart His will are ultimately futile and doomed to failure.

D7.4 Report of the Schlebusch Commission: Conclusions and Recommendations

[The following is the full text of chapter 9 of the official report of the Schlebusch Commission, which was released in May 1975. It is worth noting that most of its factual claims were disproved by the CI]

9.2 CONCLUSIONS

9.2.1 The Christian Institute is linked to the World Council of Churches as part of the ecumenical movement.

9.2.2 Since its establishment, the World Council of Churches has been active not only in the ecclesiastical sphere, but more particularly also in the social and political spheres, and South Africa was subjected to a barrage of criticism soon after inception of the organisation, in fact, at its second meeting, the World Council's attitude towards South Africa became more and more vehement, culminating in the support of violent action against the Republic in the form of assistance to terrorist organisations.

9.2.3 In this country, the Christian Institute promotes the aim of the World Council, and it is therefore understandable that the organisation operates mainly, if not exclusively, in the political, economic and social spheres. Because of this background, the organisation cannot give an independent and impartial judgement, based on Christian grounds, on political matters. In fact, the ecumenical character claimed by the Christian Institute and the right it also claims to make pronouncements in other spheres by virtue of its constitution or otherwise, have been completely overshadowed by its political activities and by the pronouncements of its mouthpieces, so much so that in appearance, in character and in function, the Institute had become a completely political body with a political destination. It was consequently necessary for your Commission to make an analysis on the principles of canon law of the ecumenical or religious claims of the Institute and its offshoots.

9.2.4 To finance its activities, the Institute works on an annual budget of about R500000. The major part of this amount is obtained from overseas. This financial support obviously results in foreign organisations being able to influence the Institute unduly.

9.2.5 The planners of the Institute's Sprocas II project have set up as an objective the substitution, through a racial conflict, of a Black-dominated socialist system for the existing order.

9.2.6 The establishment of Black Power, which was deliberately introduced by the UCM as a weapon against the existing order in South Africa, was supported by the abovementioned planners as a means of bringing about the desired change, inter alia by engineering a revolution, and the actions of the BCP and the PSC, [Programme for social change] as well as the doctrines of Black Theology form part of the technique of promoting Black Power. Where in this report, the commission expresses disapproval of Black Power, either directly or by implication, it has in mind those aspects of Black Consciousness that have been deliberately developed to foster Black Power, in which process, among other things, innocent Black people are misled and recognised Black leaders and institutions are undermined and denigrated.

9.2.7 The objectives of Sprocas II have been taken over by the Christian Institute itself, and it is actively supporting and expanding them. This means, among other things, that the Institute has concerned itself, through the PSC, with

	economic matters, with the aim of discrediting and replacing the capitalist systems, as explained above.
9.2.8	The Christian Institute, among others, Dr Beyers Naude himself and the planners of Sprocas II, have pursued these objectives and attempted to achieve them in practice regardless of the possibility that their actions might lead to the violent overthrow of the authority of the State. In fact, leaders of the Institute and, in particular, the publication *Pro Veritate*, have consistently conditioned public opinion to accept a possible, even an inevitable, violent change in the existing order.
9.2.9	In the light of your Commission's finding that a Black-dominated socialist state is aimed at, and that violence has been accepted as an element in achieving such a social state, it is clear to the Commission that the strategy adopted by the Institute to bring about the desired change is characteristic of revolutionary socialist technique.
9.2.10	In the light of the cumulative effect of the foregoing findings, the Commission has come to the conclusion that certain activities of the Institute constitute a danger to the State.

9.3 RECOMMENDATIONS

9.3.1	On the strength of its conclusions the Commission considers that certain statutory provisions may apply to the organisation under consideration and recommends that the proper authorities give the necessary attention to the organisation in this connection.

D7.5 Statement of the SA Council of Churches on the Report of the Schlebusch Commission of Inquiry on the Christian Institute

The report of the Le Grange (Schlebusch) Commission on the Christian Institute is rejected by the SA Council of Churches. It rests on the same repugnant presupposition and ramshackle logic we have come to expect from this Commission. We do not believe that the allegations contained in the Commission's report would stand up in a court of law, and we are convinced that for this very reason the Government adopted this method of dealing with uncomfortable critics. We are also more convinced than ever that the Commission's methods of working in secrecy are totally unacceptable, and that those who refused to give evidence before it are fully justified in their actions.

1. One of the presuppositions of this report is that Christians in South Africa have no mind of their own, but slavishly follow the lead of overseas organisations. For instance, on Page 93 of the Report, point 6.2.1 states that 'the idea of radical change is not of South African origin but is a concept or ideology introduced from overseas ...', one of the main sources of this 'ideology' being the World Council of Churches. This is patently absurd. Christians in South Africa do not need to be convinced by anyone outside the country of the need for radical change. Nor is there any validity in the Commission's implication that anyone supporting or having associations with the WCC is a supporter of violence because of the WCC's grants to liberation movements. If this is true, then the SACC and nine major denominations in South Africa – against which the Government has not yet taken any action – must stand charged together with the CI.

2. On this basis, we express our solidarity with and support for the Christian Institute, because if it is judged guilty of the allegations made against it, we must all be said to be guilty. Like the CI, we are 'guilty' of believing in the need for radical change in South Africa (and surely the détente policy of the Government, with its implication of change is also guilty on this count); we are also 'guilty" of supporting Black Consciousness and we are 'guilty' of welcoming the emergence of Black Theology. We must reject as absurd the finding of the Commission that these things point to the CI planning or working toward violent change or racial conflict in our society. In fact, the CI, like ourselves, are working for exactly the opposite – which explains our implacable opposition to apartheid.

3. We express our support and prayer for the director of the CI, Dr Beyers Naude, who has been subjected to the most vicious attack in the Commission's report. We question his being singled out for these attacks, when he is simply representing the views of a strong segment of Christians in South Africa. We believe, however, that to be attacked by this Commission can only add to Dr. Naude's stature. People of this stature, and there are others in South Africa, who represent the challenge of righteousness in their society, are inevitably despised and rejected by that society. But, like Alexander Solzhenitsyn in Russia, they in fact represent the hope of their countries.

4. We re-affirm that in the name of Christ we stand for, and call for, radical change in South Africa. This call has no violent implications, yet has brought persecution, intimidation and the threat of destruction to the Christian Institute. We are aware that we stand in danger of the same pressures. In the light of this we can only conclude with a word of encouragement, to both the CI and all who stand with it, spoken by our Lord

himself: 'Blessed are those who are persecuted for righteousness sake, for theirs is the Kingdom of Heaven. Blessed are you when men revile you and persecute you and utter all kinds of evil against you falsely on my account. Rejoice and be glad, for your reward is great in heaven, for so they persecuted the prophets who were before you' (Matthew 5:10; 12).

CHAPTER EIGHT

The State Versus the SACC: Eloff Commission

After the suppression of Black anti-apartheid institutions in October 1977 the political role and profile of South African churches that were aligned with the South African Council of Churches became more overt. This advance and self-reprofiling of the ecumenical movement owed much to Desmond Tutu's valiant rise as the voice of the oppressed amidst grinding State repression from the time he was installed as the Dean of St Mary's Cathedral in Johannesburg in 1975. He assumed the office of the General-Secretary of the SACC in March 1978, and effectively replaced the banned Christian Institute's Director, Beyers Naude, as the political voice and face of the anti-establishment church in South Africa.

Having worked at the World Council Churches offices in Geneva between 1972 and 1975, his confident management style and impeccable theological leadership was to radically transform the SACC. The manner in which he positioned the work of the SACC ensured that from 1978 onwards, the gathering of the annual National Conferences of the SACC became a much-anticipated item in the nation's annual political calendar.

From its inception in 1968 the SACC was theologically overshadowed by the bold and innovative Christian Institute and seemed to lack stable visionary leadership. Apart from the brief period in which it was led by Mr John Rees – a layperson who heroically saw the SACC through the stormy controversy over PCR's Special Fund – it was not until Bishop Tutu became its General Secretary that the SACC was convincingly seen to be an administratively stable organisation with a nation-wide political and ecclesiastical influence.

It cannot be denied that this transformation of the SACC was largely due to the increased participation of Black people in the leadership of its constituent denominational members, and the way their political-theological self-articulation increasingly commanded respect. Black theological thinkers like Allan Boesak, Manas Buthelezi, Simon Gqubule, Sam Buti and others emerged as formidable analysts of the South African situation whose voices were heard not only by Black people but by the entire South African theological community. Tutu, himself, was an acknowledged pioneering exponent of South African Black Theology.[98]

On the public-political level, the scale and intensity of the brutality of the Vorster regime in suppressing opposition to apartheid gradually positioned the church as the only 'safer' space to express the intolerabilities of the period. One of the resolutions of the SACC's National Conference of 1978 enunciated the organisation's emergence in this role and demonstrated its new sense of purpose. It called for a National Convention; the kind proposed by the All-In Africa Conference at Pietermaritzburg in 1961, insisting that this will be the only democratically acceptable way of settling South Africa's problem (see **Document D2.1**).

This resolution (**Document D8.2**) is emblematic of the way in which the language of struggle had changed since the emergence of Black Consciousness and the June 1976 Soweto Uprising. It had moved from the mere expression of a desire for rapprochement between races to a call for the total dismantlement of the apartheid state apparatus, replacing it with a non-racial democratic social order. To underscore that its apparent political activism is derived with Christian-theological principles of justice and liberation as its core mission, the same conference adopted 'the SACC statement of Theological Principles' (**Document D8.1**).

The novelty of the post 1978 situation was also marked by the rise to power of P.W. Botha, the erstwhile Minister of Defence under J.B. Vorster. Aware of the mounting groundswell of the questioning of the political philosophy of the National Party, Botha (Prime Minster 1978-1984; State President 1984-1989) announced a programme of reforms to apartheid upon assuming office, generating mixed feelings of scepticism and hope in the South African religious community.

The call of the South African ecumenical movement for a National Convention was thus presented as a test of the regime's readiness and willingness to change. It was soon discovered that Botha's reform programme was designed to attract Western investment to South Africa and that it was not a sincere endeavour to relieve the oppressed majority of its misery.

In 1980 the government unleashed traditionally strong-arm methods to suppress nationwide school boycotts that had sought the abolition of racially segregated and government manipulated education. Together with the consolidation of security legislation in 1982, this indicated that even as the regime spoke publicly about reform, it was consolidating and extending its repressive machinery. There was also a perceptible new wave of detentions-without-trial of several key political-community leaders during this period.

A national Consultation on Racism was held in February 1980, as a regional preparation for a WCC-PCR international consultation on racism due to be held in the Netherlands that June. The regional consultation reiterated the demand for a National Convention and instructed the South African delegation to the forthcoming PCR conference to tell the international Christian community not to take P.W. Botha's talk of reform in South Africa seriously until he talked of a democratic and sovereign National Convention (see **Document D5.5**).

The new and subtle form of repression became a rough reality for the church on 20 November 1981, when P.W. Botha announced the establishment of a commission of inquiry into the activities of the SACC, presided over by Judge C.F. Eloff,. Under the chairmanship of Justice Eloff of the Transvaal Provincial Division of the Supreme Court of South Africa, other members the Eloff Commission were Mr. T.L. Blunden, Regional Court President; Professor P. Oosthuizen, Vice-Principal of the University of Pretoria; Mr. F.G. Barrie, former Auditor-General; and Mr. S.A. Patterson, a chartered accountant. Its gazetted Terms of Reference (Government Gazette No 3343) and excepts of its final report, which was released to the public in February 1984, are as in **Document D8.3**.[99]

P.W. Botha and his Minister of Law and Order, Louis le Grange (the Potchefstroom MP who initially headed the investigation against the CI in 1972 that devolved into the Schlebusch Commission) had hoped to do to the SACC what Vorster had done to the CI in 1973. Unfortunately for Botha, he was constrained by his claim to the world that the South Africa he was now ruling was on a reformation path. Therefore, the legal powers, conduct and action in response to the findings of the Eloff Commission had to be more restrained than had been the case when the Schlebusch Commission investigated the CI.

Moreover, the SACC's leadership, having learnt from the experience of the Schlebusch Commission's investigation, left none of the proverbial stones unturned in dealing with the Eloff Commissioners. The SACC turned the whole event into a public media spectacle and a process of theological reflection on the kind of activities in which the SACC was engaged in under mandate of its member churches.

Desmond Tutu's testimony to the commission was released as a widely circulated booklet entitled *The Divine Intention*.[100] The SACC argued that its activities – the provision of financial and legal aid to the victims of state repression and welfare services to victims of apartheid, as well as the occasional public denunciation of State policy in political terms – were not alien to its nature as a Church organisation, that it derived its mandate from God alone, and that the State had neither the ability to evaluate or pass judgement on the activities of the church. Tutu reiterated this position in his address of a press conference in response to the Publication of the findings and recommendations of the Eloff Commission (**Document D8.4**).

The commission expressly recommended against the SACC being declared an 'Affected Organisation', that would have meant it being placed under the administration of a state appointed administrator and be forbidden from receiving funding from foreign donors. The rationale for this non-recommendation was ventilated in the report's Part IV, paragraphs 3.1-3.4.

This fear of clamping down on the SACC was influenced by the fact that the Soweto Uprising and massacre, as well as their aftermath, had intensely focused international attention upon South Africa and that the SACC's work depended to a large extent upon fundraising abroad, and as such involved international publicity against apartheid. The government was aware that its eventual reaction to the SACC would not fail to be noticed by the world it sought to persuade that apartheid with its repressiveness was 'dead'. Professor Oosthuizen, one of the five Eloff commissioners, prepared a separate essay[101] elaborating this argument. It was appended to the official 'Summary of Findings'.

The Eloff Commission's manoeuvre eventually backfired on the South African government. Besides attempts at scandalising some aspects of the management of the SACC, all that could be achieved was a recommendation that "adequate steps be taken to oblige the SACC to come clearly within the operations of the Fund-raising Act, 1978". The report and the SACC's politically charged theological responses to it were read and studied globally by members of the WCC constituent churches and beyond. It gave Bishop Tutu much of the international publicity that led to his winning of the Nobel Peace Prize for 1984. This intensified international attention on apartheid South Africa boosted the momentum of the efforts of the liberation movement both inside and outside the country. In September 1984 black townships, had erupted into waves of mass actions that had marks of an unprecedented resolve to render the apartheid state ungovernable. At the height of this turmoil, P.W. Botha declared a national State of Emergency in June 1985; the same year, Tutu, who then bore the title of the Bishop of Lesotho since 1972, was installed as the first Black Bishop of the Anglican Diocese of Johannesburg. Beyers Naude, whose 1977 banning order had expired, was invited to succeed him as the General Secretary of the SACC.

D8.1 SACC Statement of Theological Principles

Adopted by the SACC National Conference in July 1978.

1. PURPOSE

As an instrument of its member bodies, the SACC is committed to stimulating and strengthening fellowship and co-operation between South African churches in the light of their mission to South African society and to the world community in general. Membership in the SACC is open to church bodies who confess Jesus Christ as their only Saviour and Lord. Such confession requires churches to relate their situation to the interpretation and proclamation of the Gospel as well as to the structures and the service of church institutions.

2. CHURCH BACKGROUND

The 'historical' South African churches (e.g. Anglican, Methodist, Presbyterian, Congregational, Afrikaans Reformed and Lutheran) have roots in Europe. They were transplanted to South Africa by European settlers and immigrants who were anxious to retain their strength, the consolation and life-orientation of the churches in which they had grown up. In their countries of origin some of these churches were aware of a commitment to make provision for the religious needs of members who had settled in South Africa.

At the same time the governments of the newly emerging European communities, be it of the British colonies or of the Afrikaans Republics, were committed to forming states with a Christian orientation. They lent support to those churches which were most acceptable, and the most useful in terms of their general policy.

Under these circumstances, the process of indigenization of South African churches has been slow and difficult. Their doctrinal and polity differences – by which they frequently justify their separate existences – are developed mainly in the European context. Many Christians esteemed them as valuable heritages, to be retained at all costs in the new South African setting.

As a result, churches were slow to re-examine and re-evaluate the individual characteristics by exposing them to the demands and challenges both of the new South African environment and of their common mission obligation.

Moreover, cultural differences within individual denominations had the effect of multiplying divisions between churches. Christians belonging to the same denomination came to South Africa from different countries and spoke different languages.

In their new home country, they had intended to establish their separate church organisations according to their linguistic, ethnic and cultural characteristics. In some cases, they formed virtually separate denominations within one and the same traditional denominational group.

Church life and the relationship between South African Churches were further complicated by the tensions between the English and the Afrikaans-orientated political territories. During the second half of the nineteenth century these tensions gradually came to coincide with the tensions between the English and the Afrikaans communities in all the South African territories.

The political disagreement found its reflection in disagreements between churches working mainly in the English community and churches working primarily in the Afrikaans community. On both sides of the controversy about political hegemony in South Africa, either by the British or by the Afrikaans groups, the churches tried to justify their respective stand by theological arguments.

Mission churches

The second category of churches, the so called 'mission churches', owe their origin to mission activities of South African churches or mission societies based in Europe. For a long time, mission work in the Black communities in South Africa remained dependent on churches in Europe or on white congregations in Southern Africa. In several denominations Black congregations were incorporated with white congregations into one church organisation. In other cases, separate church organisations were established for the black community or for the different ethnic groups within the Black community, giving rise to mission churches. In both cases the leadership of the churches was for a long time was mainly in the hands of White Christians.

Church life was shaped largely according to European traditions and according to the example of European church institutions. Indigenization of church life in forms relevant to the proclamation of the gospel in a context of African culture was slow to develop.

Independent churches

A third category, the African Independent Churches emerged from the 1880's as a reaction to the predominance of white leadership in the mission churches. These churches were also a result of the neglect of specific aspects of the biblical message, which in the opinion of many Black Christians, did not have sufficient recognition in the traditional Western and in the Mission churches (e.g. healing).

A desire to express and proclaim the Christian faith in forms relevant to African culture and the concern to relate the gospel to the political oppression and economic deprivation of Black people, were other factors in the emergence of Independent Churches. They became a strong missionary movement and comprise today 23,000 groups with approximately 2-3 million adherents.

They offer new forms of fellowship and encourage mutual support among their members. In doing so they fulfil an urgent need in a society in which traditional forms of community are being uprooted.

Results in disunity
The failure of South African Churches to achieve a greater degree of unity and co-operation has had far reaching consequences. Since the resources of the churches were largely consumed in securing and protecting their own identity, decisive developments in the social and political and economic life of the country were allowed to take place without being effectively exposed to the challenge of the Gospel. Political and economic power was concentrated more and more in the hands of the Whites. A large section of the Black people were impoverished, especially in the rural areas. While industrialization led to the formation of a strong group of Black workers, the proclamation and the service of the churches, was adapted only in slight degree to the needs and the problems arising in an urban Black industrialized community. In addition, the churches largely lost their influence on the public educational system, since without much opposition on the part of the churches the State was allowed for its own ends, especially for the purpose of indoctrination.

Although church leaders have in recent years drawn attention to the injustices in the South African political, social and economic system and to the oppression and suffering to which Black people are exposed, their voices have not on the whole had much impact on the church constituency and the government.

The political authorities were anxious to obtain the ideological or religious sanction of the churches for their policies. A racist ideology intending to protect the entrenched privileged position of the white group received support from a wide section of the white population.

It is true that objections were raised by overseas partner churches against obvious injustices and practices of oppression in the South African system. But on the other hand, strong economic groups in foreign countries had an interest in the maintenance of the present South African structures.

In spite of their verbal protests against the policy of separate development they tended to support or at least not directly to challenge the power structures in Southern Africa.

Other faiths

Another characteristic of the South African context which did not receive sufficient attention in the proclamation and theological reflection of South African churches, was the encounter between Christians and members of other faiths.

From the outset South African churches received much support in finances and personnel from overseas partner churches. Since the South African situation is a reflection of the challenges facing churches on a global level, overseas partner churches have shown a strong interest in the way in which South African churches have responded to the demands of their situation.

The South African context, in fact, can be regarded as the test bench for Christian churches on a global level as they wrestle with the problems of the 20th Century.

It is in this situation that the SACC is committed to stimulating co-operation between South African churches in view of their mission to South African society and the world community at large.

3. BASIC PRINCIPLES

God has accepted man through Christ unconditionally. In relying on this acceptance the believer is enabled to love his fellowman unconditionally and to contribute towards justice and peace in human relationships.

4. OBJECTIVES

The SACC is aware that this core of the biblical message has to be witnessed in South African society in the proclamation and practice of a fellowship which transcends ethnic, racial and cultural differences between people. The practice of such fellowship is an integral part of the witness of the Church. As believers are incorporated into and nurtured within the community of Christ their Lord, they are equipped to resist the forces that cause division and strife in society and between and within the churches.

In South Africa, this message must be proclaimed, and this new life practised in a society structured on the principle that mutual rejection of each other by people of different ethnic and racial backgrounds is an inescapable fact which cannot be overcome. It is therefore maintained that peaceful relationships between people and groups of different backgrounds can be achieved only by separation.

At the same time it is said that members of the various Black racial and ethnic groups can develop their gifts only if they are separated – the rationale of the so called 'homeland policy'. This concept is used to justify withholding from Blacks a share in the political power and in the resources of the country, and thus for ensuring the maintenance of the entrenched privileges of the White people.

In view of the widespread acceptance of this belief – which denies the Gospel of man's unconditional acceptance on behalf of Christ – the SACC is committed to assisting its member churches to find forms of fellowship and co-operation which will bear witness in South African society and testify the implications of the message they proclaim.

The SACC is willing to assist its member churches in efforts to overcome the doctrinal obstacles that hinder them from practising full fellowship of altar and pulpit. The SACC is convinced that in spite of doctrinal differences, based on different interpretations of the biblical message, a greater degree of unity can be achieved by a joint search for biblical truth and its implications.

Furthermore the SACC is anxious to help churches discover structures which not only express their unity, but also, allow scope for the retention and development of valuable aspects of their different heritages through which they can enrich and strengthen each other.

Secular authorities

With regard to secular authorities responsible for justice, peace and freedom in Southern Africa and in international relationships, the SACC infers from the biblical message that God has instituted such authorities as his instruments in order to ensure the preservation, the development and wholesomeness of human life.

It therefore desires to show loyalty to the authorities. But the deepest form of loyalty is a clear proclamation of the Gospel of the unconditional acceptance of man by God. Thus, the SACC encourages member churches to make their people aware not only of the legitimate demands of political authorities, but also of the limits of authority.

The State undermines its authority by denying the limits of its power. The confessions of man's unconditional acceptance through Christ obliges the churches and their members to oppose the State in all legislation and in all measures, which harm the dignity God has accorded all men, irrespective of their influence, their education, their economic power or their cultural political background.

The SACC and its member churches do not claim a right or authority to dictate a political programme to political authorities. They are however, committed to drawing attention to the obligation of the State to provide for the protection of the weak against exploitation.

The SACC has a special interest in contributing towards a concept of human rights which will be respected and entrenched in the constitution so as to be a criterion for all legislation.

From the biblical message the SACC infers that God's unconditional love is to be extended to all mankind. God is concerned about the preservation of human life and uses man as his co-worker to ensure peace, justice and freedom in human relationships.

The SACC is thus committed to drawing attention to the interdependence of peoples and nations and to their common responsibility for ensuring peace and justice in the world community. The SACC therefore opposes a concept of the sovereignty of the state which allows political authorities to pursue policies endangering internal or international peace.

In its efforts to assist churches to recognise and practise their responsibility for contributing to peace, justice and freedom in their own country and internationally, the SACC stresses the concept and the practice of Christian love as that which always transcends the possibilities of the law.

Love cannot be embodied in legal regulations. On the other hand, the concept and the experience of God's unconditional love motivates the churches and their members to contribute, by their witness and their service, to structures which serve God's loving concern for the preservation and fulfilment of human life and which protect individuals and groups, particularly the weaker sections, against oppression and exploitation.

The SACC is aware that human selfishness will remain a powerful force in human relationships and will be uprooted ultimately with the second coming of the Lord. But precisely for this reason the SACC is under an obligation to encourage and assist member churches to relate all spheres of life, including the political and economic sphere, to the Lordship of Christ in proclamation and service.

In its concern for the preservation and the development of human life for justice in human relationships, the SACC draws attention to groups in society who tend to be neglected and overlooked because they find it difficult to make their voices heard. This applies especially to the aged, the handicapped, the mentally and physically retarded, political detainees and prisoners, as well as their families, etc.

In many cases traditional forms of Christian charity have not taken into account the harm done to the dignity of these people by making them dependent on help from fellowmen. The SACC desires to encourage a form of social responsibility for suffering fellowmen, in which their gifts are recognized and developed, and through which they are helped to fulfil, in their way, a service to the community.

The SACC is convinced that the way in which the members of the above-mentioned 'fringe-groups' are regarded and assisted by churches and their members is a crucial test, revealing whether the churches really believe what they proclaim – that man has been accepted by God through Christ without any conditions attached.
In attempting to help churches and their members to practise freedom and the new life which has been entrusted to them by their Lord, the SACC is aware of theological arguments propagated through the mass media and educational institutions to blind people to the practical implications of their faith in the South African context.

The SACC opposes anything designed to make people believe that certain spheres of life such as politics and economics lie outside the concern of the Gospel. It rejects any attempts to persuade people to accept conditions as they are, thus ignoring the fact that the Gospel of God's unconditional love in Christ emancipates the Church FOR action and responsibility.

The SACC rejects the concept of a 'Christian State' which assumes that a political programme can be the ultimate embodiment and realisation of Christian love.

It also rejects the tenet that any law or statute can oblige a Christian to desist from the duty of resisting the abuse of power by the authorities. If such laws or statutes cause harm to a society and serve the interests of some in conflict with both reason and God's loving will as revealed in the Biblical message, it is the duty of Christians to be obedient to God rather than man.

D8.2 SACC 1978 National Conference Resolution: Call for a National Convention

a. Believing that the Church cannot remain passive in this time of crisis and that the present state of separation, division and suspicion can only escalate into bloody Civil War, this National Conference of the SACC supports the many calls which have been made by South Africans for the holding of a National Convention, where all the true leaders of our people can jointly plan the future.

We believe that only by creating an opportunity for open and honest debate can the fears and hates which exist at present be explored and through God's grace be transformed into dynamic hope for a peaceful future.

Furthermore, believing that it is not sufficient to make merely verbal demands, we argue all Christians to put their faith and commitment to our Lord Jesus Christ before all racial, cultural and linguistic considerations and to prepare to suffer and to sacrifice in order to ensure that such a convention takes place.

b. The Conference requests the Division of Justice and Reconciliation to give most urgent attention to identifying ways in which Christians and member churches could strengthen, support and render effective the demand for a National Convention.

D8.3 The Eloff Commission Report: Official Summary And Recommendations

[The Eloff Commission was appointed by the P. W. Botha, on 20 November 1981, and its appointment and composition were publicised in the ***Government Gazette No 3343***, which states its terms of reference as follows:]

To inquire into and report (and if the Commission deems it desirable, to make recommendations) on –
a. the inception, development, objects and any other aspect regarding the history of and activities of the South African Council of Churches, including the way in which it functions and is managed;
b. the way in which, the purpose for which and the organisations and persons from and through whom the South African Council of Churches and persons connected with the South African Council of Churches solicited or solicit or obtained or obtain money or valuable assets;
c. all money and valuable assets that were or are received by the South African Council of Churches and the persons connected with it;
d. the organisations and persons from whom or through the agency of whom and the way in which such money and assets were or are received;
e. how and for what purpose such money and assets were or are disposed of by the South African Council of Churches and the persons concerned;
f. in the case of such money and assets having been paid over or made over to someone else by the South African Council of Churches and the persons concerned, how, to or through the agency of whom and for what purpose the money and assets

were paid over or made over and how and for what purpose that money and assets were or are being ultimately used; and
g. also, any other matter pertaining to the South African Council of Churches, its present and past office-bearers or officers and other persons connected with the South African Council of Churches, on which the Commission is of the opinion that a report should be made in the public interest.

REPORT
[The 451-page-long report of the Commission was released to the public in February 1984. The following is Part IV of the report (Report of the Eloff Commission of Enquiry on the SACC, RP.74/1983, Government Printers, Pretoria, pp. 427-443). Following are excerpts, with only irrelevant repetitions omitted]

1. The historical review of the SACC in this report, and the detailed examination of some of its activities, indicated the emergence of the following trends:

   1.1 From an organisation whose main activity originally was the co-ordination of efforts to spread the Gospel, and whose principal interests lay in spiritual matters, the SACC developed into one largely concerned with political, social and economic issues, and having specific objectives in those fields.

   1.2 This development went hand in hand –
      1.2.1 with the growth and acceptance of ecumenism, with its emphasis on the essential unity of man and the idea of the involvement of the Church in all of the activities of mankind, including political, social and economic matters; and
      1.2.2 the domination by Black Christians of member churches of the SACC, and the emergence of liberation or Black

theology, with its close relationship with Black Consciousness and Black Power, and a concomitant political involvement.

1.3 While the SACC initially confined itself to strong criticism and even condemnation of the policies of Government, it increasingly gave practical effect to its stance by adopting and pursuing 'strategies of resistance to the Government'.

1.4 The main feature of the afore-mentioned actions is that they were designed to force the pace and direction of change which the SACC considered the Government should adopt; the SACC opted for a revolutionary rather than an evolutionary process.

1.5 In the process of planning the above-mentioned actions and giving practical effect to its stance, the SACC increasingly identified or aligned itself with the struggle termed the 'liberatory struggle', waged on many fronts by several organisations having the common aim of achieving radical socio-political and economic changes in South Africa.

1.6 The 'strategies of resistance' designed or adopted by the SACC for the furtherance of its 'liberatory struggle' include –

1.6.1 An extensive propaganda campaign described by the General Secretary as 'massive psychological warfare', designed:
– internationally, to persuade foreign governments or organisations to bring political, economic or diplomatic pressure to bear on the Government;

- locally, to 'conscientise' Whites and to politicise Blacks; and
- generally, to endeavour to discredit the State and its institutions such as the Defence Force and the Police Force, as embodiment of the capitalist system.

1.6.2 An extensive campaign of civil disobedience and non-co-operation with the State.

1.6.3 Support for the disinvestment campaign.

1.6.4 Support for those who seek to avoid the performance of compulsory military service.

1.6.5 The ceaseless prognostications of imminent violence if the Government does not rapidly abandon 'apartheid' or the policy of separate development.

1.6.6 The display of sympathy and solidarity with, and at times even the granting of aid to, those who in some way or another come into confrontation with the State or its institutions, such as striking school teachers, militant Black consciousness movement and militant Black trade unions.

1.7 While the SACC failed to secure significant grass-roots support for the above-mentioned activities from its constituents, and to obtain anything but minimal financial support from its member churches or indeed any other local source, it had little difficulty in obtaining extensive funding for its activities from overseas churches, church bodies, government and other organisations.

1.8 In the course of time the SACC distanced itself significantly from its constituent member churches, becoming in the process an independent bureaucratic body, with its staff playing a dominant role.

1.9 In the past few years the members of the SACC staff whose contributions were the most significant, were its General Secretary, Bishop D. Tutu, and the Director of its Division of Justice and Reconciliation, Dr. W. Kistner. The former was conspicuous for his efforts to conduct propaganda, mainly by his speeches and other public pronouncements. The latter was responsible for the planning of many of the 'strategies of resistance' of the SACC.

1.10 With the rapid expansion of its activities and inflow of funds from abroad, the SACC increasingly neglected its financial administration, particularly from 1975 onwards ...

1.11 Secret and covert operations increasingly characterised the activities of the SACC: it endeavoured to conceal the origin of certain of its funds, and the manner in and purpose for which some of those funds were expended; and in its involvement in the civil disobedience campaign its Director of Justice and Reconciliation planned the use of 'underground groups' whose actions would be inconspicuous.

1.12 The afore-mentioned policies and strategies of the SACC and its involvement in the 'liberatory struggle' were intended also to obstruct the Government in its declared endeavour to effect change by a process of evolutionary development, in which the emphasis is to be on the rights of minorities. Any moves by the Government to carry out its intentions are denigrated, except in rare instances involving minor issues.

2.1 The commission considers that –

2.1.1 the civil disobedience campaign of the SACC has a potential for destabilisation; and that –
2.1.2 the covert encouragement of disinvestment by certain SACC officials; and
2.1.3 the SACC's support of those who resist participation in compulsory military service, are not in the national interest.

2.2 Specifically with regard to the encouragement of disinvestment, the Commission recommends that consideration be given to the question whether the Internal Security Act, 1982, is capable of entertaining as an offence the commission of acts of economic sabotage, including the sort under discussion in this report, which are perpetrated in order to achieve a political aim. In order to remove all doubt, the Commission recommends that consideration be given to the creation of a specific offence of economic sabotage.

3. The commission does not recommend that the Government should take any steps in terms of the Affected Organisations Act, No 31 of 1974.
In the opinion of the majority of the members of the Commission the following reasons exist for not invoking the provisions of this Act:

3.1 To render the SACC ineffective by a declaration under the Act is not likely to cut off the bountiful flow of funds from abroad to assist 'the victims of apartheid' or to halt member churches of the SACC in their pursuit of substantially the same sort of objectives as those endorsed by the SACC. There was cogent proof before the Commission of a strong overseas commitment to provide assistance. To debar the SACC from receiving such funds will not present serious or insuperable obstacles to achieving the same result in some other way, for example by way of donations direct to member churches.

3.2 The invocation of the provisions of the Act will be seen by many Christian constituents of the SACC's member churches as an unwarranted action by the State against the Church and as a restraint on religious freedom.

3.3 Of importance is the fact that no overseas donor of the SACC coupled its financial contribution to the SACC with any endeavour to influence its political stance, or the thrust or direction of its policies. The clear uncontradicted evidence before the Commission was that the SACC itself at all times laid down its policy and formulated its credo long before it began to become overly dependent on overseas financial support. It was furthermore established by the evidence that the SACC itself prepared its own budget, and determined its projects and priorities before it approached its overseas partners. There was no evidence of the SACC being manipulated by overseas donors.

3.4 The SACC performs acts to help the needy and deserving, and although the amount of money spent in this direction can only be described as meagre when compared with that used for mainly political purposes, innocent people will suffer if the SACC were to be rendered largely ineffective...

4. The member churches of the SACC should take note of the fact, as found by the Commission, that the confrontationist stance of the SACC tended over the years to harden, and that with the passage of years additional strategies to give practical effect to its stance were planned. Should this tendency increase, the State may feel obliged to apply restrictive measures.

5. The Commission considers it advisable that statutory control should be imposed on the finances of the SACC.

   5.1 There are at present two statues which establish control over the raising of funds by organisations and persons, and on the application of funds so collected.
   5.1.1 The Fund-raising Act, No.107 of 1978 ...
   5.1.2 In terms of section 2 and 3 of the Act an organisation intending to collect contributions must apply for authorisation so to do to the Director of Fund-raising, who may grant written authority 'subject to the prescribed conditions and such other conditions as may be specified...'It then becomes a fund-raising organisation ...
   5.1.7 It seems to be reasonably clear that, unless it can be said that the exempting provisions of section 2 apply to the SACC, it would, by reason of its collecting contributions in the RSA and overseas, have had to apply to become a fund-raising organisation, and would have been subjected to disciplines imposed by the Act. It in fact never applied, nor does it seem that any steps were taken to enforce the provisions of the Act as far as the SACC is concerned. It is probable that, had such steps been taken, the SACC would have contended that it fell within the ambit of the above-quoted exempting provision. It might claim that it is a religious body which collects funds in terms of its written authority and that this is done exclusively for the purpose of promoting the religious work of the body. If the SACC were to be faced with the contention that the application of funds for such purposes as, for example, the financing of the defence of persons charged with political offences or the support of Black workers on strike, is not religious, it might answer that according to its biblical perceptions it is religious work. It is part of "caring for the least of our brethren". It in fact in 1982 exempted itself from the

provisions of the Act "on grounds that it is not answerable to secular authority" (EOC Minutes, 17 June 1982).

In his evidence before the Commission Bishop Tutu also said:
> And the position is that we believe that everything we do is religious, and that it therefore falls within the rubric of that particular clause in the Fund-raising Act.

Having regard to the rather vague dictionary meaning of 'religious work' a court having to adjudicate on such a question might conclude that 'religious work' means different things to different people, and might find that it is at least uncertain whether the SACC falls within the operation of Part I of the Act. In the only case of which the Commission became aware where a prosecution under the Act was instituted for activities connected with the SACC, S v. Begbie, 1982 (that was when a Methodist minister was charged because he had collected funds to finance the defence of Mr J.C. Rees) the accused was acquitted on the basis that he on reasonable grounds believed that the collection was legitimately organised by a church.

5.1.8 The second statute which should be mentioned is the National Welfare Act, No. 100 of 1978, which requires the registration of welfare organisations... However, all that need be stated for present purposes is that while the definition in the Act of 'social welfare services' is rather confined and limited, it will embrace at least some of the supporting functions exercised by the SACC ...

6.1 The Van Rooyen Commission, whose report led to the creation of the Act, recommended that the exemption should be restricted to bona fide churches which collect money from their members...There would only be confrontation with the churches (said the Minister) if they began to become political organisations. And so the exemption was cast in its present form.

Enough is said elsewhere in this report regarding the SACC and many of its member churches to show that its involvement in what is by many said to be purely political matters is considered to be biblically justified; but it is equally clear that when the Minister presented the Bill to Parliament he had a more conservative idea of what the proper sphere of interests of religious bodies should be. He probably would not have proposed the present wording of section 33 in order to exempt an organisation such as the SACC from the provisions of Chapter I of the Act in order to enable it to assist political offenders and strikers.

6.2 In view of the SACC's unfortunate history...of allowing a state of affairs to continue in which large sums of money could be misappropriated, and of omitting to have part of its application of the Asingeni Fund audited, and also by reason of the size of the funds involved, it is necessary that more effective controls be introduced. It is true that the SACC has done much to improve its administration, but what happened before can happen again ...

6.4 The principle that organisations such as the SACC, and organisations performing functions such as it does, should be subjected to some sort of State control is well established in Western countries ...

11. The Commission accordingly recommends that adequate steps be taken to oblige the SACC to come clearly within the operation of the Fund-raising Act, 1978 ... we recommend that the State law advisers prepare a suitable

amendment reflecting the idea that only truly spiritual purposes are not included. The substitution of the word 'spiritual' for 'religious' might be adequate.

D8.4 SACC Response to the Findings of the Eloff Commission

A Response to the Publication of the Findings and Recommendations of the Eloff Commission by SACC General Secretary, Bishop Desmond Tutu, 15 February 1984

[The following is a transcript of an address Bishop Tutu delivered at a press conference in Johannesburg as the SACC's response of the findings of the Eloff Commission.]

When I appeared before the Eloff Commission I said I did not wish to impugn the integrity of the Commissioners. I want to reiterate as vehemently as I can what I then went on to say: That Commission had no competence at all to sit in judgement on the SACC and its member churches. I said then and want to repeat for all to know that no secular authority, not even the Government of the land, has any authority to sit in judgement about how churches are to fulfil their God given mandate to work for the extension of God's kingdom of justice, peace, reconciliation, compassion, laughter, joy and goodness to serve Our Lord Jesus Christ by serving those He has called the least of His brethren.
I want to agree whole-heartedly with the honourable Commission on at least one point. They have little understanding, as they declared, of theological verities. And how in the name of everything that is good could they be expected to make a judgement that would be even remotely fair if they had little or no theological expertise? The whole matter of our existence, the raison d'être of the Council, is theological through and through. The Commission did not boast a single professional theologian in its membership and how could it be expected to pass fair judgement on an organism and organisation whose every reason for existence is theological from beginning to end. It really was like

asking (speaking respectfully) a group of blind men to judge the Chelsea flower show.

No one can understand why we exist as a Council and why we do and say the things we do unless they understand our theological, biblical justification for doing so. We are not and have never before been inspired by an ideology, political or otherwise. It is not politics that impels us to speak up against the vicious and iniquitous policy of forced population removals exemplified so aptly today by the forced uprootal of a stable and settled community in Mogopa, something that has outraged the world.

It is not a political philosophy that makes us declare apartheid to be wholly immoral, unbiblical, evil and unchristian without remainder, to say that it is the most vicious policy since Nazism and (Stalinist) Communism; it is not politics that makes us say that Bantu Education is designed to be inferior and an abomination, a system intended to turn blacks into perpetual serfs no matter how much more money is being spent on it; it is not politics that compel us to condemn the migratory labour system which forces married men to live unnatural lives for eleven months of the year in single-sex hostels helping to destroy black family life not accidentally but by the deliberate policy of a Government that declares itself to be Christian; it is not politics that say we cannot remain silent when such a government dumps God's children in arid poverty-stricken Bantustan homelands making them starve not accidentally but by their deliberate government policy.

No, my friends, no South Africa, we are constrained by the imperatives of the Gospel of Jesus Christ. Until my dying day I will continue to castigate apartheid as evil and immoral in an absolute sense and I will burn my bible as I have promised before, and cease to be a Christian if anyone can prove to me that I am wrong in my view about apartheid. This Commission did not have the theological nor the moral competence to pass judgement on us on that score. We are not answerable to a secular authority, not even the government of the land, to give an account of how we have sought to obey the injunctions of God alone and then to our member churches. To the latter we have given adequate reports on a regular basis of our stewardship and to our donor partners and they alone have the right to call us to book – not the government of this land or any other land. We have said that this Commission was totally superfluous. If we have contravened any laws of this land, then we should have been charged in an open court. This government has a formidable phalanx of draconian legislation on the statute book which they could use. In any case they have not been known to be bashful about passing new legislation to deal with awkward customers.

And I want to challenge them even now on the basis of the findings of their own Commission to bring charges against us for having contravened any of their laws and to make those charges stick in an open court. That a former employee of the Council, a man who helped develop this Council into this impressive instrument for good in the hands of God was found guilty in a court, does not discredit the Council. If that were so certain banks whose officials were guilty of fraud would have to be similarly condemned. Recently a member of the SADF was found guilty of malfeasance in dealing with a certain SADF Fund. That conviction was not used to malign and discredit the SADF and have it accused of being criminal. Equally therefore if Council employees or officers should be convicted of criminal offences that should not be used as a stick with which to beat the SACC, for it is mainly the SACC that is being criticised in this report, it is the SACC that must therefore be brought to court, arraigned and convicted. I challenge the Government to do that.

This Commission had no competent theologian. What is more is it was sitting in judgement on an organisation which was largely (i.e 80 per cent) black. Was there a black Commissioner among them? He was invisible to me. The perspective of the commission was an entirely White perspective. With due respect, all the Commissioners are people who benefit daily from the vicious socio-political dispensation which we want to see changed. They have spoken like whites threatened by the fear that their privileges would disappear or be significantly modified if we were to have a more just and more democratic setup in South Africa. Have anyone of them or their families been part of the three and half million blacks uprooted in the forced population removal schemes; have they lived in squatter resettlement camps such as Winterveld and Onverwacht? Have their wives been arrested and harassed having to sit in the cold winter rain with plastic covering that the police callously destroyed at Crossroads? Have their homes been demolished at 2 a.m. as happened recently in Bekkersdal; have they lived in single sex hostels; have they had to pay school fees for a travesty of an education with overcrowded schools and underpaid and ill trained teachers?

What do they know about starvation in the homelands as a personal experience; what do they know about being stopped on the way to work and being thrown into a police van because your pass was not in order; have they been in solitary confinement or detention without trial; have they been banned without a chance to know the charges facing them or being granted opportunity to defend themselves and to cross examine their faceless accusers? Or have any of those they hold dear suffered these indignities? What do they know of that humiliation and anguish? What do they know of living in a match box house in a drab ghetto even when they could afford to live elsewhere more luxurious? What do they know about being declared an alien in your own motherland because those who at the moment wield power say you are no longer a South African citizen but the citizen of a spuriously independent pawn of apartheid you have never seen before in your life? What do they know about the agony of a mother whose children have gone into exile and she does not know where and whose husband is serving a life sentence for having the audacity to think that he was a human being and who has not had a contact visit with her husband for twenty one years of his incarceration? Have they visited a resettlement camp or a black ghetto?

They have vested interest to keep things as they are with a white minority enjoying the vast privileges of their whiteness, benefiting from the oppression and exploitation of blacks. Have they asked black people who have received legal assistance when facing serious charges? Have they asked the families of political prisoners who have had virtually their only support from the SACC what they thought of the SACC? Have they asked the high school and university students who have received the opportunity of an education only because of a grant from the SACC what they thought of the SACC? I refer to the 1,000 new high school students each year who have obtained SACC bursaries to go to government schools. I refer to the 100 new University students each year who have obtained SACC bursaries to enable them to go to University. Have they asked even one of these what they thought of the SACC? Have they asked the old people who receive blankets to protect them against the winter cold from the SACC what they thought of the SACC; have they asked those who got clean water supplies, self-help project grants, health education, help with growing their own food through the auspices of the SACC what they thought of the SACC? I can say almost without fear of contradiction: 'No', if they have spoken to blacks it will have been with stooges who would say what they thought their white master wanted to hear.

My dear friends, have they asked striking workers whose families received relief assistance form the SACC what they thought of the SACC – No because virtually all the blacks would say the SACC has helped us to keep body and soul together, the SACC has given us hope, the SACC has helped us get an education. The SACC has helped us believe in a God who cares about injustice, about unemployment, about hunger, about harsh laws, about vicious forced population removals. My dear friends, these are the activities that the Commission has considered subversive, confrontational, etc. With respect I may say, that is adulterated and arrant nonsense. I told the Commission that they should tell those who appointed them that I myself do not fear them. I have said it before and I say it again that those who think they are in immense power today, must take a lesson from history. I warned them that if they took on the SACC then they must know they are taking on the Church of God and other tyrants before them have tried to destroy the Church: Nero, Amin, Hitler, Bokasa, etc. Where are they today? They have bitten the dust ignominiously. I warned the South African government again – they are not gods, they are mere mortals who will end up as mere marks on the pages of history, part of its flosam and jetsam. I am not afraid of them. The worst I said that they could do to us when their disgraceful efforts to discredit us have failed as they have, is to kill me, but who said death is the worst thing that can happen to a Christian?

They are unscrupulous and ruthless men as we can see from their treatment of those they uproot and what they do to those they have at their mercy when they detain them without trial. The late and unlamented Mr Jimmy Kroger by innuendo and suggestion (very much as was done before the Eloff Commission in the half truths and guilt by association tactics produced by General Johan Coetzee) tried to link the SACC with fomenting violence and so-called terrorism. I repudiated his silly allegations then and challenged him to debate the workings of the SACC publicly, he failed to take up my challenge. Then Mr Le Grange, now Minister of Law and Order and successor to Mr Kruger, made some quite asinine remarks about how our self-help projects were exacerbating a tense situation and he too, I dealt with gently and I hope effectively, suggesting he need a course in elementary logic, because he really was saying much that was mind-boggling nonsense; then Mr P.W. Botha spoke at the Rand Afrikaans University at a Republic Day rally accusing the SACC of using its vast funds for subversive purposes.

The Commission's own auditor stated before the Commission that the financial affairs of the Council since we appointed Mr Stevenson had improved remarkably, why was this fact not mentioned prominently? They claim that I have little ability to control vast funds. That is a gratuitous insult. I was not appointed for my financial skills. In any large organisation the head is not expected to know everything; he appoints those with the necessary skills. Does the head of, e.g., SADF have financial ability? If he has why are the SADF finances in such a mess? I said then that he was a liar and that he knew that he was lying. I want to reiterate those statements using their own Commission to support my statements. The Government has lied about the SACC. But we are not surprised. They generally lied without batting eyelids as shown in the Info Scandal, as shown in what they told the country about their first incursions into Angola. If they are so concerned about financial probity why are they appointing a commission to look into the financial administration of the SADF which has received scathing reports from the Auditor-General for two years running and which in one year has lost inexplicably more funds than the SACC will hope to use in a decade? Why are they so coy about all the shoddy underhand things concerning the Salem affair which has cost this country about R30,000,000? Why have they not made public in South Africa what is common knowledge about this affair in other lands? They won't do these things because they cannot stand the light of day and the searching scrutiny such as that which SACC has been subjected to for two years.

Let me say again we in the SACC operate openly and above board. We do not act clandestinely. Not even their masterspy Lt. Williamson with whom I had extensive conversations overseas when I did not know that he was a Government agent could say that I have any other view than that I am opposed to violence. I have said before and I will say it again – I support the ANC wholeheartedly in its aim to work for a truly democratic and non-racial South Africa; but I do not support its methods. I have never hidden the fact that I meet with the leaders of the liberation movements when I go abroad. It is one of the first things I announce when I return to South Africa. How are we going to persuade them to come to the negotiating table if we have not kept in touch with them? Whether the Government and whites like it or not, I won't have the South African Government dictate to me who my friends are going to be. The ANC have a long history of working peacefully for change and it was this Nationalistic Government that banned them in 1960 forcing them to opt for the armed struggle.

Our operation is transparent and above board. We have said before we did not hide even unpalatable truths from our donor partners and our member churches, not even when we received an audited report about material irregularities. Can the Government match that kind of transparency?

We do not use the methods of the Government revealed in the Info Scandal. I have offered myself as a go-between to the Government and the ANC to suggest possibilities of a negotiated settlement because, stop kidding yourselves, one day whites must negotiate with the ANC amongst others. I do not have a brief for the ANC, Ton Vosloo, former editor of the *Beeld* has said as much.

It will not do for whites nor for their Government to fulminate when I say that those they call terrorists are our brothers and sisters, our fathers and our mothers, our sons and daughters. Nothing can change that biological fact. If my brother should commit murder that will not alter the fact that he is my brother. White South Africans must know whether they like it or not that just as much as they have their 'boys' on the border so the black community too has their boys on the other side of the border. That is not sedition, that is not treachery, that is stating just plain truth.

The SACC seeks to place before the public facts relating to the important aspects of South African life so that they can make informed decisions.

We are accused of being separated from our membership and of relying heavily on overseas funding when 10c per member would raise large sums internally.

The Commission respectfully shows its woeful ignorance of many things in this assertion. None of our churches can claim that as individual denominations their Synod and assemblies are not often viewed by the person in the pew as remote from them. All churches complain of a gap between the leadership and their rank and file membership. This is conventional wisdom in all our churches. But all our major churches through their leaders testified before the Commission. It is surely to run in the face of facts to say we are separated from our constituency when Archbishop Hurley, Archbishop Russell, President Mgojo of the Methodist Church, the General Secretary of the United Congregational of Southern Africa and its chairman, the General Secretary of Presbyterian Church in Southern Africa, the presiding Bishop of the Evangelical Lutheran Church in Southern Africa and other church leaders came to testify for the SACC. Why should they have inconvenienced themselves to such an extent for a body they thought to be of little consequence? The Commission chose to ignore a vast body of evidence which contradicted what some powerful people wanted said about the SACC.

All our member churches receive substantial materially and in person from their overseas partners as a matter of course, so the SACC is not peculiar in this matter. The Commission knows very little about the theology of the nature of the church. Because we are churches, as our overseas partners testified before the Commission last March, they regard it as a privilege to share with us in our ministry.

We are members of the Body of Christ and there is a mutuality in our relationship that the Commission appears to know nothing about. There is a give and take which are part and parcel of being what it means to be a church. Can the Commission point to any self-respecting overseas church that supports the white Dutch Reformed Church? Is this purely accidental? Why did such high-powered delegations from right round the world come to testify about their fraternal relations with the SACC and be keen to see these maintained and strengthened whereas the NGK has its membership suspended from the World Alliance of Reformed Churches?

We want to point the Commission to the fact that the White Dutch Reformed Church has often given substantial subsidies to her black sister churches. Is the fact that these churches have not been able to be self-sufficient evidence of a distance between them and their members?

We have been accused of fomenting unrest. We must point out that the Gospel of Jesus Christ is subversive of evil and injustice and the Church will always confront evil to work for real reconciliation. But have the Commission ignored the fact that we served as mediators helping to end a long drawn out strike in Cape

Town? Have they forgotten my intervention to save the life of a policeman at Mr Mxenge's funeral in King Williams Town? Have they forgotten how I have tried to stop stone throwing at Regina Mundi on June 16th last year?

Have they forgotten our appeal to President Rene which helped to secure the release of those condemned to death in the abortive coup? Have they forgotten our attempts to bring peace on the black University campuses and in black schools? All this evidence was before them. They chose to ignore it. But this Commission was a thinly veiled part of the Government's strategy to vilify and discredit the Council. They are part of a blasphemous act to put the church and Christ on trial, for our faith believes that all life belongs to God not just the spiritual aspect. And at the very time that we are under attack so viciously and maliciously at home, the SACC has been nominated for the Nobel Peace Prize, testimony to the fact that some in the world think we are a powerful instrument for justice and peace.

We may act confidentially but our policy is that we do not say anything by which we would not stand if it became public. The police intercept our mail, our telexes and several of our documents, as became evident when Gen Coetzee gave evidence before the Eloff Commission. They wasted valuable time because they speculated hopelessly wrongly about what we said, wrote or did.

We repeat our offer to the authorities:
(a) If we have contravened any of your multifarious and hideous laws, charge us and let it stick;
(b) If you want to know what we are planning to do, stop trying to bribe SACC staff to spy for you. It is despicable. We have nothing to hide. Ask us and we will tell you;

(c) I am willing to provide you with advance copies of my speeches if you will observe my embargo.

But know that I will always condemn apartheid as evil and unchristian. Know too that nothing you can do will stop liberation coming to this country for all its people black and white. We shall be free whatever you try to do. We are committed to justice and peace and reconciliation and are opposed to all forms of violence.

I want to pay a warm tribute to our legal team led by Adv S Kentridge including Advs Unterhalter and P Solomon and our attorney Mr O Barrett of the firm Bowens. I am deeply grateful to the leaders of our member churches and overseas partners for their prayerful and other support and I want to express my admiration for my SACC colleagues for the joyous commitment and conscientious application to duty during a difficult time.

Bishop Desmond Tutu
General Secretary – SACC
15 February 1984

CHAPTER NINE

The Demise of Afrikaner Civil Religion

Despite the rebuke of a theological rationalisation of apartheid by the 1968 Lunteren Reformed Ecumenical Synod (see **Document D4.4**), the official position of the NGK, as reiterated at its national General Synod of 1978 (**Document D9.1**), continued to support 'separate development' and to uphold an interpretation of Calvinism[102] that rendered undue authority to the state[103]. With the rise of Black political protestation against their experience of apartheid, and the concomitant formulation of Black Theology in the late 1970s, this theological and ecclesiastical *status quo* came under relentless attack from both inside and outside the Reformed Church's own structures.

Led by Allan Boesak[104] of the 'Coloured' N.G. Sending Kerk (Dutch Reform Mission Church), and Sam Buti, Elias Tema and Piet Moatshe of the 'African' NGK in Afrika, the leadership in these 'daughter churches',[105] including the 'Indian' Reformed Church in Africa, started to be more and more vociferous of their criticism of the racism in NGK structures, and on the justification for political change.

At a colloquium held in October 1981 in Hammanskraal, these Black Reformed clergy and leading lay persons form these churches launched the Alliance of Black Reformed Christians in Southern Africa (ABRECSA) (**Document D9.2**). This included other non-Lutheran Black Christians from the reformed tradition – the Presbyterian churches and the United Congregational Church of Southern Africa.

At the same time, signs of dissatisfaction with attempts to provide a rational defence of apartheid had begun to surface within the theological leadership of the NGK 'mother church'. On 31 October 1980, the so-called 'Reformation Day', a statement signed by eight leading Afrikaner academic theologians was publicised in the national Afrikaans press.[106] It was the first of what was to become a series of similar statements from Afrikaans-speaking theologians. This was soon followed by the publication in 1981 of an unusually critical collection of essays written in the Afrikaans language by twenty-one leading Afrikaner theologians, edited by the already noted 'rebels': Prof Nico Smith, Dr F.E O' Brien Geldenhuys, and Dr Piet Meiring. This widely circulated and debated volume bore the evocative title *Storm-Kompas: Opstelle op Soek na 'n Suiwer Koers in die Suid-Afrikaanse Konteks van die Jare Tagtig*[107] (Storm compass: In search of the right direction in the context of the South Africa of the nineteen eighties).

In June 1982 an open letter written by a group of 123 ministers, among them its theological educators, was publicised widely after the General Synod of the NGK had refused to recognise its message that March. In the letter, the signatories proclaimed their disavowal of any defence of apartheid on biblical grounds, and a call for the de-racialisation of the church structure, that is, "with immediate effect ... all member churches within the family of the Dutch Reformed Churches (NGK) should be welcome at any meeting of any of these churches" (**Document D9.4**).

Ironically, this emergent internal Afrikaner rumblings was fomented by P.W. Botha's declarations on assuming power as Prime Minister in 1978, stating that his government was intent on reforming apartheid. Intellectuals who were imbedded within the community structures of Afrikanedom exploited the political space created by this claim. For the first time, apartheid could be freely appraised from within the Afrikaner world. However, the motives behind Botha's rhetoric of 'reform' were not examined with the critical rigour which Black political activists and theologians generally urged.

It had become clear that Botha's moves were tactical, aimed at regaining international acceptance of South Africa following the world's shock at the Soweto 16 June 1976 events. The intensification of the United Nations arms embargo, and the increasing adoption of trade and economic sanctions by various countries, and financial institutions, meant that the outside world's perception of and interest in South Africa could no longer be ignored. Pronouncements on South Africa by the World Council of Churches (WCC) and other influential international religious bodies could no longer be dismissed in the way they had been during the Vorster years.

In 1977, at its General Assembly held in Dar-es-Salaam, the Lutheran World Federation had made an important theological statement to the effect that any one's personal attitude toward the racism of apartheid was definitive of one's standing as a Christian or at least as a Lutheran (*Status confessionis*[108]).

This statement included a formal declaration of what was now a common position since the Lunteren Reformed Ecumenical Synod of 1968 – that the theological justification of apartheid is a malicious and heretical contradiction of Christian doctrine. Inspired by this, the possibility of a Confessing Church movement, along the lines of the German anti-Nazi theological resistance movement, began to be widely debated and explored in the Black Dutch Reformed Churches, who happened to have taken up membership of the SACC, as an alternative to the prevailing structural relationship between their 'mother church' and the apartheid state.

The kind of intricate relationship this church had with ideology and practices that were facilitating social evils and political brutalities of the government of the day was leading to the conclusion that this could not be allowed to portray itself as a 'Church of Jesus Christ'. It was an errant indulgence in the heresy of apartheid.[109] The formation of the *Belydenekring* ('Confessing Circle') in about 1983 by a network of theologians from all the racial compartments of the Reformed-tradition churches was a calculated expression of this judgement, that a church which succoured racism and the kind of inhumanity found in South Africa was guilty of apostasy[110] (see **Document D9.5**).

The Hammanskraal 1981 colloquium where ABRECSA was launched was conducted with an eye to the Assembly of the General Council of the World Alliance of Reformed Churches (WARC) which was to be held in Ottawa in August 1982. Both the NGK and the NHK (The Nederduitse Hervormde Kerk, the smaller and more conservative product of an earlier schism within the NGK) were members of WARC. Noting that the WARC Conferences had passed statements critical of racism since 1974, the ABRECSA founding conference passed a resolution to the effect that the South African Black delegation to Ottawa should ensure that the General Council of WARC translate these declarations into some form of action. They even suggested that WARC should be urged to establish within its international secretariat a department like the World Council of Churches'

Programme to Combat Racism, which would embark upon concrete projects commensurate with the WARC's stand against racism.

The General Council of WARC in Ottawa exceeded the expectations of both ABRECSA and the South African regime: Dr Allan Boesak, ABRECSA's chairman, was elected the World President of WARC, and the assembly resolved to suspend the NGK and NHK from membership 'until such time as the WARC Executive Committee has determined that these two churches in their utterances and practice have given evidence of a change of heart' (**Document D9.3**).

At its synod in September 1982 following the WARC Assembly, Boesak's NG Sending Kerk drafted and adopted a confession of faith in which it dissociated itself definitively from the NGK, and accused it of theological heresy and idolatry. This statement (*Byledenis van Belhar*) which developed into what was internationally adopted by other reformed churches on *Status confessionis* against apartheid became known as 'The Belhar Confession of Faith' (**Document D9.5**, and **Document D10.6**).

The events of 1982 had serious ramifications for the NGK. The cracks in the edifice of its theological defence of apartheid were now laid bare. In addition, the National Party ideologues appeared to be more attentive to the pragmatism of avoiding further international sanctions than to the religious counsel of the *dominees*. Also, the largely non-Afrikaans capitalist class that ran the South African economy were more stridently articulating their concern that apartheid was eliminating the majority of its population from meaningful economic participation, as skilled labour, property owners and a credible consumer market.

'Petty apartheid' legislation that thwarted the emergence of a Black consumer class could be removed without any structural social change. For the first time the possibility of a divorce between the Afrikaner church and the Afrikaner State became manifest. The Afrikaner church began to feel that a new enemy, secularism, had entered the decidedly religious terrain of Afrikaner political culture.

The most traumatic blow, aggravating the injury caused by WARC at Ottawa, came during the same September in 1982, when a spilt in the ruling National Party was formalised and the hardline conservatives who were unsettled by P.W. Botha's reform (*verligte*) rhetoric formed their *Konserwatiewe Party* (Conservative Party). The splitting *verkrampte* faction was led by a former dominee and NGK theologian, Dr Andries Treurnicht.

The NGK church leadership was left in the dilemma of choosing one of these factions. In 1986, they published a Synodical document, '*Kerk en Samelewing*' ('Church and Society'),[111] declaring support for the removal of 'hurtful discriminatory measures'. Like the regime's rejection of any fundamental political reconstruction in its programme for 'reform', the NGK could not contemplate a change deeper than the superficial repeal of so-called 'petty apartheid' laws. Even this nuanced indecision led the NGK to split along the set political camps of *verligtes* versus *verkramptes* of wider Afrikaner political community. Part of its membership left it to form the Afrikaanse Protestant Kerk (Afrikaans Protestant Church), which supported the preservation of classical apartheid, as promised by the Conservative Party.

The rise to power of P.W. Botha coincided with a marked revival of the exiled ANC which became increasingly visible inside South Africa. In 1979 P.W. Botha had announced his Twelve Point Plan, as the charter of his government, a mixture of the re-affirmation of apartheid's "multinationalism" and of "South Africa's determination to defend itself against outside intervention with all practical means at its disposal".[112] The ANC proclaimed the same year as 'The year of Umkhonto we Sizwe' (its military wing) in commemoration of the Battle of Isandlwana in Natal a hundred years earlier – when the Zulu army successfully defeated British colonial forces.

The year was marked by a display of unprecedented political decisiveness by the ANC, which was by then assuming the hegemonic position as the custodian of the democratic aspirations of the oppressed of South Africa following the squashing by the regime of the Black Consciousness Movement in October 1977. The youth that had fled the country during and after 1976, trained by the ANC, were now ready for military missions against the regime. Under P.W. Botha (as the former Minister of Defence) and under Vorster, the regime responded by formulating an ideological system that subordinated the rationalisation of apartheid as a cultural and political system to considerations of 'state security'. As the ideology of the National Security State became more vital, the dependence on Afrikaner nationalism, which the Afrikaner church served, receded in importance.

D9.1 NG Kerk: Human Relations and the South African Scene in the Light of Scripture, 1974 General Synod

[Original: *Ras, Volk, en Volkereverhoudinge in die Lig van die Skrif* (Cape Town, NG Kerk Boekhandel, 1974), paragraphs 49.1 to 49.7]

THE CHURCH AND SOCIAL JUSTICE: POLITICAL ASPECTS

Our study of the data contained in the Bible has led to the following conclusion with regard to state and church as separate institutions and instruments of God, each with its own authority, structure and functions, and the relationship between them.

Task of the church
In the first instance, it is the function of the church to preach to its adherents the gospel of personal salvation in Christ in order to strengthen them in holy faith and to prepare them for service in the broad sphere of the church as organism (Eph. 4:11-16). This aspect of the church's function is of the utmost importance, because through the life and testimony of its spirituality equipped members the church fulfils its calling to be the salt of the earth and the light of the world, to see that justice is done in all spheres of life (Col. 4:1), to carry the norms of God's Word into all spheres of human endeavour, including that of the central authorities charged with the complex and demanding function of governing a multinational and multiracial society . The church also has an external function – to preach the Word of God in all spheres of life and, consequently, also to the authorities. This aspect of the church's task is not set out in many words in the New Testament, but it is part and parcel of the essential being of the church, i.e. as aspect and instrument of the kingdom of God, on the basis of

which it is called upon to preach the supremacy of Christ in all spheres of life, including that of the state.

In a multinational situation the calling of the church vis-à-vis the state is two-fold: it must preach the norms of God's Word for the mutual relationships of various groups of people and for the duties of authorities in this situation, and it must warn when injustice is being done in the implementation of national policy and the application of laws.

The church must be both bold and cautious in the fulfilment of these functions. The manner in which the church addresses itself to the central authorities is determined by the following considerations: recognition of the fact that the authorities are an institution of God and have competency in their own sphere (Rom. 13:1–7). The actions of the church vis-à-vis the authorities are therefore circumscribed by the fact that the church shall honour and acknowledge the different character and competency of the authorities: acknowledgement of the believer's function in the sphere of the state; the fact that it is not part of the church's calling to dictate to the authorities, for instance, exactly how they should regulate intercourse and relationships between the various groups in a multinational or multiracial situation, precisely because the Bible does not provide a clear indication on the nature of the structures by which the mutual relationships should be regulated; the nature of the church's contact with the authorities which should preferably be established and maintained through the various official church bodies; acknowledgement that in its dealings with the authorities the church should be sure of two things: the accuracy and the expertise of its facts; and that, in each case, it is indeed giving expression to the demands of the Word of God. The church not only has a preaching, but also an intercessionary function, with a view to the coming of the kingdom of God (according to 1 Tim. 2:1–4).

Function of the state
It is the duty of the state to preserve public order within its own particular area of jurisdiction, to reconcile and regulate legal interests of the various groups for the sake of public order, to combat evil and to preserve justice. For without this, an orderly society is not possible (cf. 1 Tim. 2:2–4). In all this the state should act in accordance with Biblical norms, i.e. love of God and neighbour as guide-line for the public administration of justice (cf. 2 Chron. 19:6). The state may use institutions of power and even the sword to keep in check the pervasive influence of sin (Rom. 13:4). While this system of authority is essential for the regulation of various aspects of everyday life, it may never degenerate into a totalitarian system in which the state usurps the sovereignty of other institutions in their own particular fields in order to regulate all aspects of human existence. The golden rule of sovereignty for each institution in its own sphere, of justice and of love, should be sufficient to preserve the state from revolutionary chaos and political absolutism and tyranny.

Limited responsibility of the state
Because the state alone does not regulate the internal activities of all institutions of society, it cannot be held solely responsible for all abuses resulting from a given political system. Industry is a separate sphere of human endeavour in our modern society. The manner in which it organises and utilises its labour and capital should also be tested by the norms of the Bible and should, in terms thereof, be called to account for its own Christian bias so that it may realise the norms of justice within its own sphere.

Conduct of church vis-à-vis state
An institution the church submits itself to the authority and law of the state, as far as its participation in the normal processes of justice and exercising of its civil rights are concerned, provided the legal order does not conflict with the Word of God (Church order

65.2). It is the duty of the church to preach the Word of God to the authorities, in particular the norms of the Bible in respect of mutual relationships and social justice, and the duties of the authorities in this connection.

Human Rights
We cannot accept, purely according to the teaching of the Bible, that man has rights in the sense of claims on the basis of his own merits, as the term is generally understood today. Human rights are those rights which God has bestowed upon man as the bearer of his image so that he may be able to fulfil his duties and calling as a human being. In order to be able to fulfil his calling as a human being, man has a right to life and the propagation thereof through marriage and the creation of communities and associations, to property and to freedom of religious practice and of conscience. It is self-evident that the exercise of these rights can never be divorced from the community in which the individual lives his life. For, as an association of people, the community has collective rights on the basis of which it must fulfil its divine calling. When it comes to the acknowledgement of rights, privileges must at all times be accompanied by responsibility. Rights and privileges may not be withheld when the claim is just.

Autogenous separate development
A political system based on the autogenous or separate development of various population groups can be justified from the Bible, but the commandment to love one's neighbour must at all times be the ethical norm towards establishing sound inter-people relations.

The Christian and politics
Since the Christian must apply the principles of the kingdom of God in the sphere of politics as well, he must enjoy the freedom of political thought and action, exercised in a responsible manner

under the guidance of the Word and Spirit of God. The message of reconciliation of the Bible implies that there should at all times be channels for effective communication and consultation in a multinational situation.

The Christian must at all times seek to ensure that his political thinking and actions are based on justice and righteousness.

D9.2 Alliance of Black Reformed Christians In Southern Africa, 1981, ABRECSA Charter

1. **DEFINITION**

    A broad movement of Black Reformed Christians based on church affiliation and open to individual members to join. We understand black to mean a condition and an attitude and not merely the pigmentation of one's skin. We recognise that in South Africa the oppressors who enjoy social privileges, wield political power and possess economic advantages are white and that the oppressed who are socially underprivileged, politically powerless and economically exploited are black. At the same time we also recognise that there are blacks whose attitude and condition is such that they have clearly opted to be on the side of the oppressor and that there are whites whose attitude and condition is such that they have clearly opted to be on the side of the oppressed.

    Membership is subject to acceptance of the Theological Basis, the Declaration and Commitment.

    1.1 Theological Basis

    a. The Word of God is the supreme authority and guiding principle revealing all that we need to know about God's will for the whole existence of human beings. It is this Word that gives life and offers liberation that is total and complete. Christ is the Lord of all life even in those situations where his Lordship is not readily recognised. It is our task in life not only to recognise the Lordship of Christ but also to proclaim it.

    b. We as Christians are responsible for the world in which we live, and to reform it is an integral part of our discipleship and worship to God.

c. God institutes the authority of the State for the just and legitimate government of the world. Therefore, we obey government only in so far as its laws and instructions are not in conflict with the Word of God. Obedience to earthy authorities is only obedience in God.
d. The unity of the Church must be visibly manifest in the one people of God. The indivisibility of the body of Christ demands that the barriers of race, culture, ethnicity, language and sex be transcended.

1.2 Declaration
We, as members of ABRECSA, unequivocally declare that apartheid is a sin, and that the normal and theological justification of it is a travesty of the Gospel, a betrayal of the Reformed tradition, and a heresy.

1.3 Commitment . . .

2. MOTIVATION
There are important and imperative reasons why an Alliance of Black Reformed Christians in Southern Africa should be formed:

2.1 The Black Reformed Churches in Southern Africa are by tradition 'mission Churches', struggling to find their own authentic identity, autonomy and independence, and also to give expression to their own theological understanding of their faith in the South African context.

2.2 Being 'mission Churches', they have been divided into separate denominations by the 'mother' missionary societies even though they share the same confessional base, and these divisions are not of their making.

2.3 As heirs of the Reformed tradition they are faced with a crisis because the system of apartheid has been and is still justified theologically mainly by people of that very tradition. Yet the people of these Churches, representing the victims of apartheid, reject the system as evil and contrary to the Word of God. The question that this poses is whether they are also rejecting their confessional heritage from which so much support for the system stems.

2.4 To answer the above questions, it has become absolutely necessary for Black Reformed Christians to come together and struggle with the question: 'What does it mean to be Black and Reformed in Southern Africa today?'

2.5 It is also important for Black Reformed Christians to make a more positive and specifically Southern African contribution to the witness of the World Alliance of Reformed Churches in the ecumenical field. An initial opportunity is available to them in preparing for the WARC Assembly to be held in Ottawa, Canada, in 1982.

3. AIMS

3.1 To bring together Black Reformed Christians from the different Churches:
The NG Kerk in Afrika
The NG Sending Kerk
The Reformed Church in Africa
The Evangelical Presbyterian Church in South Africa
The Presbyterian Church of Africa
The Presbyterian Church of Southern Africa
The Reformed Presbyterian of Southern Africa
The United Congregational Church of Southern Africa
and other existing Black Reformed Churches.

3.2 To promote the unity of these Churches in organisation, in action and in witness.

3.3 To strengthen the prophetic witness of these Churches by challenging both their leadership and their membership to live out of the Gospel in the context of the struggle for a just society in South Africa.

3.4 To promote the understanding of involvement in the struggle for liberation as an act of obedience and theological necessity.

3.5 To provide supplementary and alternative theological understanding by action/reflection models of theologizing.

3.6 To create an ecumenical network with other Reformed Christians who share the same commitment and vision and thereby to form groups of solidarity. This is important not only with regard to South Africa, but also to those minority groups struggling in Western Churches.

3.7 To create a network of understanding and support for those blacks in Reformed Churches elsewhere who find themselves in minority positions.

3.8 To create possibilities for co-ordination of efforts in Reformed circles across Southern Africa and the world to support each other in our different struggles but especially concerning the struggle in South Africa.

3.9 To be better able to give content to the awareness of ecumenical bodies and/or Churches who concern themselves with the South African situation.

D9.3 World Alliance of Reformed Churches, Ottawa, 1982. Statement on Racism and the South African Afrikaans Churches

This is the second part of a tripartite statement adopted by the General Council of the World Alliance of Reformed Churches in Ottawa on 25 August 1982.

1. The General Council of the WARC affirms earlier statements on the issue of racism and apartheid ('separate development') made in 1964 and 1970, and reiterates its firm conviction that apartheid ('separate development') is sinful and incompatible with the Gospel on the grounds that:
   (a) it is based on a fundamental irreconcilability of human beings, thus rendering ineffective the reconciling and uniting power of our Lord Jesus Christ;
   (b) in its application through racist structures it has led to exclusive privileges for the white section of the population at the expense of the blacks;
   (c) it has created a situation of injustice and oppression, large-scale deportation causing havoc to family life, and suffering to millions. Apartheid ('separate development') ought thus to be recognized as incurring the anger and sorrow of God in whose image all human beings are created.
2. The General Council express its profound disappointment that, despite earlier appeals by WARC General Council, and despite continued dialogue between several Reformed Churches and the white Dutch Reformed Churches over twenty years, the Nederduitse Gerefermeede Kerk (in the Republic of South Africa) and the Nederduitsch Hervormde Kerk van Afrika have still not found the courage to realize that apartheid ('separate development') contradicts the very nature of the Church and

obscures the Gospel from the world; the council therefore pleads afresh with these churches to respond to promises and demands of the Gospel.

3. The General Council has a special responsibility to continue to denounce the sin of racism in South Africa as expressed in apartheid ('separate development'). It is institutionalized in the laws, policies and structures of the nation; it has resulted in horrendous injustice, in the suffering, exploitation of millions of black Africans for whom Christ died; and it has been given moral and theological justification by the white Dutch Reformed Churches in South Africa who are members of the WARC and with whom we share theological heritage in the Reformed tradition.

4. Therefore, the General Council, reluctantly and painfully, is compelled to suspend the Nederduiste Gereformeede Kerk (in the Republic of South Africa) and the Nederduitsch Hervomde Kerk van Afrika from privileges of membership in the WARC (i.e. sending delegates to General Councils and holding membership in departmental committees and commissions). Until such time as the WARC Executive Committee has determined that these two churches in their utterances and practice have given evidence of change of heart, they will be warmly welcomed once more only when the following changes have taken place:
    a. Black Christians are no longer excluded from church services, especially Holy Communion;
    b. Concrete support in word and deed is given to those who suffer under the system of apartheid ('separate development');

c. Unequivocal synod resolutions are made which reject apartheid and commit the Church to dismantling this system in both Church and politics.

The General Council asks the Executive Committee of the WARC to keep this whole issue regularly under review.

D9.4 A Statement on Rejection of Apartheid Theology By 123 Ministers of The NG Kerk, 8 June 1982

AN OPEN LETTER TO THE NGK LEADERSHIP AND FAMILY

We, ministers and ordinands of the NGK, state as our conviction that genuine reconciliation in Christ between individuals and groups is the greatest single need in the Church and so also in our country and society. We believe that the Church of Jesus Christ in South Africa has a particular contribution to make in this connection by:
(1) giving ever more explicit expression to reconciliation and the unity of the church,
(2) by exercising its prophetic calling in respect of society.

1. *Concerning reconciliation and the unity of the church*

1.1 We are convinced that the primary task of the church in our country is the ministry of reconciliation in Christ.
1.1.1 In the first place this means that it is the inalienable privilege of the church to proclaim the message of reconciliation between God and man. Without this aspect of reconciliation, the issue at point would lose its deepest meaning and significance.
1.1.2 It is likewise the inalienable privilege of the church to proclaim simultaneously the message of reconciliation between people – even between those who had formerly been enemies – and to bear witness that for believers Christ has put an end to human enmity and has united us by creating 'in himself one new man' (Eph. 2:15, 16).
1.1.3 We confess that the unity of the church is both a gift and an injunction of God. Like reconciliation, it was brought into being by God and it is therefore a fortiori our

responsibility to give it visible expression. The church will therefore oppose factors which threaten her unity. This includes factors like heterodoxy, lovelessness, self-righteousness, exclusivism, prejudice and the giving of preference to personal or group interests.

1.1.4 There is space within the unity of the church for a diversity of languages and cultures. Specifically, because of the reconciliation this diversity provides mutual enrichment and not division.

1.1.5 The unity, however, belongs to a different category than diversity. Unity is primary, diversity secondary. The unity is normative and is confessed (the Apostles Creed and Nicene Creed), the diversity not so.

1.2 This has the following implications, among others, for the concrete existence of the Church in South Africa:

1.2.1 That no particular church (denomination) can afford to do without discussion and fellowship with other churches or close its doors to others.

1.2.2 that the church may lay down no condition for membership other than the confession of true faith in Jesus Christ (Belgic Confession, Art. 27).

1.2.3 that the various churches within the family of the Dutch Reformed Churches (NGK) who in any event adhere to the same Confession of Faith and historically emanated from the same church, ought to do everything within their powers to give visible expression to the unity which they confess

1.2.4 that with immediate effect, while negotiations for clearer structural unity are under way, all members of churches within the family of Dutch Reformed Churches (NGK) should be welcome at any meeting of any of these churches

1.2.5 that members of the one Body of Christ accept one another as brothers and sisters without questioning one another's Christianity, concern themselves with each other's welfare, esteem the other higher than oneself, bear one another's burdens, show mutual love in word and deed and intercede for one another in prayer.

2. *Concerning the prophetic calling of the church*

2.1 We are convinced that the calling of the church extends beyond the ministry of reconciliation within the four walls of the church. We therefore reject the opinion that the church ought to concern itself only with so-called 'spiritual matters' and withdraw from other areas in society.

2.1.1 Reconciliation includes a prophetic witness in relation to the entire life of society and therefore the church dares not remain silent concerning such matters as moral decay, family disintegration and discrimination.

2.1.2 The church will always bear witness that an arrangement of society based on the fundamental irreconcilability of individuals and groups cannot be accepted as a basic point of departure for the ordering of society.

2.1.3 The church has a wonderful opportunity to be God's experimental garden in the world. This means that God wants to demonstrate something to the world, through the life of the church, concerning that unity, mutual love, peace, understanding, sharing and justice, which God intends to be present in the whole of society.

2.1.4 Naturally all this is also realized in the church only in a defective manner! This state of affairs must not, however, give rise to the prophetic task of the church in relation to society being made into a responsibility of the distant future when the church's integrity has been fully established.

2.2 For the concrete situation in South Africa society, the above comments mean, inter alia, the following:

2.2.1 that the church may exercise its prophetic witness with great boldness in South African society; we in fact live in a state which explicitly calls itself Christian and therefore wishes to listen to the Word of God together with the church

2.2.2 that a social order which elevates irreconcilability to a principle of societal living and which alienates the different sections of the South African population from one another is unacceptable

2.2.3 that such a system makes it virtually impossible for the inhabitants of South Africa to really learn to know one another, to trust one another and to be loyal to one another

2.2.4 that the laws which have become symbols of this alienation – among these being those concerning mixed marriages, race classification and group areas, cannot be defended scripturally

2.2.5 that justice, and not simply law and order, shall be the guideline and point of departure for the ordering of society. We believe that the incidence of the forced removal of people, the disintegration of marriage and family ties as a result of migrant labour, the inadequate expenditure on black education, insufficient and inadequate housing for black people and the low wages paid to such people cannot be reconciled with biblical demands for justice and human dignity

2.2.6 that all people who regard South Africa as their fatherland ought to be included in the process of negotiating a new order of society

2.2.7 that this system ought to enjoy equal treatment and opportunities.

3. *Our solidarity*

In the above statement we do not only want to place on record what is, in the light of Scripture, our deepest conviction concerning the concrete South African reality, but we also want to

3.1 confess to our deepest guilt before God that we ourselves have also failed to manifest adequately the unity of the church of Christ in our lives and that we too have contributed to many of the societal evils which we have identified

3.2 explicitly declare that we have neither spoken concerning the church nor the government from an attitude of self-righteousness. Our witness emerges out of a deep solidarity with the church and awareness of co-responsibility with regard to the present order of society

3.3 confess that we believe in conversion, the forgiveness of sins, and a new life in obedience to God

3.4 pray that our letter will contribute to the church of Christ in South Africa having a clearer version concerning its calling, and that the realization of a new societal order in South Africa may be expedited

3.5 bear witness that the Gospel of Jesus Christ – God's good news to the world – also gives hope to the people of South Africa in these specific circumstances

3.6 gives the assurance that we will earnestly continue in prayer for the Church, as well as for the government in its extremely difficult task.

D9.5 Nederduitse Gereformeerde Sendingkerk, 1982 Synod Statement on Apartheid: Belhar Confession of Faith

[The NG Sending (Mission) Church was the 'Coloured' partner of the racially exclusive NG Kerk. At its 1982 General Synod in Belhar, Cape Town, it adopted the following expository statement, which is part of the confession of faith known as the Belhar Confession (**Document D10.6**). The following extract is its statement on apartheid.]

RECONCILIATION AND APARTHEID

Proposition
The political and ecclesiastical order of South Africa is an order within which irreconcilability has been elevated to a fundamental social principle within which, in spite of supposed good intentions, the greed and prejudice of the powerful and the privileged are entrenched at the cost of those who are powerless and without privileges.

Responsibility
Apartheid is a system within which people are separated from one another and kept apart from one another.

The possibility that these groups can be brought together, and that peaceful co-existence can replace tension and conflict is ruled out as a matter of principle. Therefore, ethnic groups, to the extent that this is possible, must be compelled, by law if necessary, to remain separate from one another, because the bringing of these groups of people together will necessarily result in conflict and the mutual threatening of one another.

The use of the phrase 'separate development' in an attempt to replace the hated word 'apartheid' in essence results in no change to the basic point of departure: the development of each group must still take place apart from that of other groups, because the development of one group is regarded as a threat to that of the other. Similarly, communal development is regarded as a threat to individual development.

In light of this unchanged point of departure, it is not surprising that when we are requested to give more attention to the positive aspects of apartheid, this repeatedly breaks down in the face of reality, which is that the white section of the population always benefits most from such development.

The choice of the term 'irreconcilability' in the decision of the Synod of 1978 was intentional. The Synod translates its witness into its own language, that of the Church and theology. Irreconcilability always stands in contradiction to reconciliation; the main artery of the Christian Gospel is also the main artery of the existence and the proclamation of the Church.

The visible effect of reconciliation between God and man is the existence of the Church as a reconciling community of people, a unified community. The message of reconciliation is entrusted to this Church. The invitation is extended to the world and to all people who inhabit it to reconcile themselves to God and to one another. In Christ, the Church says, there is new hope, there are new possibilities for the world. Sinfulness and hatred, enmity and separation need not be the last word, but rather reconciliation and peace. Christ has made this possible.

The Church will always bear witness to the fact that no order of communal living which fundamentally affirms the irreconcilability of people and groups of people can be regarded as acceptable. Such a point of departure binds people to their past history of enmity and hate – it invalidates the Gospel.

We do not simply present one or more Bible texts. It is always too easy to use biblical texts to one's own ends, even to the extent that it was possible for many years for it to be said that apartheid is Scriptural, and, indeed, on the ground of only two texts: the story of the Tower of Babel (Genesis 11:1–9, and Acts 17:26)

No! The Touchstone for apartheid is the essential biblical message of reconciliation. If is fails here, a few disparate biblical texts cannot save it. In fact, the traditional exposition of these texts then needs to be fundamentally questioned.

The Decision of the 1978 Synod with regard to Apartheid
In addition to the theological proposition regarding irreconcilability, the Synod went further to say that the system which necessarily results from such a policy must inevitably lead and has led to an increasing polarization between people. It does more than merely keep them apart from one another. It moves them further apart from one another. It polarizes and creates conflict. In turn, this conflict is then used as an alibi to maintain this separation at all costs. So, everyone is drawn into this vicious circle – which can only be broken by changing the point of departure.

The Demand of Justice and Self-concern
The decision of the Synod goes further to demonstrate that, in practice, it can be shown undeniably that 'within the system one section of the population, the whites, is privileged, and that as a result of this the Gospel demand of justice for all has not been satisfied'. In a system within which concepts such as the 'own' (*eie*) and the 'separateness' (*afsonderlike*) receive so much attention, people are indeed going to concern themselves essentially with their 'own'. The result is that the powerful and privileged are not

willing to share their power and privilege, but rather tempted to acquire still more for themselves. In conclusion the Synod shows that through the system of apartheid 'it is not only the humanity of the underprivileged sections of the population that is affected but also the humanity of everybody involved within the system'.

Racism and Apartheid
Racism is an ideology of racial domination which includes a belief in the inherent, cultural and biological inferiority of certain races and racial groups. It is also a political and an economic system that determines the unequal treatment of these groups at the level of law, structures and institutions. Racism does not merely concern the attitude of people, it is also structural. It does not merely concern the feeling of inferiority in relation to another person or group, but the system of political, social and economic domination. In a racist situation certain groups of people are excluded because of their race from participation in the political decision-making process, from participation in the economic decision-making processes, and as a result, they are discriminated against both economically and socially. This exclusion is, however, not merely on the basis of race and colour, it is exclusively aimed at the domination of the other. Where this racism is regimentally imposed in Church and communal structures it denies, the community of believers the possibility of being human and it denies the reconciling and humanizing work of Christ.

In South Africa apartheid in the Church and in society leans to a significant extent on the theological and moral justification of the system. Apartheid is therefore a pseudo-religious ideology as well as a political policy. It allows itself to be validated within the realms of both Church and state, and in so doing it influences and structurally controls the entire South African society.

Article 9 of the Apostle's Creed

The specific character of the pseudo-religious ideology of apartheid makes it practically impossible for the confession 'I believe in one holy, Catholic Church, the community of the saints' to determine the structures of the Church. In reality, the secular Gospel of apartheid structures the way in which the Church is realized and the way in which Church unity is manifest within the Dutch Reformed Churches in South Africa.

Resolutions

Because the secular Gospel of apartheid threatens in the deepest possible way the witness of reconciliation in Jesus Christ and the unity of the Church of Jesus Christ in its very essence, the NG Mission Church in South Africa declares that this constitutes a *status confessionis* for the Church of Jesus Christ. (a *status confessionis* means that we regard this matter as a concern about which it is impossible to differ without affecting the integrity of our communal confession as Reformed Churches).

We declare that apartheid (separate development) is a sin, that the moral and theological justification of it makes a mockery of the Gospel, and that its consistent disobedience to the Word of God is a theological heresy.

The decision of Ottawa and the decisions with regard to racism and therefore apartheid (separate development) cannot be regarded as an alternative to the decision of the Synod of 1978, but rather as a consequence.

According to the conviction of the Synod the NGK believes in the ideology of apartheid, which is in direct conflict with the evangelical message of reconciliation and the visible unity of the Church. Therefore the 1978 decision of the Mission Church (as argued on the level of principle at the beginning of this statement) makes it clear that we can do no other than with deepest regret accuse the NGK of theological heresy and idolatry. This is done in the light of her theological formulated standpoint and its implementation in practice.

The NG Mission Church makes this statement in deep humility and self-examination so that we may keep ourselves 'from being disqualified after having called others to the contest' (I Cor. 9:27).

CHAPTER TEN
Call To Prayer for an End to Unjust Rule

The show piece of P.W. Botha's government's 'reform programme' was the unveiling of a notion of constitutional reform, a new Constitution to be adopted during 1984. This was to be accompanied by the traditional referendum among the racialistically proscribed White electorate, scheduled for November 1983. This was an express attempt at creating a new form of apartheid that was adapted to new social and international economic pressures, intended to appease the world community whilst guaranteeing continued White minority domination.

Botha's proposed reform programme ignited the kind of invigorated and organised mass opposition that had not been witnessed in South Africa since the 1952-1955 Defiance Campaign. It was also subjected to an unprecedented theological attack of a political project by almost all sections of the South African ecumenical movement.

Document D10.1, a 1983 Pastoral Letter of the Southern African Catholic Bishops Conference, is an exemplary summary of the main points of theological objection to this constitutional programme of the apartheid regime, at the other end of the historical spectrum, the SACC's 16 June 1985 'Theological Rationale and a Call to Prayer for an End to Unjust Rule' (**Document D10.3**) is an indication of the consciousness this rejection of Botha's reforms eventuated into.

The unveiled 'Tri-cameral Constitution' would create segregated Indian and Coloured houses of parliament, subordinated to the dominant White minority chamber, while excluding the African majority from parliamentary politics. The United Democratic Front (UDF) was launched in August 1983 as an organised non-racial expression of the rejection of this violently imposed dispensation of further racialisation of South African society. The Rev. Allan Boesak, the President of the World Alliance of Reformed Churches (WARC) and Rev. Frank Chikane, then General Secretary of the Institute for Contextual Theology, were among its founding leaders.

The Republic of South Africa Constitution Act 110 of 1983 was eventually passed by a self-serving racist parliament under a storm of brutal suppression of popular opposition to its promulgation. P.W. Botha was no longer the Prime Minister, he was now the State President. In tandem, the post-1976 Black political consciousness had by this time already mutated into a tangible quest for the overthrowal of the apartheid regime as the ANC's military wing had been revived and resourced by hundreds and thousands of youth who had been forced into its ranks by state brutality at home since the Soweto Uprising.

The post-1983 state of mind of the White electorate and its government, as exposed by the *kragdadig* (authoritarian, Might over Reason) institution of this new 'constitutional dispensation' induced a resolve to render the country ungovernable. 'Peoples power' would be pitted again the 'State power' that was deemed illegitimate. The end of the apartheid regime was inevitable.

The promotion of this new constitution, in tandem with a programme of systematic repression under the refined ideological paranoia of the national security apartheid state, crystallised the reality that the National Party, and all those who were still arguing for the 'reform of race relations in South Africa', had run out of alternatives to apartheid rule. This buttressed the argument of the international anti-apartheid movement that it was time for more sanctions to be imposed on the Botha regime to force it to a negotiated non-racial democratic settlement.

In ecclesiastical circles, there was a sense of despair that was mixed with a spirit of crisis at this exposure of the moral-political bankruptcy of the National Party. Indicative of this new consciousness, the Catholics Bishop pastoral letter referred to earlier marked a significant step in the development of South African Catholic social thought and teaching. It indicates how the severity with which this new face of apartheid was viewed, and how its rejection catapulted the broad spectrum of religious institutions that identified with the theological perspectives and actions of the SACC into a position of a more radical challenge against the government.

The events beginning in the year 1983 would culminate in the tumultuous and grim developments that reached their nadir point in 1988. The widespread scale and intensity of mass uprisings in Black townships and the defiance of the regime's urban Bantu Administration structures forced President Botha to declare a partial State of Emergency on 20 July 1985, which had to be extended nationally on 13 June 1986.

Dealing with the impact of this multi-faceted drama of conflict between the State and its Black population launched the churches into a fundamental process of transformation. The 'Urgent Message to the State President from the Southern African Catholic Bishops Conference' on August 20, 1986 (**Document D10.5**) details the grimness of the situation, as does an earlier Memorandum to the State President that was prepared and signed by thity-three members of MUCCOR (Ministers United for Christian Co-Responsibility) (**Document D10.4**).

Under this State of Emergency, township life was militarised, with police given unlimited powers to act without regard for the lives of perceived opponents of the state. Scores of influential anti-apartheid leaders were either placed under house arrest or detained with thousands of others under national security laws.[113] Millions of young activists roamed across the country from town to town in order to evade arrest, whilst continuing their acts of resistance wherever they were hiding or displaced.

What acted as the game-changing catalyst for the transformation of the church into an unequivocal voice for the end of the oppression of the unworkable apartheid system, whilst being itself a reflective product of the prevailing political crisis, was the construction of a 'kairos theology'. Its basic proclamation and tenets are codified in the 'official summary' of the *Kairos Document, Challenge to the Church: A Theological Comment on the Political Crisis in South Africa* (**Document 10.2**) – a 30-page treatise produced and signed by a group of theologians and Christian activists. The signatories initially met in Soweto and ended up at the release of the booklet on 25 September 1985 with an endorsement by 156 signatories claiming affiliation with about 20 different church denominations from across South Africa. Its publication and promotion were facilitated by the Institute for Contextual Theology.

The 'Moment of Truth' invoked by the Kairos theologians was a consensus that apartheid could not be reformed, and that all actions aimed for its replacement by a non-racial, free and egalitarian democracy were morally and theologically legitimate. Many Christians were being convinced that the words of St Augustine of Hippo that "a government without justice, is merely a group of bandits"[114] were applicable to the conduct of the South African government, and it could not continue to hold rule unchallenged.

In the run-up to the annual commemoration of the 1976 Soweto Uprising, the Western Province Council of Churches issued a 'Call for an End to Unjust Rule', a theological rationale and injunction for all to pray for the fall of the government on 16 June 1985[115]. This statement and campaign, which was originally issued under the title 'A call for the *Removal* of Unjust Rule', was to have its title diluted as the SACC Executive Committee adopted it for consideration by its member churches (**Document D10.3**).

The call, with its detailed explication of how classic Christian political thought cohered with the position of the oppressed in South Africa seeking to bring about an end to unjust rule, presaged the more overt declaration three months later by the Kairos Document, that the government of South Africa had become "an enemy of the people, tyrant, totalitarian regime and reign of terror".[116]

Significantly, it was in the hubris of this period that the final nail was hammered into the coffin of the NG Kerk's state theology. As the Belhar Confession of Faith (**Document 10.6**) that declared association with apartheid a sin, a *status conffesionis*, was adopted by the Synod of the Dutch Reformed Church in Africa and offered by adoption by Reformed tradition churches in South Africa and abroad.

D10.1 Pastoral Letter of the Southern African Catholic

BISHOPS' CONFERENCE ON THE PROPOSED NEW CONSTITUTION FOR SOUTH AFRICA, 20 JULY 1983

1. At the present time there is a matter before the people of South Africa that deserves serious consideration, namely the proposed new Constitution. Since it affects the lives of all, we consider it our duty as pastors of the Church to voice our guidance on this issue. It is particularly opportune during this Holy Year, to consider how as a society we can receive and welcome the redeeming action of Christ. The theme for the year is 'Open the doors to the Redeemer', to let the light and saving purposes of Christ enter every dimension of our lives. In particular, we wish to examine whether the new constitution enables us to go beyond the conflicts and divisions of our country. Does it open doors to the redeemer, to let the light and saving purposes of Christ enter every dimension of our lives? In particular, we wish to examine whether the new constitution enables us to go beyond the conflicts and divisions of our country. Does it open doors for redemption or does it close them off?

2. Our concern is that the people of South Africa might live in peace, a concern that is shared by many people of goodwill through this country. But before peace can prevail it must dwell in the heart of each inhabitant and it must be prompted by the constitution and laws regulating our lives. As Pope John XXIII pointed out in a letter called Peace on Earth, relations between people must be founded on truth, justice, love and freedom. This holds for the relations between individual people, between citizens and the state, between different states and throughout the whole world community.

3. In this light, realizing that the love of Christ our Redeemer helps us overcome division and conflict, we wish to consider the new constitution proposed for South Africa. Our concern is for human rights and the morality of what is proposed. We are concerned as citizens and as spiritual leaders.

4. The preamble of the proposed constitution is good in that it speaks of protecting 'the human dignity and rights and liberties of all in our midst'. But it does not say what these rights and liberties are, nor does it specify what duties each person has in protecting them. This omission causes us great concern, since people are left vulnerable and unprotected. Work for peace cannot succeed unless every inhabitant of South Africa is seen as a person endowed with rights and duties. These need to be clearly and legally specified and recognized as belonging to all persons, and hence not subject to violation and suppression by the state or any individual. Some of the consequences of disregarding human rights and duties are evident in the proposed constitution.

5. In the first place more than two-thirds of the population, that is, the whole African section is disregarded. Africans will still have no representation in the central government, which will continue to make laws affecting them. This is a serious moral failure. It is an affront to the people concerned and ensures that racial discrimination will continue. Pope John XXIII said that 'any government which refused to recognize human rights or violated them would not only fail in its duty: its decrees would be wholly lacking in binding force'.

6. Racial discrimination will also continue in the establishment of three houses: one for Indians, one for so-called Coloured people and another for whites. We cannot accept a

constitution that prevents people from crossing racial barriers and working together for unity and peace in parties and associations of their own choosing. The maintenance of racial discrimination runs counter to the redemptive work of Christ, who sought through his death and resurrection to break down all walls of division and make one new people from our divided human race.

7. We have no confidence in the proposed machinery of government. It seems extremely cumbersome. Besides, it is likely to create a gap between the president and parliament. This may cause people to have little confidence in parliament, since its power will be substantially reduced.

8. The proposed constitution puts vast power in the hands of the president and his council, which the elected representatives of the people in parliament will be unable to control. This could lead to a feeling of helplessness or apathy even among people who have parliamentary representation. Within parliament the opportunity for the opposition to play a creative role seems to be lessened. All the inhabitants of the country have a right and duty to express and show concern about how the country is run. But instead of increasing the people's role, the new constitution lessens it. This will make the chance of achieving consensus on how South Africa should be governed even more remote. Moreover, the judiciary will have no power to curb the government.

9. In light of Catholic social teaching we are forced to conclude that the proposed constitution is not a satisfactory step on the road to peace in South Africa. It falls far short of what is required in terms of truth, love and freedom. It fails in regard to justice by not spelling out the rights and duties of all. It fails in regard to the truth because it does not recognise the

great majority of people. It fails in regard to love because it ensures that racial discrimination will continue. It fails in regard to freedom because it puts too much power in the hands of the president.

10. In conclusion, we ask for a constitution with a much broader vision embracing the real interests of all the people of South Africa. We cannot support the proposed constitution, so we have sent a memorandum to the parliamentary select committee setting out our view. We point out that the present bill represents the mind of only one section of a particular population group. So, we have asked for it to be seriously reconsidered and reformulated to meet legitimate aspirations of all.
11. We wish now to make our views known through this pastoral letter for the information of all and as a special act of pastoral guidance for the Catholics of our country.

12. As the debate on the proposed new constitution goes on and the time for a decision draws near, we call for humble and constant prayer for God's guidance and help, not only in regard to this matter but also in regard to all that affects the future of our country and its growth in justice and respect for human rights.

Signed on behalf of the Southern African Catholics Bishops conference.

Denis E. Hurley, OMI
Archbishop of Durban

President

D10.2 The Kairos Document: Official Summary

Challenge to the church

The political crisis in South Africa today is the KAIROS or moment of truth not only for apartheid but also for the church. A KAIROS is a critical decisive moment, a time of grace and opportunity, a challenge to decision and action.

What this moment of truth shows up first of all is that we are a divided Church and a Black Church. Both the oppressor and the oppressed, who are in mortal conflict at the moment claim loyalty to the same Church and the same faith and participate at the same table of the same Lord. How is that possible?

In relation to our political crisis there are three different theologies or ways of understanding Christian Faith.

State theology
The apartheid State misuses biblical texts and Christian beliefs to justify its oppression of the people. This we call 'State Theology'.

1. The State appeals to Romans 13:1–7 where Paul says that we should obey the State. That would be true in normal circumstances, but Paul does not tell us in this text what we should do when the State becomes unjust, oppressive and tyrannical. When this happens, we must say with Peter that we shall 'obey God rather than men' (Acts 5:29). We should also read Revelations 13 where the State is described as a diabolical beast.

2. When we oppose the State and resist its oppression, the State makes use of the idea of 'law and order' to try to make it feel guilty and sinful. But 'law' here is the unjust and

discriminatory laws of apartheid and 'order' here is the disorder of oppression and exploitation.

3. In 'State Theology' the symbol of all evil is communism. Everyone who disobeys and opposes the State is called godless, an atheistic communist take-over. They use this in an attempt to frighten people.

4. And finally, the god that the State preaches to us is not the God of the Bible. It is an idol. It is the god of the gun, the god of oppression. In fact, this god is the devil in disguise – the antichrist.

We must reject this heretical theology and its false prophets who can even be found among the ranks of those who profess to be ministers of God's Word.

'Church theology'

Many church leaders, who make statements and pronouncements about apartheid, appeal to certain abstract Christian ideas like reconciliation, peace, justice and non-violence. This we call 'Church Theology' and we offer here our critique of this theology too. It is inadequate, irrelevant and ineffective.

1. Reconciliation: There can be no true reconciliation and no genuine peace without justice just as there can be no forgiveness until there is repentance. If we call for reconciliation and negotiations now before repentance and justice and equality have been established, we will be calling for reconciliation between good and evil, justice and injustice, God and the devil. We must not come to terms with evil, we must do away with it.

2. Justice: True justice cannot come from the 'top', from the oppressor in the form of concessions and reforms. Why then

do Church leaders so often address their appeals to the 'top', to the State and to the white community? They (the top) must indeed repent but true justice will be determined by all the people together – as equals. Should the Church not address its appeals to the oppressed, encouraging them to take up their own cause and to struggle for justice?

3. Non-violence: violence is a loaded word. What a person calls 'violence' and what they call a 'legitimate use of physical force in self-defence', depends upon which side a person is on. When Church statements call physical force 'violence' no matter which side does it, they are trying to be neutral and to avoid saying who is right and who is wrong, who is the aggressor and who is the defendant. Of course, that does not mean every or any use of physical force by the oppressed is justifiable but it cannot be condemned for the same reason and in the same way as the violence of the aggressor.

4. The Fundamental Problem with this kind of 'Church Theology' is that it is still influenced by a type of spirituality that tends to be other-worldly. It is only recently that the Church has come to face the realities of this world and it has not yet developed an adequate analysis of our society and an appreciation of the need for politics and political strategies. A new biblical and prophetic spirituality is needed today.

Towards a prophetic theology

What we need now is a prophetic theology that takes a clear and unambiguous stand in the present crisis. This will have to be based upon a reading of the signs of our times, that is to say, a social analysis of the conflicting forces or interests that make up our situation of oppression.

Then we will have to go back to the Bible to find out what God has to say about oppression and what it means to say that God is always on the side of the oppressed. In the Christian tradition we will find this same theme expounded in terms of tyranny. A tyrannical regime is one that has become the enemy of the common good because it governs in the interests of some of the people and not in the interests of all the people – the common good. The apartheid regime is clearly a tyrannical regime. It is therefore a morally illegitimate regime and should be replaced by a government that will govern in the interests of all the people.

A prophetic theology, however, will not only point out what is wrong and sinful in our society, it will also present both the oppressor and the oppressed with a relevant and explicit message of hope. There is hope because God has promised us in Jesus Christ that justice and truth and love will triumph over all injustices and oppression in the end.

Challenge to action

God sides with the Oppressed: We are a divided Church and there is only one way forward to unity and that is for those Christians who find themselves on the side of the oppressor or sitting on the fence, to cross over to the other side to be united in faith and action with those who are oppressed. We must be united in Jesus Christ and in god 'who is always on the side of the oppressed' (Ps 103:6).

Participation in the Struggle: The present crisis challenges the Church to move beyond an 'ambulance' ministry to a ministry of participation in the struggle for liberation by supporting and encouraging the campaigns and actions of the people.

Transforming Church Activities: The usual activities of the Church like Sunday services, baptisms, funeral and so forth must all be re-shaped to promote the liberating mission of God in our present crises. The evil force we speak of in baptism, for example, must be named. We know what these evil forces are in South Africa today.

Special Campaigns: The Church should also make its contribution to the struggle by having special programmes, projects and campaigns. However, this should be done in consultation with the political organisations that truly represent the grievances and demands of the people. Otherwise there will be a serious lack of co-ordination and co-operation.

Civil disobedience: The Church must not collaborate with tyranny and oppression. It should encourage all its members to pray and to work for a change of government. In the process the Church may sometimes have to confront the apartheid regime and even advocate civil disobedience.

Moral Guidance: It is also the role of the Church in the present crisis to provide moral guidance by helping the people to understand their rights and their duties, especially the moral duty to resist tyranny and to struggle for a just society. While it is necessary to curb the excesses of those who act wildly and thoughtlessly, the Church should be experienced as the community that challenges, inspires and motivates people.

It is hoped that this document will become the basis of discussion, reflection and action and that it will be further developed and improved by those who can hear what the Spirit has to say to the Churches in our day.

D10.3 A Theological Rationale and a Call to Prayer for an End to Unjust Rule, 16 June 1985

[The statement was prepared by the regional Western Province Council of Churches and issued by the SACC's Executive Committee to all its regional councils and member churches]

Introduction

Soweto, 16 June 1976, is South Africa's most potent symbol of black resistance, approximately 700 people were killed and hundreds more wounded in unrest which soon extended beyond that day and place to encompass the entire country. These events have come to constitute a fundamental crisis in South African Society which the authorities are apparently incapable of resolving. They present a phase of resistance which began on 21 March 1960 when the police killed 69 people and wounded a further 180 people in the notorious Sharpeville shooting ... Now, on 16 June 1985, twenty-five years after the dawning of this phase of resistance it is right to remember those whose blood has been shed in resistance and protest against an unjust system. It is also right that we as Christians reassess our response to a system that all right-thinking people identify as unjust.

Declaration

We have prayed for our rulers, as is demanded for us in the Scriptures. We have entered into consultation with them as is required by our faith. We have taken the reluctant and drastic step of declaring apartheid to be contrary to the declared will of God, and some churches have declared its theological justification to be a heresy. We now pray that God will replace the present structures of oppression with ones that are just and remove from power those who persist in defying his laws, installing in their place leaders who will govern with justice and mercy.

A Firm Theological Tradition

We do this conscious of a broad and compelling tradition of faith that unites us in a loyalty to the sole lordship of Jesus Christ. The Scriptural record is clear. Civil authority is instituted of God, in order to rule with justice, goodness and love (Romans 13). This same record is equally God (Revelation 13). In this awareness Christians have through the ages prayed that they may be godly and quietly governed.

With Tertullian, in the spirit of the early church, we recognise that if civil law is not the source of social justice it is tyranny, and that such authority has no right to exist. In the same spirit Augustine defines the objective of 'government' to be human peace and 'the republic' as the welfare of the people. St. Thomas taught that 'human law has the true nature of law only in so far as it corresponds to right reasons, and therefore is derived from the eternal law. In so far as it falls short of right reason, a law is said to be a wicked law; and so lacking the true nature of law, it is rather a kind of violence'.

In this tradition the Reformers addressed themselves to the nature of legitimate government. Luther counselled people themselves willing to accept injustices, but warned of the obligation to oppose injustice shown towards one's neighbour. He also warned the tyrant that people would not accept their presumption indefinitely, and allowed that it was not their duty to obey such authority which contradicted the rule of God. In calling the people to turn to prayer to God in their need, he believed that God would not tolerate such rule for long. Calvin recognized the obligation of citizens to be subject even to the wicked ruler, while at the same time rejecting unjust laws as no laws at all. He stressed that obedience to civil authority should never be allowed to contradict obedience to God, who is the Lord of all and the King of kings. He understood the hunger for justice to be implanted in the human soul by God himself. 'And this feeling, is it not implanted in us by the Lord?' he asked. "It is then the same as though God hears himself, when he hears the cries and groanings of those who cannot bear injustice.'

In more recent times Karl Barth spoke of the obligation of the church to pray for the state, never as an object of worship, but on its behalf, that it might be legitimate, governing according to the rule of God. In so doing he recognized that such prayer cannot be offered without a corresponding commitment to work for good and legitimate government. He left us with no doubt in this regard that the Church is obliged to be unconditionally and passionately for the lowly and against the exalted. The Dutch Calvinist, Abraham Kuyper, has also spoken of the obligation of government: 'In order that it may be able to rule people, the government must respect this deepest ethical power of human existence. A nation consisting of citizens whose consciences are bruised, is itself broken in its national strength.' For this reason, he continued, 'we must ever watch against the danger which lurks, for our personal liberty, in the power of the state.' Indeed, 'the struggle for liberty is not only declared permissible, but is made a duty for each individual in his own sphere.'

It is this affirmation that stands central to the contemporary emphasis of the Roman Catholic Church, which proclaims a preferential option for the poor. It is this option, which requires the theologian to analyse the process of authority from the perspective of the poor, the marginalized and the oppressed – an opinion reaffirmed by Pope Paul II in his recent commentary on Latin American theology. Pope John XXIII, has stated that 'if civil authorities legislate for or allow anything that is contrary to that order and therefore contrary to the will of God, neither the laws nor the authorizations granted can be binding on the conscience of the citizens, since God has more right to be obeyed than men'. Paul VI, in turn, recognising that government can be tyrannical, declared: 'There are certain situations whose injustices cries to heaven ... whole populations destitute of necessities live in a state of dependence barring them from initiative and responsibility, and all opportunity to advance culturally and share in social and political life'. 'We want to be clear', he concluded, ' the situation must be faced with courage and the injustices linked with it must be fought against and overcome'.

It is this affirmation which forms the basis of Vatican II theology which states: 'Where citizens are oppressed by a public authority which exceeds its competence, they should not on that account refuse what is objectively required of them for the common good, but it must be allowable for them, within the limits of the law of nature and the gospel, to defend their rights and those of their fellow citizens against this abuse of authority.'

The Church in South Africa

The considered judgement of every synod, assembly and conference of the Roman Catholic and mainline protestant Churches (with the exception of the Afrikaans Reformed Churches), has been that the present regime, together with its structures of domination, stands in contradiction to the Christian Gospel to which the churches of the land seek to remain faithful. We have continually prayed for the authorities, that they may govern wisely and justly. Now, in solidarity with those who suffer most, in this hour of crisis we pray that God in his grace may remove from His people the tyrannical structures of oppression and the present rulers in our country who persistently refuse to heed the cry for justice, as reflected in the word of God as proclaimed through His Church both within this land and beyond.

In constant and solemn awareness of the responsibility we take on ourselves in this regard, we pray that God's rule may be established in this land.

We pledge ourselves to work for that day, knowing that this rule is good news to the poor, because the captives will be released, the blind healed, the oppressed set at liberty, and the acceptable year of the Lord proclaimed (Luke 4:18–19).

A Call to Prayer

We invite Christians, and all people of goodwill, to join consistently in prayer for a new and just order in this land. In so doing we share in a community of those who believe throughout this world, who will pray on June 16, in commemoration of those who died in Soweto and other places such as Sharpeville, Crossroads and Uitenhage, in commitment to a new South Africa for all its people.

D10.4 A Memorandum to T\the State President, P.W. Botha, 17 March 1986

This memorandum was prepared and signed by 33 members of MUCCOR (Ministers United for Christian Co-Responsibility), a group of clergy and lay persons based around the Johannesburg area which engaged in pastoral and theological reflection. MUCCOR is one of the projects facilitated by the institute for Contextual Theology.

The State President

The war in the country, which has now reached such frightening proportions and cost so many human lives and deep suffering in the homes of thousands of people particularly in our black townships, has made it more than necessary for us, Soweto ministers of religion and other ministers representing neighbouring townships of Randfontein, Kagiso, Alexandra and the Vaal Triangle, to meet in order to prayerfully consider what our role should be under the current conflictual circumstances. Our Christian conscience does not allow us to sit back while many of our people lose their precious lives almost on a daily basis. Their blood challenges us to sit up and take stock of the meaning of our God-given vocation as ministers of the Most High God.

We as servants of God feel that our role and mission is to save lives and not just to bury the victims of this war. We have agonized and earnestly sought God's guidance in this matter and thus feel constrained to express the following points to you.

There is every sign that the present violent confrontation between our people and your Government is escalating instead of decreasing. We are convinced that the only reason for this worsening of conditions in our country is the system of apartheid, which is the basis of all we perceive as being repressive legislation:

bannings, detentions, influx control, differential schooling, group areas fragmentation of the land, etc. Apartheid is the root cause of our current problems. We are painfully aware of the many delegations, especially from the church leadership, that have sought to meet and deliberate with you on these issues. But almost all of them have come back empty handed to their respective communities because they found themselves having to deal with everything within the framework of apartheid (or what you, Sir, call 'self-determination'). This is obviously dangerous because it proves that the path of talking or negotiation with the Government is fruitless and renders the route of violent confrontation the only viable and practical option!

We feel that to the extent that you cling to the ideology of 'separate freedom' for the people of this sub-continent, you are, by implication, not yet ready to talk meaningfully to the true and genuine leaders of the disadvantaged black masses of this country. Unless and until you are prepared to go beyond the framework of 'separation' there can be no meaningful talks with you and therefore no lasting resolution of this country's immense problems.

For instance, we are greatly disappointed, Sir, that we find very little recent speeches and those concerned Governmental departments regarding the resolution of our black schools' problems. We are greatly concerned, particularly as we approach the end of March. We feel that the Soweto Parents Crisis Committee and the consultative meeting it held in the December of 1985 deserve to have been taken more seriously than has been the case. These people represent a genuine black effort to bring about some sanity in the whole black education situation, but we continually got the impression that their efforts were not appreciated if not downright discouraged.

Sir, there is no knowing exactly what the situation is going to be at the end of March particularly in the black schools. Unparalleled and deep violent confrontation is likely to rattle this country decisively! But one thing is certain, you alone have the solution. Break out of the apartheid framework. Dismantle apartheid. Abandon security legislation and let the people of South Africa sit together to produce their own Constitution, a Constitution devoid of all racial traits. That is the only way out of the present political impasse.

We beg of you. Do not be afraid to follow this way. Almost all the churches and religious groupings in our country have called the apartheid way 'heresy' and 'sin'. This means that the majority of the people of this country believe that God is not on the side of apartheid. And that therefore those that uphold apartheid have no 'moral power' or 'soul power' on their side. And people who are devoid of such power will never win, our faith tells us. No amount of military power can subdue a people who are possessed of such 'moral power' and the determination to be free. We, the Servants of God in Soweto, Kagiso, Randfontein, and the Vaal Triangle want to make it unequivocally clear that at this junction in our people's sad history and this daily confrontation we have no choice but to take a stand on the side of the disadvantaged black masses who struggle to be free. It is on this basis that like the prophets of old we appeal to you in the name of God to turn your weapons of war into ploughshares and make it possible for the people of this country to build a new nation together, a nation where persons will simply be persons fashioned and made in the likeness and similitude of God.

A government can only be just if it actively promotes the common good of all the governed. We feel your Government cannot be perceived in this light, Sir. And we are God's servants, firmly taking sides with the politically, economically and socially disadvantaged people of this country, feel constrained not only to pass God's judgement on your Government but also to let it be known that henceforth we cannot be expected to co-operate with it until it repents and governs in the name of all the people and for the common good of all the people.

To this end the true leaders of the people must be released from prison and the exiles must return home, and a completely new start, new spirit must be created. We hereby publicly declare our stand with the people, and with God's own help may the people's struggle soon succeed, and may a new nation be born.

N.B. If this message of the 'Prophets' warning, is not heeded, and there be more bloodshed, your Government must take the full responsibility for the situation of death! The blood of the dead, God will place on you, Sir, and your Government!

To The Embassies

We want to express our Indignation to the Embassies of other countries as well!

We feel that the countries represented by these embassies benefit from the apartheid-created injustices and inequalities.

We therefore urge the international community to act against apartheid and decisively!

If this is not done, we declare them co-responsible for our miseries, and are therefore accomplices in our death, oppression and exploitation! This is a warning from God's servants.

D10.5 Urgent Message to the State President from the Southern African Catholic Bishop's Conference, 20 August 1986

Mr. State President

1. We members of the Southern African Catholic Bishop's Conference find ourselves compelled to express our views on the present situation in South Africa. It is a situation of conflict, of violence, of bloodshed. The state Bureau for Information maintains that there has been a lessening of conflict since the imposition of the state of emergency. Be that as it may, the state of emergency cannot last indefinitely and when it is lifted or becomes inoperative, it will be found not to have effected a cure. While apartheid remains in force its consequence will be with us. As long ago as 1957 our conference wrote:

   > To all white South Africans we direct a plea to consider carefully what apartheid means: its evil and anti-Christian character, the injustice that flows from it, the resentment and bitterness it arouses, the harvest of disaster that it must produce in the country we all love so much (Statement on Apartheid, July 1957).

2. The word of God is concerned with peace between people. As hearers and ministers of that word peace is our greatest concern too and so we express our views in an endeavour to make a contribution to promoting peace in South Africa in the context of the great prayer of Jesus for his disciples: 'May they all be one, Father; may they be one in us, as you are in me and I am in you' (John 17:21), in the context too of his special legacy: 'Peace I leave with you: my peace I give you' (John 14:27).

3. Peace in any human society exists only if there is general observance in society of the values that ensure good relations between its members. These values are truth, justice, love and freedom. We see these values as goals to be pursued by the whole human family in terms of God's will in creating us. We find them proclaimed in his word in the Bible, most especially in the preaching of the kingdom by Jesus. We recognise that sinfulness has disfigured human conduct but thank God for the gift of redemption in Jesus by which disfigurement is healed and people are given the grace to struggle bravely and vigorously to express those values in their personal and social life.

4. Social life embraces four important dimensions: the religious, the political, the economic and the cultural. In all these dimensions human society should seek to emphasise the values of truth, justice, love and freedom to achieve peace: peace between religious and political dimensions, peace between members of society, peace between government and citizens, peace between the societies that make up the human family.

5. Since this is our interpretation of God's will for his people in terms of the mysteries of creation and redemption, we must obviously be concerned to play our part in bringing this vision of peace into the society in which we live and in which we exercise our ministry.

Apartheid versus liberation

6. South African society is being torn apart by the consequences of apartheid. A fierce confrontation has arisen between the structures of apartheid and the forces of liberation. We recognise that the government has committed itself to the

dismantling of apartheid and has taken some measures towards this end, but much more needs to be done. We urge that the total dismantling of apartheid be pursued without further delay and as a matter of priority.

7. The present tempo and scope of the dismantling process does not appear to take into account the needs of this time in our history. A piecemeal abolition of unjust and discriminatory structures of the past is not enough to meet the critical situation in our country. A firm undertaking to dismantle apartheid totally will not only give credence to the government's stated desire for justice and peace for all, but it should in some measure alleviate the suffering, anger and injustices experienced by the majority of our people and open the way for meaningful negotiations.

8. We are perturbed at this suffering and anxiety. We deplore the escalation of the state, the security forces, those who experience oppression and even among the people themselves. We are saddened by the deterioration of the quality of life of all, especially the blacks.

9. We are especially concerned for the youth of our country. They are caught up in this spiral of violence. Black youth are trapped in situations obstructing their normal development to adulthood. With their personality development damaged, what hope is there for the South Africa of tomorrow? Youth serving in the security forces are faced with ever-increasing crises of conscience.

10. We all know that a spirit of liberation cannot be quenched, it cannot be suppressed for ever. The history of South Africa provides a vivid example of the eventual triumph of the Afrikaner people, of their spirit of national liberation. They, as

well as their English-speaking counterparts, should be able to recognise the spirit of liberation when they see it in their black compatriots.

The longer the present struggle takes, the worse the final condition will be.

The state of emergency

11. The state of emergency has been declared to control the striving for liberation. Our assessment of the state of emergency is born of personal knowledge of and experience of its effects, of exchanges with church personnel, of reports from various parts of the country, especially those areas where the repression and reaction to it have been most intense. We are conscious too of the practical implications of the regulations proclaimed for the state of emergency. They are hampering us and our co-workers in the communication of information and of normal guidance to our people, for instance, in the matter of public pronouncement and pastoral letters which may be declared 'subversive'.

12. The picture that emerges from personal or reported knowledge of the effects of the state of emergency is very disturbing: increased, even extreme, repression is its major feature.

13. Especially deplorable are the actions of the security forces in general against persons who are opposed to government policy and in particular against church personnel, for example, the suspension of civil liberties such as the right of assembly and the right to information, also physical assaults, destruction of property, detentions, deportations, unjustified arrests and intimidatory raids. The detention net has been cast very wide, enveloping countless persons far removed from political

activism and has imposed on them long periods of imprisonment, frequently in most uncomfortable and humiliating conditions with very poor diet and all too often subjected to the psychological torture of solitary confinement. We are dismayed too by instances of the violation of religious freedom, such as interference with church services, disregard for the sacred character of church buildings and the detention of whole congregations.

14. A second major consequence of the present state of emergency is the people's reaction to primary violence on the part of the state. Inspired and impelled by the unquenchable spirit of liberation, the people, especially the youth, are unyielding in the face of increased repression and respond with counter-violence against state institutions and personnel and against persons, both black and white, seen to be active in this latest form of repression. We deplore in the strongest possible terms the summary trial and 'execution' of those suspected of collaborating with the state. Sadly, the unspeakable cruelty of the 'necklace' continues. These tragic developments emphasise how mistrust grows and polarization intensifies.

15. A third effect of the state of emergency is the suppression of information and the blocking of communication. As a result of the restrictions on the free flow of information there is a proliferation of rumours, often grossly exaggerated. Confusion intensifies in a public already confused and uncertain. The result of ignorance or misinformation is at the root of growing fear and suspicions which in turn is fuelling already strong feelings of insecurity and hopelessness among a nervous and frightened people.

16. The state of emergency is at best a misguided concept to crush the urge for liberation which has irreversibly taken hold of the black, oppressed people of South Africa. The state of emergency is not a solution. It constitutes rather a formidable obstacle to the search for a true and lasting peace because:
    a. it heightens the impression that the government's intention is to hold on to power no matter what the consequences;
    b. it exposes more and more people to the repressive might of the state;
    c. it aggravates the feelings of frustration, anger and bitterness; it makes it impossible for the leadership to emerge that in due course must represent the people at the conference table.

17. In short, we see the state of emergency as being one of the principal obstacles to the process of rapprochement and negotiation between contending parties. As an interim measure, it may suppress conflict to some extent. But essentially it is treating the symptoms, not the disease.

Negotiation

18. Since the beginning of this year the government has admitted the need to negotiate with representatives of the black opposition. No progress can be made as long as those who have a major claim to leadership are excluded from meaningful participation in the political process. We see the problem in the criteria the government applies to these negotiations: only representatives of groups who renounce violence are to be considered as partners in negotiations, and a number of vital issues – such as the introduction of the universal suffrage – are non-negotiables.

19. As regards the first criterion, the call for a renunciation of violence, under normal circumstances this would be a valid point. However, it cannot be denied that the longstanding repression of the majority of South Africa's people under the system of apartheid has provoked the oppressed to adopt violence as a last resort to express their total rejection of an unjust system. The declaration of a state of emergency twice within a year has only compounded the impasse: massive repression on the part of the security forces is seen by the black majority as state-sanctioned violence and finds its response in widespread outbursts of counter-violence against any symbols of power vested in the state.

20. As regards the non-negotiables, the government itself has based to a large extent the 1983 Constitution of the Republic of South Africa on the process of negotiation, preferring consensus wherever possible to the imposition of majority rule. We believe in the creative momentum that negotiation can unleash for the good of all the people in the country. Through it, the non-negotiables of both parties in conflict can give way to mutual trust and understanding. This negotiation process must not exclude any of the accepted leaders of the oppressed majority in our country, whether they are residing in it at the moment or living in exile abroad.

21. We take the liberty of quoting here from a letter sent to us in April 1986 by the Cardinal President of our Justice and Peace Commission:
    May I bring to the fore some aspects of the problematic that concerns your country:

    a. The complete elimination of apartheid and a new social fabric that guarantees the participation, on an equal footing, of every citizen for the development of South

Africa, must be sought after without resorting to further acts of violence which could fatally compromise the very results that it is seeking to obtain.

b. The various ethnic groups that make up the South Africa society must be able to negotiate this new fabric and, to that end, their leaders who are banned or in prison must be given back their freedom of movement.

c. During the process of negotiation, all the above mentioned groups must seek to understand one another's positions and be open to a fruitful collaboration by eliminating prejudices and gradually overcoming the obstacles that interfere with the formation of a South African community proud of the rich variety that exists amongst its different components.

22. Many have urged the release of political prisoners and the unbanning of their organisations as a prerequisite for meaningful negotiations on the future of our country between the government and its extra-parliamentary opposition. We strongly support this proposal. We are convinced that the longer such unconditional negotiations are delayed the greater will be the danger that these persons and their organisations will, in despair, increasingly turn to Moscow and other communist centers of power for ideological and material support. Repression is more a stimulus than an antidote to communism.

Namibia

23. As we join our voice to other voices calling for negotiations on the future of South Africa we come back again to the question of Namibia. We made a strong appeal in our Report of Namibia of 1982 'for a creative, human and Christian effort on

the part of South Africa to conclude a just and peaceful settlement, and for sustained fervent prayer that, with the help of God, this will be achieved'. Unfortunately, peace has not yet come to Namibia. If South Africa had the will the way would surely be found. While continuing to maintain its armed occupation of Namibia, South Africa remains responsible for the death and disruption that plague that unhappy country, Once again, we urge the acceptance of Resolution 435 of the United Nations Security Council.

Sacrifice in the cause of peace

24. Both in the case of South Africa and Namibia we realize the obstacles to negotiation. We realize that in terms of human politics it will be extremely difficult to open negotiations. So, in concluding this expression of our views, we return once again to the vision given to us by the word of God and our Christian faith. The will to negotiate must be inspired by the Christian values that we cherish and that we accept as normative for our personal and domestic life and consequently should accept as normative too for our social life. There must be a compelling desire for peace. There must be a willingness to make sacrifices in the cause of peace including sacrifices that involve a too exclusive view of one's own nation or people. From the Bible we learn that Israel received its special calling as God's chosen people and was granted liberation from slavery in order ultimately to be at the service of other nations in the mystery of redemption. 'I have given you as a covenant to the people, a light to the nations' (Isaiah 42:6).

25. The life and teaching of Christ impress upon us that the cross is part of every human life and of all dimensions of human life, including the political. This has a special significance in the pursuit of peace. Jesus has taught us that it must be the mark

of the Christian, no matter how painful, to take the first step in seeking peace. 'So if you are offering your gift at the altar, and there you remember that your brother has something against you, leave your gift there before the altar and go; first be reconciled to your brother, and then come and offer your gift' (Matthew 5:23–24). This may be painful indeed. It may seem humiliating in political life but even in regard to political life the words of Jesus are relevant: 'Truly, truly, I say to you, unless a grain of wheat falls into the earth and dies, it remains alone; but if it dies, it bears much fruit. He who loves his life loses it, and he who hates his life in this world will keep it for eternal life' (12:24–25)

26. The will to negotiate must be characterized by hope, another of the great values taught by Christ. In the matter of negotiation there must by Christian hope for a sufficient degree of trust and communication between the contending parties to produce a result conducive to peace.

27. The assurance can be given that a great volume of prayer will rise up to God so that the will to negotiate may triumph over the whole unfortunate heritage of the past with its fears and suspicions, divisions and hatreds and so that it may open the way to a peaceful resolution of the present conflict and the birth of a new South Africa.

D10.6 Belhar Confession of Faith, Drafted In 1982, Adopted In September 1986

A STATUS CONFESSIONIS

Because the secular Gospel of apartheid threatens in the deepest possible way the witness of reconciliation in Jesus Christ and the unity of the Church of Jesus Christ in its very essence, the NG Mission Church in South Africa declares that this constitutes a *status confessionis* for the Church of Jesus Christ. (A *status confessionis* means that we regard this matter as a concern about which it is impossible to differ without it affecting the integrity of our communal confession as Reformed Churches.)

We declare that apartheid (separate development) is a sin, that the moral and theological justification of it makes a mockery of the Gospel, and that its constant disobedience to the Word of God is a theological heresy. The Decision of Ottowa and the decisions with regard to racism and therefore apartheid (separate development) cannot be regarded as an alternative to the decision of the Synod of 1978, but rather as a consequence.

According to the conviction of the Synod the NGK believes in the ideology of apartheid, which is in direct conflict with the evangelical message of reconciliation and the visible unity of the Church. Therefore the 1978 decision of the Mission Church makes it clear that we can do no other than with the deepest regret accuse the NGK of theological heresy and idolatry. This is done in the light of her theologically formulated standpoint and its implementation in practice.

The NG Mission Church makes this statement in deep humility and self-examination so that we may keep ourselves 'from being disqualified after having called others to the contest' (I Cor.9:27).

HE CONFESSION OF FAITH

We believe in the triune God, Father, Son, and Holy Spirit, who gathers, protects, and cares for his Church by his Word and his Spirit, as he has done since the beginning of the world and will do to the end.

We believe in one holy, universal Christian Church, the communion of saints called from the entire human family.

We believe that:

- Christ's work of reconciliation is made manifest in the Church as the community of believers who have been reconciled with God and with one another; that unity is, therefore, both a gift and an obligation for the Church of Jesus Christ; that although the working of God's Spirit is a binding force, yet simultaneously a reality which must be earnestly pursued and sought: one which the people of God must continually be built up to attain;
- this unity must become visible so that the world may believe; that separation, enmity, and hatred between people and groups is sin which Christ has already conquered, and accordingly that anything which threatens this unity may have no place in the Church and must be resisted;
- this unity of the people of God must be manifested and be active in a variety of ways: in that we are obligated to give ourselves willingly and joyfully to be of benefit and blessing to one another; that we share one faith, have one calling, are of one soul and one mind; and we have one Father, are filled with one spirit, are baptized with one baptism, eat of one bread and drink of one cup, confess one name, are obedient to one Lord, work for one cause, and share one hope; together come to know the height and the breadth and the depth of the love of Christ, to the new humanity; together know and bear one another's burdens, thereby fulfilling the

law of Christ; that we need one another and upbuild one another, admonishing and comforting one another; that we suffer with one another for the sake of righteousness; pray together; together serve God in this world; and together fight against all that may threaten or hinder this unity;
- this unity can be established only on freedom and not under constraint; that the variety of spiritual gifts, opportunities, backgrounds, convictions, as well as the various languages and cultures, are by virtue of the reconciliation in Christ, opportunities for mutual service and enrichment within the one visible people of God; that true faith in Jesus Christ is the only condition for membership of this Church.

Therefore, we reject any doctrine:

- which absolutizes either natural diversity or the sinful separation of people in such a way that this absolutization hinders or breaks the visible unity of the church, or even leads to the establishment of a separate Church formation;
- which professes that this spiritual unity is truly being maintained in the bond of peace while believers of the same confession are in effect alienated from one another for the sake of diversity and in despair of reconciliation; which denies that a refusal earnestly to pursue this visible unity as a priceless gift is sin;
- which explicitly or implicitly maintains that descent or any other human or social factor should be a consideration in determining membership of the Church.

We believe that

- God has entrusted to his Church the message of reconciliation in and through Jesus Christ; and the Church is called to be the salt of the earth and the light of the world;

- that the Church is called blessed because it is a peacemaker;
- that the Church is witness both by word and by deed to the new heaven and the new earth in which righteousness dwells;
- that God by his lifegiving Word and Spirit has conquered the powers of sin and death, and therefore also of irreconciliation and hatred, bitterness and enmity; that God by his lifegiving Word and Spirit will enable his people to live in a new obedience which can open new possibilities of life for society and the world;
- that the credibility of this message is seriously affected and its beneficial work obstructed when it is proclaimed in a land which professes to be Christian, but in which the enforced separation of people on a racial basis promotes and perpetuates alienation, hatred, and enmity;
- that any teaching which attempts to legitimate such forced separation by appeal to the gospel and is not prepared to venture on the road of obedience and reconciliation, but rather, out of prejudice, fear, selfishness, and unbelief, denies in advancing the reconciling power of the gospel, must be considered ideology and false doctrine.
- therefore, we reject any doctrine which, in such a situation, sanctions in the name of the gospel or of the will of God the forced separation of people on the grounds of race and colour and thereby in advance obstructs and weakens the ministry and reconciliation in Christ.

We believe that

- God has revealed himself as the one who wishes to bring about justice and true peace among men; that in a world full of injustice and enmity he is in a special way the God of the destitute, the poor, the wronged and that he calls his Church to follow him in this;

- that he brings justice to the oppressed and gives bread to the hungry; that he frees the prisoner and restores sight to the blind; that he supports the downtrodden, protects the stranger, helps orphans and widows, and blocks the path of the ungodly;
- that for him pure and undefiled religion is to visit the orphans and the widows in their suffering; that he wishes to teach his people to do what is good and to seek the right;
- that the Church must therefore stand by people in any form of suffering and need, which implies, among other things, that the Church must witness against any form of injustice, so that injustice may roll down like waters, and righteousness like an ever-flowing stream;
- that the Church as the possession of God must stand where he stands, namely against injustice and with the wronged; that in following Christ the Church must witness against all the powerful and privileged who selfishly seek their own interests and thus control and harm others.

Therefore, we reject any ideology, which legitimates forms of injustice and any doctrine which is unwilling to resist such an ideology in the name of the gospel.

We believe that, in obedience to Jesus Christ, its only head, the Church is called to confess and to do all these things, even though the authorities and human laws might forbid them and punishment and suffering be the consequence.

Jesus is Lord.

To the one and only god, Father, Son and Holy Spirit, be the honour and the glory for ever and ever.

CHAPTER ELEVEN

Sanctions: The World's Moment of Truth

A recognition that, to a significant degree, the apartheid regime owed its political sustenance to its participation in global trade and financial institutions goes as far back as the call in 1959 by iNkosi Albert Luthuli, the President of the ANC, for sanctions against apartheid South Africa. Various studies since the 1960s showed how South Africa's economic vitality as enabled by foreign investments produced wealth through harsh exploitation of Black labour, how this wealth is distributed in favour of the privileged White minority, and in turn, directly enhances the minority regime's ability to repress all forms of resistance to its rule.[117]

The 1981 Synod of the United States Presbyterian Church noted that "the record of the past twenty-five years shows that during that period when the economy of South Africa grew rapidly, and US investment increased, the politics of apartheid were enacted into law and made ever more repressive". Over time, the enunciation of the culpability of foreign investors and their shareholders in the perpetuation of apartheid had become a perennial ethical statement by the World Council of Churches, in particular.[118]

For the Christian community in South Africa and abroad, the discussion of an international trade embargo and corporate disinvestment from South Africa was initially nested within the fierce debates around the moral efficacy of political violence that had followed the announcement of the Special Fund of the PCR in 1970 (See Chapter 6). Those who argued that only non-violent means of protest is the ethically legitimate way of bringing change in South Africa were impelled to concede that only a measure as drastic as mandatory international economic sanctions, as the extreme form of non-violent pressure, would move the apartheid regime.

From the beginning the debate was hampered by two factors. The first was that Black workers, the people who would be most severely affected by a withdrawal of foreign companies from South Africa, were not, until 1979, organised extensively enough to allow their collective opinion to be canvassed reliably. Secondly, the government began to treat the promotion of economic sanctions as sabotage. The consolidation of the Internal Security Act in 1982 formalised this, making the promotion of sanctions an act of sedition.

The debate within South Africa on the assessment of the medium-term socio-economic effects of sanctions was not only skewed, but paralysed. Only those who supported the government's denunciations of threats of sanctions (chief among whom was Prince Mangosuthu Buthelezi – leader of the Kwazulu Bantustan) could freely canvas their views. They could do so in the knowledge that the government would deal harshly with those who argued against them.

In 1980 Desmond Tutu, the General Secretary of the SACC, had his passport withdrawn after a trip to Scandinavian countries where he called for a boycott of South African coal. In August 1985 Allan Boesak was detained for three weeks and unsuccessfully charged with treason after a speaking tour of Australia.

By 1985, however, the situation hand changed dramatically. The South African economy was beginning to feel the effects of economic isolation, and the country was in a state of a fiscal crisis that was compounded by a violent political crisis. The regime's brutal response to widespread civil disobedience that erupted across Black townships during 1984, and its flagrant aggression against neighbouring states, produced a broad consensus that any form of succour for the regime was tantamount to collusion in a threat to international peace and stability.

The point began to be made in religious circles that opposition to the regime was not merely a matter of pragmatism but of faith and morality. Any support for apartheid, even the purchase of goods produced in South Africa, or ownership of shares in companies with ties to the South African government or its parastatal institutions, was increasingly considered religiously reprehensible among the ecumenical community (see **Document D11.3**).

Acting out of this conviction of a moral responsibility, the delegates at the 1985 National Conference of the SACC formulated a carefully worded motion that supported disinvestment by foreign companies from South Africa without infringing the Internal Security Act (**Document D11.1**). The motion sent a signal to the international community that the oppressed people of South Africa were consciously willing to accept the discomforts entailed by sanctions.

The motion instructed the SACC'S Division of Justice and Reconciliation to conduct further studies and consultations on the issue of international economic ethics in relation to the conduction of apartheid state. During implementation of this resolution, the SACC held a series of consultations with trade union officials to benefit from the experiences of black workers, and other sectors to take systematic account of the aspirations of South Africans yearning for change.

The resolution of the SACC'S National Conference, held in June 1985, was widely viewed by both international ecclesiastical and the anti-apartheid solidarity movement as a signal and mandate to push for sanctions against the regime. The most dramatic and vigorous formal support for this position was displayed at the Commonwealth Leaders Summit held at Nassau in October 1985, when all the Commonwealth leaders (bar Margaret Thatcher of Great Britain) collectively called for mandatory economic sanctions against South Africa. In reaction, supervening the official stance of their government, the British Council of Churches, meeting in its scheduled General Assembly three weeks after Mrs Thatcher's option of 'constructrutive engagement' with the Botha regime at the Commonwealth Summit, issued a most comprehensive and categorical call for the British public to disengage from all linkages with the apartheid economy (**Document D11.4**).

In September 1985, the unimaginable had happened: Ronald Reagan had on the 4th of that month signed an executive order declaring South Africa's apartheid policy an "unusual and extraordinary threat to the foreign policy of the United States"[119], and duly prohibited trade and a plethora of commercial transactions between South African and United States companies.

As the post-1984 violent crisis in South Africa intensified and the death toll of victims of state violence mounted, the WCC General Secretary,

Dr Emilio Castro, called an Emergency World Church Leaders Meeting with South African church leaders to work out the most appropriate response to events in South Africa. The meeting was held in Harare, Zimbabwe, on 4-6 December 1985. It noted that the situation in South Africa constituted a kairos, a challenging moment of truth, not only for South African Christians but for the entire world. It was proclaimed that events prevailing in South Africa challenged the churches of the world to review their traditional responses to political problems and called them to a renewed dedication to the cause of liberation in South Africa.

The meeting enjoined the international community to apply immediate and comprehensive sanctions on South Africa, and significantly, called on international banks to deny the regime's pleas for debt-standby arrangements on its loans. It was also resolved that 16 June 1986 be observed internationally as a world day of prayer and fasting for rededication to ending of unjust rule in South Africa **(Document 11.2).** The latter sentiment, in effect, extended the process that had been ignited by the SACC's National Executive Committee's adoption of the theological rationale and call for prayer for the end to unjust rule a year before (See Document 10.3). Towards the end of 1985, the apartheid regime was clearly in trouble. P.W. Botha authorised his Minister of Justice, Kobie Coetsee to visit Nelson Mandela in prison.[120]

D11.1 SACC National Conference Resolution on Disinvestment, 28 June 1985
RESOLUTION NO. 5: DISINVESTMENT

The National Conference of the South African Council of Churches, being deeply concerned at the violent conflict in which the people of South Africa are now embroiled:

1. reiterates the statement which the Council has made in the past, that foreign investment and loans have been used to support prevailing patterns of power and privilege in South Africa;
2. recognises that many church leaders and Christians in South Africa are in favour of (selective) disinvestment and economic sanctions because they believe that the situation is now so serious that economic action must be taken to strengthen political and diplomatic pressures on South Africa to force the South African government to take seriously the need for fundamental change in South Africa;
3. has agreed that fundamental change would include the dismantling of apartheid and the democratic involvement of all South Africans in the planning of new political, economic and social structures which would seek to guarantee for all people justice, development, freedom and peace;
4. welcomes the concern and support of our fellow Christians in other countries who are working to assist us in finding non-violent ways in which fundamental change can be brought about in South Africa;
5. believes that the pressure in Western countries for disinvestment has been most effective in moving white South Africans into a more serious consideration of the cause of the political conflict of this country;

6. concludes from the evidence placed before it that foreign investment does not necessarily create new jobs and that the contrary is often the case because new investment is frequently in the form of sophisticated technological equipment;
7. draws attention to the fact that the churches have for many years tried to address the problems of structural unemployment in black communities and have not been aware of any serious concern being shown by the business sector, foreign or South African, or by government until recent months when economic sanctions have become a legislative probability in the United States;
8. confesses that in the churches there has been no proper debate and consideration of the disinvestment question because we have allowed ourselves to be restrained by the severity of laws designed to prevent open discussion of economic sanctions. This has meant that the only arguments being heard in South Africa are those in opposition to disinvestments.

This Conference therefore resolves:

a. to express our belief that disinvestment and similar economic pressures are now called for as a peaceful and effective means of putting pressure on the South African government to bring about those fundamental changes this country need;

b. to ask our partner churches in other countries to continue with their efforts to identify and promote effective economic pressures to influence the situation in South Africa, towards achieving justice and peace in this country and minimizing the violence of the conflict;

c. to promote fuller consideration of the issues by placing the case for the imposition of economic sanctions and disinvestment before the Executive Committee of the SACC and the regional councils, and the councils of our member churches and organisations with the request that they encourage congregations to study and debate them;

d. to ask the executive to appoint in consultation with the Director of Justice and Reconciliation, a task force to examine the whole question of economic justice as well as issues of disinvestment and economic sanctions, to review and co-ordinate the responses from the churches, and to assist the church leaders by making available to them information and analyses;

e. to call member churches and individual Christians to withdraw from participation in the economic system that oppresses the poor, by reinvesting money and energy in alternative economic systems in existence in our region.

D11.2 The Harare Declaration, WCC World Church Leaders Emergency Meeting on South Africa, 4–6 December 1985

We, leaders of churches from Western Europe, North America, Australia, South Africa and other parts of Africa, along with representatives of WCC [World Council of Churches], WARC [World Alliance of Reformed Churches], LWF (Lutheran World Federation] and AACC [All Africa Conference of Churches] met here in Harare, Zimbabwe, from 4th to 6th of December 1985, on the invitation of the World Council of Churches.

We have come together to seek God's guidance at this time of profound crisis in South Africa and have committed ourselves to a continuing theological reflection on the will of God for the Church.

We affirm that the moment of truth (kairos) is now, both for South Africa and the world community.

We have heard the cries of anguish of the people of South Africa trapped in the oppressive structures of apartheid. In this moment, of immense potentiality, we agree that the apartheid structure is against God's will and is morally indefensible. As we await a new democratic and representative government in South Africa,

1. We call on the Church inside and outside South Africa to continue praying for the people of South Africa and to observe June 16th – the tenth anniversary of the Soweto uprisings – as World Day of Prayer and fast to end unjust rule in South Africa.
2. We call on the international community to prevent the extension, the rolling over, or renewal of bank loans to the South African government, banks, corporations and para-state institutions.

3. We call on the international community to apply immediate and comprehensive sanctions on South Africa.
4. We call on the Church inside and outside South Africa to support South African movements working for the liberation of their country.
5. We welcome and support recent developments within the Trade Union movements for a united front against apartheid.
6. We demand the immediate implementation of the United Nations Resolution 435 on Namibia.

We gathered here, commit ourselves to the implementation of the Harare declaration as a matter of urgency. We are confident that the liberation of South Africa will be liberation for all the people in the country, black and white.

D11.3 United Church of Christ (USA): 1985 General Synod Resolution

FULL DISINVESTMENT OF ALL FINANCIAL RESOURCES FROM ALL CORPORATIONS DOING BUSINESS WITH SOUTH AFRICA

A PROPOSAL FOR ACTION

Whereas the Fifteenth General Synod had adopted the pronouncement on United Church of Christ Full Divestment of All Financial Resources from All Corporations Doing Business with South Africa, and whereas this pronouncement calls the Church to fulfil our Statement of Faith through this action; therefore, the Fifteenth General Synod:

1. Calls upon all instrumentalities, agencies, national bodies, conferences, associations, congregations and members of the United Church of Christ to begin immediately the process of divestment, and to complete divestment within two years.

2. Defines as entities to be divested those corporations with direct investment in South Africa and banks and other financial service institutions engaged in loans, credit or services to the Government of South Africa or its instrumentalities or agencies.

3. Calls upon the President of the United Church of Christ to inform the major corporations involved and investing in South Africa of the passage and implementation of this pronouncement and proposal for action, and to encourage the withdrawal of these corporations and their financial resources from South Africa.

4. Calls upon the President of the United Church of Christ to call upon the President and the Congress of the United States to terminate all US government economic, scientific and military support of the apartheid regime of South Africa.

5. Calls upon the United Church of Christ, in co-operation with the National Council of Churches, the World Council of Churches, and other denominations to participate in full divestment of financial resources from South Africa.

6. Calls upon agencies, instrumentalities, national bodies, conferences, associations, congregations and members of the United Church of Christ to combine divestment with other forms of economic pressure to maximize our effectiveness as instruments of change by:
    a. Engaging in acts of public witness directed at corporations supportive of the apartheid system such as prayer vigils, demonstrations and letter and postcard writing campaigns;
    b. Withdrawing bank accounts and investments from financial institutions which continue to lend to the Government of South Africa or its agencies or instrumentalities or which make strategic loans to the private sector for the provision of products, services or technology that helps maintain the apartheid systems;
    c. Abstaining from buying gold, Kruger Rands (South African gold coins), diamonds and other products from South Africa;
    d. Supporting the campaign of the Interfaith Centre on Corporate Responsibility to bring pressure on key corporations assisting the apartheid system in their demands that these corporations cease immediately all sales and service relationships with the South African Government and government-owned corporations and

inform the South African government that the dismantling of the apartheid systems is a prerequisite for their remaining in South Africa.

7. Calls for a major effort to educate members of the UCC regarding the role of US investment in South Africa in supporting the apartheid system.

8. Calls for action by the Congress of the United States to limit economic relations between the US and South Africa and impose economic sanctions on the apartheid regime.

9. Calls for members, congregations and agencies of the United Church of Christ to support state and municipal legislation limiting investment and business relations with corporations with direct investment in South Africa and financial institutions making loans to the public sector or strategic loans to the private sector in South Africa.

10. Asks that individuals, congregations, agencies and instrumentalities of the United Church of Christ take into account whether corporations have direct investments in South Africa as they make consumer decisions and whenever possible, abstain from the purchase of products manufactured by corporations continuing to do business in South Africa.

11. Calls for the development of a United Church of Christ pastoral letter, 'South African Apartheid and Full Divestment and other forms of Economic Pressure' by a drafting committee representing the United Church Board for World Ministries, United Church Board for Homeland ministries, Pension Board, Office for Church and Society, Commission for Racial Justice and Council of Conference Ministers, and to widely circulate the document throughout the United Church of Christ and the nation for discussion and theological reflection.

12. Calls upon the President of the United Church of Christ to strengthen our ecumenical partnership with the United Congregational Church of South Africa and to initiate planning for a Day of Prayer for the people of South Africa, inviting church bodies to join us in that solemn observance, in faith and hope that repentance and redemption might be revealed through the healing love of God in Jesus Christ.

13. Requests the United Church Board for World Ministries and Commission for Racial Justice to coordinate this proposal for Action and calls upon the instrumentalities of the United Church of Christ to make a detailed report to the Sixteenth General Synod of the UCC.

D11.4 British Council of Churches, November 1985 General Assembly Resolution on South Africa

... aware that the policy of 'constructive engagement' has not contributed to the participation of black South Africans in the government of their country:

reaffirms the BCC's policy (November 1979) that 'progressive disengagement' from the economy of South Africa is the appropriate basic approach for churches to adopt until all the people share equally in the exercise of political power;

requests member churches to urge their financial authorities to cease, where they have not already done so, to invest in companies which have a substantial stake in the South African economy; and

calls on all Christian people to identify personally with the peaceful struggle against apartheid by refusing to buy or sell South African products ...

resolves that, given the deepening crisis in South Africa and the Christian duty to promote its just resolution, BCC policy will be a strong advocacy of all and full support for carefully targeted sanctions.

CHAPTER TWELVE
Pilgrimages to Lusaka

A major complicating factor for the apartheid regime around the mid-1980s was that as its economic vulnerabilities exacerbated, and the conflagration around mass action to render the country ungovernable became an endemic part of South African life, the stature of the African National Congress as the credible voice and leader of the direction of the liberation sought in South Africa grew. As the desperation for a search for the alternative out of the violent gridlock increased, the imperative to seek the views of the ANC, or to consult with the organisation from its headquarters in Lusaka Zambia even trumped the fact the ANC was a banned organisation, contact with which was an offence.[121]

From the church front, the Southern African Catholic Bishops Conference took the pioneering step when in April 1986 their delegation, led by Archbishop Denis Hurley, journeyed to Lusaka for a meeting with the ANC President, Oliver Tambo. Besides the bravery of the defiance of the bishops, which *de facto* installed the status of the ANC as the representative of the struggling masses in the country, the most dramatic development was the content of the communique released by President Tambo and Archbishop Hurley at the conclusion of the meeting (**Document D12.1**).

The bishops declared on 16th April 1986, from Lusaka, their "common commitment [with the ANC] to bring a speedy end to the evil system of apartheid and to transform South Africa into a united, democratic and non-racial country", and "that the Pretoria regime cannot be an agent for change. Rather, it is the principal obstacle to the emergence of a democratic government representative of all the people of South Africa". By this time, of course, the country was under a tightened national State of Emergency, troops were patrolling township streets, and police cells were overflowing from mass detentions. The regime's alternative more brutal 'third-force' units were let loose in their extra-judicial missions and schemes to eliminate key anti-government activists.

It was against this background of grim repression and the desire to dialogue with South Africans both inside the country and those in exile that the World Council of Churches staged its Emergency Leaders Consultation in Harare, Zimbabwe in December 1986 (see Document D11.2). The choice of the venue was in part designed to allow for elements of the liberation organisations to make some kind of an input in the deliberations.

Arising from this momentum and the perspective on the apartheid regimes strategy of brutalising and destabilising the neighbouring states that were providing operational bases ('Frontline States'), especially for the ANC, a decision was taken to convene a broader and more overt consultation between the world church leadership, all the exiled South African liberation organisations and the South West African People's Organisation (SWAPO) in Lusaka the following year.

At the invitation and facilitation of the Programme to Combat Racism of the WCC representatives of churches, trade unions, women's, youth and anti-apartheid groups from South Africa, Namibia and other parts of the world, met in Lusaka, Zambia, 4-8 May 1987 under the theme 'The Church's Search for Justice and Peace in Southern Africa'. Of the 250 delegates from all over the world, forty-two delegates from South Africa and twenty-eight from Namibia (author was an attendee).

There were emotional and historically iconic scenes at the opening ceremony of the conference as the leader of the South African delegation Beyers Naude, Secretary General of the SACC, met and fondly embraced Oliver Tambo, and later John Mlambo (President of the Pan Africanist Congress of Azania), and Sam Nujoma (President of SWAPO). The entire top leadership of the liberation organisations were in attendance. In parallel to the official programme of the conference a plethora of private briefings were held between delegates from South Africa and Namibia and their respective exiled political leaders and comrades.

Following the precedent set by the Catholic bishops, this principally protestant summit effectively recognised the legitimacy of the ANC, the PAC and SWAPO as the rightful means through which the people of South Africa and Namibia should seek their freedom. This was a daunting step not only for the international Christian community but also for the South

African protestant churches which formed a constituency of the SACC. There were still concerns about the plight of the minority White population and of those sections of the body-politic who did not subscribe to the vision and actions of these armed liberation movements.

Beyond the expected condemnation of the apartheid regime and the call for the intensification of sanctions, in its summative Lusaka Statement (**Document D12.2**) the conference pronounced its recognition "that the nature of the South African regime, which wages war against its own inhabitants and neighbours, compels the movements to the use of force along with other means to end oppression," and continued, "We call upon the churches and the international community to seek ways to give this affirmation practical effect in the struggle for liberation in the region and to strengthen their contacts with the liberation movements".

A revealing indication of the intensity of the deliberations at this conference emerged in a statement prepared by the West European delegates, stating:

> The Churches have declared sanctions to be the last non-violent pressure for change. Increasing repression within South Africa, and continuing lack of political will by some governments to impose sanctions, requires us to support the Movements when they exercise the right of the oppressed to take up arms against the unjust state. At certain times in history the Church finds it possible and indeed mandatory to provide support to groups who have found it necessary to resort to armed struggle.[122]

Uncharacteristically, the Lusaka Statement confessed the frequent failure of the churches "to move from resolution to practice". It reaffirmed the declaration of world church leaders who had met in Harare the previous year and urged the WCC to establish a machinery to monitor and encourage the implementation of that declaration and its precursors. For its part it adopted a Lusaka Action Plan as an appendix to the Lusaka Statement in order to counteract the tendency of statements and declarations ending being just mere words.

The Lusaka conference amplified the radical theological attack against the Pretoria regime that had been initiated by the Kairos Document in 1985. The most important consequence of the Lusaka Statement was its translation of the postulations of the 'Kairos theology' into a workable set of proposals. The Statement's unequivocal and categorical positions on the illegitimacy of the South African government and the consequent moral right of the oppressed to seek liberation through the outlawed and armed ANC and PAC were now presented to the councils of the various churches.

The SACC delegates attended the Lusaka conference without being official representatives of their churches. This meant that the Lusaka Statement and resolutions had to be considered by the SACC itself and its respective member churches. Media publicity surrounding the Lusaka conference had already created considerable interest in the Lusaka Statement. A wide variety of role players, including the state, were waiting anxiously to see how the churches were going react to the statement, given their ambivalence towards violent resistance and notions of the 'removal' apartheid government. Among the more progressive church groups and theologians, the statement was seen as a theological litmus test. The challenge of its radical positions would test if the churches had just been paying lip-service or had been serious on ending apartheid in a manner that would eventuate into a political dispensation that is dominated by the ANC, which had by now clearly assumed the widely supported vanguard of the aspirations of the oppressed.

The first opportunity for an official ecclesiastical consideration of the Lusaka Statement came at the SACC's annual conference in 1987, six weeks after the Lusaka meeting. A fierce debate erupted on the motion calling for the adoption of the statement. Ultimately, procedural technicalities were used to block outright adoption of the Lusaka Statement as the SACC's official policy.

The conference was reminded that the SACC is a federated forum that cannot adopt a position of such magnitude before it had been debated within the individual synods of its member churches, and that it should not adopt principles of action concerning which its membership had been unable to achieve consensus. In the end, the conference adopted a watered-down version of the original motion whereby the SACC 'received' the Lusaka Statement instead of 'adopting' it. The council would merely present the statement to its member churches for study. Following this, however, the Church of the Province of Southern Africa (the main stream Anglican Church in South Africa), the second largest constituent of the SACC, became the first church to formally the Statement. It did so at its 1987 synod.

In the largest member church of the SACC, the Methodist Church of South Africa (MCSA), the Lusaka Statement sparked one of the most memorable disputes in the history of the Methodist Connexional Conferences ever since the 1970 WCC-PCR grants to the liberation movements (**see Documents D6.1 and D6.4**). The outcomes of the Lusaka conference were presented and discussed at the general conference of the MCSA held in Benoni in October 1987. The import of the political positions adopted in Lusaka fell upon a theological-political climate which, in response to the lingering Kairos Document debates, had coagulated into movement of White Methodists who were campaigning that the MCSA declare itself a 'peace church'. The drive was that the MCSA should take a feather out of the quakers' cap and declare that a commitment to pacifism was constitutive of Methodist identity. The ensuing debate, which sharply revealed the persistence of a Black-White divide within the South African theological community, prevented any specific response to the Lusaka Statement.

In frustration, members of the Black Methodist Consultation (BMC), the informal Black caucus within the MCSA, held a series of fringe meetings during the Benoni conference disgusted at the stark divergence along racial lines of perspectives on the reality facing the majority of the South African population. They noted that the church was still not restructured in a way that allowed the opinion of the oppressed Black majority to be heard. (According to the Official Government Census, in 1980 there were 1,554, 280 Africans, 140,120 Coloureds, 4,320 Asians, and only 414,080 White members of the Methodist Church.[123]

They issued a letter to the newly elected President, enclosing a statement announcing the formation of the Alliance of Radical Methodists

(ARM), and a letter which the ARM had already written to the World Methodist Consultation. In the letter they stated that "an increasing number of people find themselves alienated by the inadequate response of our church to the Black struggle for liberation from inequality, exploitation and oppression in both church and nation". They would, therefore, bring these concerns to international and local public attention and ask the World Methodist Conference to review its relationship with the MCSA. Furthermore, they declared that unless there was a significant change of direction in the church, they would be obliged to reconsider their own position within the Methodist Church of Southern Africa.[124]

On the other stream, the Institute for Contextual Theology, which facilitated the production of the Kairos document and acted as the centre of all the debates bearing upon it, and whose former Executive Director, Frank Chikane had just assumed the office of the Secretary General of the SACC in July 1987, held a special theological conference on 'Theology and Violence' in the South African context on 26 November of the same year.

The conference, attended by around 120 participants, emerged with a consensus that after 1985, and as shown by the institutional Church's ambivalent and equivocal response to the Lusaka Statement, it was a mistake to speak of the South African Church as a single unit bound together by opposition to the evil of apartheid. The conference statement styled 'a working document' concluded that "the institutional Church in South Africa is divided and therefore cannot be an unambiguous agent for the liberation of the poor and oppressed. The church, however theologically defined, is a reflection of the structure of our society" (**Document D12.3**).

These theologians and lay Christian activists appealed to those identified as 'the remnant', that is, those in the mainline churches who were deemed committed to the liberation struggle, to ensure "that the Church which has been partly responsible to giving legitimacy to colonial and other oppressive regimes since the 4th century BC, adopt the Lusaka Statement and declare the South African regime morally illegitimate".

The conference was also planned to serve as an occasion to launch a collection of essays edited by Charles Villa-Vicencio, professor of

Theological Ethics at the University of South Africa (UNISA) titled *Theology and Violence*[125] which had been commissioned by the ICT the previous year. The introductory essay to the book had argued that it would not be out of keeping with the history of Christian tradition for the churches in South Africa to accept the Lusaka Statement. It suggested that the church, acting as the instrument of the oppressors, had given theological support to the political programmes of these oppressors and to their use of military means over the centuries. It pointed to the duplicity of an attempt to change the rules of the game now that the oppressed, hitherto silenced, were now able and prepared to break the power of the oppressor with whatever means available to them. Through their conference statement, the ICT theologians stated that "the individual must choose their means of struggle according to their informed conscience, and the situation in which they are."

Those who had been forced into exile or who were deprived of the legal space to engage in non-violent political struggle could not be expected to give up the struggle on the debatable grounds that violence against a state that had unleashed a reign of terror against those it is denying citizenship in the land of their birth was taboo. They had to do what was practicable for them to do. Finally, they argued, those with the space for non-violent resistance should move beyond preaching and should go out and confront the regime non-violently.

D12.1 A Communique of the Southern African Catholic Bishops Conference, Jointly With The African National Congress, 16 April 1986

Delegations of the Southern African Catholic Bishops Conference (SACBC) and the African National Congress (ANC) met in Lusaka on the 15th and 16th of April 1986. The delegations were led by Archbishop Denis Hurley and Oliver Tambo, presidents of the SACBC and the ANC respectively.

The bodies met as a result of their common commitment to bring a speedy end to the evil system of apartheid and to transform South Africa into a united, democratic and non-racial country.

They recognised that apartheid cannot be reformed but must be ended in its entirety. Accordingly, they agreed that the Pretoria regime cannot be an agent for change. Rather, it is the principal obstacle to the emergence of a democratic government representative of all the people of South Africa.

The SACBC recognised the fact that the ANC is playing an important role in this struggle and that it will occupy a similar position in a free South Africa. It therefore considers it vital that there should be a continuing contact between the ANC and the SACBC. The SACBC also recognised that it is necessary for the Catholic Church to engage in specific actions to increase the pressure for genuine change in South Africa. Mere condemnation of the apartheid system is not enough. The delegations agreed that the international community has a responsibility to increase its own pressure for a speedy end to the apartheid systems.

Moved by a common concern to see all the people of South Africa, both Black and White, living together in peace and as equals, the SACBC and the ANC agreed that they would continue to maintain contact with each other.

D12.2 Lusaka Statement, 8 May 1987

We, representatives of churches, trade unions, women's, youth and anti-apartheid groups from South Africa, Namibia and other parts of the world, met in Lusaka, Zambia, 4–8 May 1987 at the invitation of the Programme to Combat Racism of the World Council of Churches under the theme 'The Churches' Search for Justice and Peace in Southern Africa'.

The Context

We have met together eighteen months after leaders of churches around the world committed themselves to the implementation of the Harare Declaration. In Lusaka, we have reviewed the activities undertaken since Harare. Churches, countries, regions recorded varying degrees of progress in implementing the Declaration.

During the period following the Harare meeting, the situation in South Africa has considerably worsened. In the last eleven months more than 20 000 opponents of the apartheid regime have been detained, among them black children as young as 7 years of age. The emergency powers of the South African regime have placed the country under virtual martial law. During the same period, South Africa's detention, killing and violent oppression of the Namibian people has also escalated.

Our meeting was especially significant because of the opportunity it afforded us for discussions and exchange of views with the liberation movements of South Africa and Namibia.

We began our meeting on the ninth anniversary of the Kassinga Massacre remembering the 800 Namibians, mostly women and children, who were killed by the South African army in their refugee camp in Angola. A few days prior to the meeting, South Africa attacked Livingstone, Zambia, killing four innocent persons –

yet another reminder of South Africa's policy destabilisation and aggression against the Frontline States.

We have heard the moving testimony of the victims of apartheid. The cruel reality of life in the townships of South Africa and the horrors of occupation in Namibia have been brought home to us in the most graphic terms. Anguish, suffering, unimaginable pain and heroic resistance are the hallmarks of the struggle for justice in South Africa. Against such a background, our duty to ensure that the resolutions that follow are translated into early action is in no doubt.

The Theology
It is our belief that civil authority is instituted by God to do good, and that under the biblical imperative all people are obliged to do justice and show special care for the oppressed and the poor. It is this understanding that leaves us with no alternative but to conclude that the South African regime and its colonial domination of Namibia is illegitimate.

We recognise that the people of South Africa and Namibia, who are yearning for justice and peace, have identified the liberation movements of their countries to be authentic vehicles that express their inspirations and self-determination.

We as churches also recognise and repent of our failure to work as vigorously as possible for the implementation of the Harare Declaration, and so to work for the removal of the present rulers who persistently usurp the stewardship of God's authority.

The Challenge
1. We call on the churches and the international community to recognise the overwhelming material sacrifice and suffering of the people of the Frontline States in combating apartheid and

the destabilising influence of the Pretoria regime in the region. This necessitates an immediate and enhanced programme of aid and assistance to the Frontline States through the South African Development Coordination Council and other agencies in order to reduce their dependence upon South Africa and to enable them to continue support for both refugee victims of apartheid and those movements actively engaged in the struggle for liberation.

2. We affirm the unquestionable right of the people of Namibia and South Africa to secure justice and peace through the liberation movements. While remaining committed to peaceful change, we recognise that the nature of the South African regime, which wages war against its own inhabitants and neighbours, compels the movements to the use of force along with other means to end oppression. We call upon the churches and the international community to seek ways to give this affirmation practical effect in the struggle for liberation in the region and to strengthen their contacts with the liberation movements.

3. We affirm that the end to the conflict in Namibia and the attainment of self-determination by the Namibian people lies in the implementation of UN Security Council Resolution 435 (1978). We therefore condemn the attempt by the United States, in collusion with other members of the Western Contact Group and with the minority government of South Africa, to bypass this resolution by linking the independence of Namibia to extraneous issues such as the withdrawal of Cuban troops from Angola. We recognise the willingness of SWAPO, the sole and authentic representative of the people of Namibia, to enter into an immediate ceasefire on the basis of UN Security Council Resolution 435. We call upon the churches to mark the 10th Anniversary Year of the UN Security

Council Resolution 435 with a programme of action to end the colonial domination of Namibia. We further call upon the churches to observe 4th May as a World Day of Prayer for a free Namibia.

4. We urgently call upon the churches in countries which through economic and political cooperation with South Africa and Namibia, support the apartheid regime, to exert increased pressure upon their governments to implement sanctions, and upon banks, corporations and trading institutions to withdraw from doing business with South Africa and Namibia. We especially call upon the international community not to engage in newly-devised deceptive forms of disinvestment which maintain the status quo, but instead to apply immediate and comprehensive sanctions to South Africa and Namibia.

5. We note with the gravest concern the growing number of those imprisoned, tortured, on trial, under sentence of death, and bereaved as a result of the actions of the apartheid regime. We call upon the churches especially those outside Namibia and South Africa, to respond with prayer and increased efforts to publicise and meet with material assistance the needs and concerns of those who bear this particular burden of apartheid.

6. We condemn the censorship of the media and the concerted campaign of misinformation directed by the apartheid regime and its collaborators against the opponents and victims of apartheid. We call upon the churches and the international community to take steps to secure the freedom of information about and within South Africa through their own, and if necessary, new mechanisms, thus ensuring the fair and objective reporting of events in the region.

7. We recognise, at this crucial time (kairos) in the history of Southern Africa, the need for unity of purpose and action on the part of all those concerned with the process of liberation in the region, not least among the churches themselves whose failings in this respect are a cause for repentance. We see the suffering that results where unity is not present. We commit ourselves to further the cause of unity in our churches, and in our ministry to the movements for liberation operating to bring an end to the illegitimate regime in South Africa and Namibia.

8. We call upon the WCC, in the light of the Harare Declaration and the previous resolutions, to establish with urgency a mechanism whereby the progress of member churches and others in implementing the Harare Declaration and these resolutions can be monitored, and through appropriate advice and encouragement, made more effective. Special attention should be given to the implementation of economic sanctions. This monitoring process should occur at national, regional and international levels. We recommend that further meetings of churches, liberation movements, and others be held within eighteen months to review the result of the monitoring process.

In the past, we have often failed to move from resolution to practice. We recognised that it is God's obedient instrument in the struggle for justice and peace in Southern Africa. We pray for God's grace and covenant together to accompany our brothers and sisters in Namibia and Africa on their journey to liberation.

LUSAKA ACTION PLAN

This plan was produced and adopted at the 4–8 May Conference as part of the Lusaka Statement in order to ensure that the statement be translated into action.

1. The WCC should send a delegation of Eminent Church persons on a mission to the United States, United Kingdom, Federal Republic of Germany, Japan and the European Community Secretariat in Brussels, permanent members of the Security Council of the United Nations and the Contact Group nations on Namibia. This group should:

1.1 Call for the immediate and unconditional implementation of UN Security Council Resolution 435 (1978) and underline the critical urgency for the churches and people of Namibia of an end to the prevailing impasse which generates increased pain and suffering:

1.2 Call for the immediate implementation of comprehensive economic sanctions against South Africa. Churches should specifically press for:

   a. EEC countries to include coal in their sanction package:

   b. an end to trade in oil, a crucial import for South Africa, by endorsing and supporting the international Shell Oil boycott;

   c. ways to boycott South African Airways and end its landing rights at international airports;

   d. pressure on banks to stop the granting of credit to the government of South Africa, its institutions, private banks and the rest of the private sector in South Africa, as well as to the public and private sectors in Namibia; banks should also refrain from scheduling South African loans and making such rescheduling dependent on the resignation of the Botha government;

e. withdrawal of multinational corporations based in the countries visited who maintain trade and investment with South Africa and Namibia. Particular emphasis should be put on refraining from the exploitation of the resources of Namibia in accordance the UN Decree I;

f. increased and effective measures to comply with the UN Security Council Arms Embargo against South Africa (1977) and the prosecution of those who break it.

1.3 urge the diplomatic isolation of the Afrikaner National regime and its expulsion from all United Nations agencies;

1.4 urge Western governments to sign and ratify the International Convention on the Elimination and Repression of the Crime of Apartheid adopted by Resolution on the UN General Assembly in 1973 and ratified by some 8-member states;

1.5 promote a climate of solidarity with the struggling peoples of Namibia and South Africa in the countries visited by meeting with South African Liberation movement representatives in these countries.

2. **Namibia**

2.1 PCR should embark upon a programme of Information on Resolution 435, its provisions and its implications for the future of Namibia. An information packet should be disseminated to all member churches for wide distribution and discussions at all levels.

2.2 The 4 May 1988 should be observed as a World Day of Prayer for a free Namibia; and the 10th Anniversary of the Kassinga Massacre on 4th May 1978 should be marked by a special focus on the continuing brutality and atrocities being committed in Namibia.

3. South Africa

The WCC should embark upon and intensify the campaign to expose the moral and theological illegitimacy of the South African regime by:

3.1 encouraging member churches to recognise, support and relate to the liberation movements; actively endorsing the Lusaka statements and working for its implementation as well as the Lusaka action plan;

3.2 campaigning for the recognition of the liberation movements of Namibia and South Africa's legitimate representatives of their countries;

3.3 encouraging Trade Unions to boycott the transport of goods to South Africa and Namibia and seeking ways of working closer with unions on campaigns and boycotts;

3.4 facilitating the production of educational and informational resources on the liberation movements to be widely distributed to local congregations;

3.5 establishing a coordinating mechanism for implementation of the Lusaka and Harare Declarations by churches and anti-apartheid groups, especially all actions on sanctions mentioned under Point I of this document.

4. The Frontline States

4.1 This consultation commends the work of the Frontline States in their care for refugees, noting especially the commitment of the Zambian government and the Zambian Church Council, our hosts in Lusaka, as well as other church agencies working among refugees.

4.2 Member churches should promote awareness of the pernicious consequences of apartheid policies on the economy and well-being of Frontline Sates especially insofar as it means that scarce resources have to be diverted towards the defence of the countries.

4.3 The churches are encouraged to continue to campaign for a radical reform of the world economic order and to give as much political and economic support as possible to the newly established Africa Fund of the Aligned Movement.

4.4 The All Africa Conference of Churches should encourage its member churches to monitor the use being made by the South African regime or its agents in African states to violate sanctions especially with regard to oil shipments and the arms embargo, and to become more actively involved in anti-apartheid activities such as the Shell Oil boycott.

4.5 Churches should oppose all support for UNITA in Angola and RENAMO in Mozambique, which are South African funded groups, and work to end US support for UNITA.

4.6 Churches should elicit moral and material support for the Frontline States, in particular by increasing aid to the SADCC in its efforts to lessen dependency on South Africa.

4.7 Churches should support the call for sanctions/withdrawal/ disinvestment from South Africa and Namibia and instead support investment in the SADCC countries.

4.8 The WCC should support and call on churches to
   b) make financial contributions to the Documentation and Information Centre in Harare, and
   c) participate fully in the radio transmission venture by preparing religious programmes with a Kingdom-oriented approach on all aspects of liberation theology in order to counter right-wing religious propaganda.

5. *Southern Africa*

5.1 Churches should provide mechanisms for Southern African students to study abroad.

5.2 Churches should increasingly work to encourage international youth groups to incorporate the issues of South Africa and Namibia in their ongoing activities.

5.3 Churches should raise the visibility of the plight of women in Southern Africa by convening seminars and workshops.

D12.3 Theology and Violence: A Working Document of the ICT Theological Conference, Cape Town. 26 November 1987

The struggle

The issue is not violence and non-violence but the struggle for the liberation and the dismantling of apartheid, capitalism and sexism, because without justice, there will never be peace and an end to war in South Africa.

There is not always clarity as to what violence is and what non-violence is. The word is often used to mean reform or passivity, but it can also mean active resistance to oppression. There is not exclusive choice between armed struggle and non-violence; the two complement each other. In the struggle the individual must choose their means of struggle according to their informed conscience, and the situation in which they are.

The Church

The Institutional Church in South Africa is divided and therefore cannot be an unambiguous agent for the liberation of the poor and oppressed. The church, however theologically defined, is a reflection of the structure of our society:

1. The dominant tradition has played a significant role in supporting the wealthy and powerful.
2. This tradition has tended uncritically to accept the institutionalized violence of the state.
3. The churches fail to find ways of excluding from membership those working for the apartheid regime.
4. The church has little political analysis of itself and its role.

5. It does, moreover, play a political role in legitimizing actions, policies and organizations in society.
6. It must, therefore, be seen as every other institution in society, as a site of the struggle.
7. We also need to recognize that there are forces actually fighting for the soul of the Church on the side of the oppressor.

Appeal to the remnant

There is, however, a remnant in the Church (and in each of its denominations), as there was in Israel, which understands the Word of God from the perspective of the poor and oppressed and challenges the existing institutional structures of the Church.
We appeal to the remnant to remind the Church continuously of its calling to take sides in the struggle against oppression, even at the risk of causing further divisions.

We appeal to this remnant to analyse the Church and the interest, especially the economic interest, that determines the decisions that are made by the Church.

We appeal to the remnant to ensure the following:
1. That the Church which has been partly responsible to giving legitimacy to colonial and other oppressive regimes since the 4th century BC, adopt the Lusaka Statement and declare the South African regime morally illegitimate for the following reasons:

    a) It has no mandate from the majority of the people and has never been recognized as legitimate by the colonized people of South Africa.
    b) It is deliberately destabilizing South Africa and its neighbouring countries.

- c) It has, in effect, declared war on the inhabitants of South Africa.
- d) It is not serving the common good and the interests of all South Africans and does not allow all to participate in these.
2. That the Church show critical solidarity with the liberation movements and alternative structures, offering resources: venues, accommodation, volunteers, finances, etc.

CHAPTER THIRTEEN
Standing for the Truth

Arguably, at the dawn of the year 1988 the ANC as a revolutionary movement whose success could only be measured by the levels of the intensity of the social conflict within South African society and the apartheid government, was at its strongest position. Under the pen of Oliver Tambo, it was proclaimed that "there is no doubt that we enter this year [1988] with the prestige and authority of the ANC and Umkhonto we Sizwe higher than they have ever been before".[126] The organisation's Message to the People of South Africa, delivered on its 76th anniversary on 8 January 1988, would stand out as its most confident and directed command to the multifaceted forces which were increasingly conscious that they were throwing in the last punches against the apartheid regime.

In November 1987, the unthinkable happed. Govan Mbeki, one of the Rivonia trialists sentenced to life imprisonment in 1964 was released from prison. P.W. Botha's two-years long national State of Emergency had failed to quell the culture of the intent to render the country ungovernable. A co-ordinated internal 'mass-democratic movement' was honing its mass defiance campaigns. Internationally, the enactment of a web of economic and other sanctions against Pretoria was growing.

On the other hand, the scale of the pain and disruption of social life by the apartheid regime's systematic national security management system under P.W. Botha's 'Total Onslaught' strategy was overwhelming. Addressing a regular National Church Leaders forum on 2 February 1988, SACC General Secretary Frank Chikane gloomily lamented that "the last twenty months since May 1986 have been the darkest part of the tunnel in life of the people of South Africa". He narrated about "... the detention of more than 30 000 peace-loving South Africans, the detention of thousands of children ... the emergence of vigilantes and assassination squads, the deliberate creation of the so-called 'black-on-black' violence ...".[127]

Paradoxically, the ANC's triumphant January 8th Statement, too had pragmatically reflected that "in the 75 years of struggle under the banner of the ANC, we have never known a campaign or repression as coldly calculated and systematic as we experienced this past year".[128] Still, a clarion call was made:

> We must remain on the attack, maintain our offensive posture and, in struggle, win new ground in our advance towards people's power. To wrest that new ground from the enemy requires that we plan for action, organise ourselves for action, and on the basis of those plans and relying on our organised strength, attack the enemy on all fronts as a united force. To achieve a further advance to people's power, these must be our watchwords – plan, organise, attack![129]

In what appeared to be a knee-jerk reaction to this resilient determination to sustain the now evident unravelling of the apartheid body politic fight on Wednesday 24 February 1988 a fresh set of Emergency regulations were proclaimed. Seventeen mass-based organisations, including some that were known to have tirelessly promoted non-violent protest, were barred "from carrying on or performing any activities or acts whatsoever". The restricted organisations included the United Democratic Front (UDF), an umbrella organisation of some 400 community-based organisations, including the Release Mandela Committee (RMC).

The Azanian People's Organisation (AZAPO) was also included in the banning order. The Congress of South African Trade Unions (COSATU) whose head office had been bombed by state agents in May 1987 was specifically prohibited from engaging in what the government would elect to perceive to be political activities. As part of this clampdown, restriction orders were imposed on eighteen respected leaders of these organisations, including Mrs Albertina Sisulu. Rev. Simon Gqubule, a Methodist theological educator and past Vice President of the SACC, was listed among these prominent leaders, restricted to the Pietermaritzburg magisterial district and placed under house arrest. This action was immediately seen inside and outside religious circles as a sign that the regime would not tolerate even non-violent opposition and appeared to be more determined to react with greater repressive force.

At their regular forum on 2 February 1988, meeting under the aegis of the SACC, leaders from all the main churches had agonised on the deepening political crisis and deliberated intensely on the nature of the intervention they felt the church was impelled to take. According to Frank Chikane they "agreed in principle to engage in effective non-violent action to persuade or pressure those in power to abandon violence and negotiate with the legitimate leaders of the Black majority in South Africa".[130]

Having believed that there was still scope for non-violent persuasion of the apartheid regime, the church hierarchy was thus shocked and angered by the 24 February proscriptions on what they considered to be organs of a pursuit for peaceful change. In response, an emergency meeting of church leaders, was held the following day, on 25 February 1988, at the SACC's Khotso House in Johannesburg. This time, the meeting included leaders from the Catholic Church and a broadened representation from the Council of African Independent Churches.

At this emergency church leaders' meeting, the clergy went beyond the ritual of condemning the behaviour of the government. Uncharacteristically, the unequivocally declared their intention to defy and violate the new repressive order: "We must make it quite clear, that whatever the consequences, we will continue as a matter of course to campaign for the release of prisoners, to call for clemency for those under sentence of death, to call for unbanning of our political organisations, to call for negotiations involving the true leaders of our country to bring about a transfer of power from a minority to all of the people of our country, to commemorate those who have died in what the state calls 'riots', and to call upon the international community to apply pressure to force the government to the negotiating table."**(Document 13.1).** To make good on their intention, they also resolved to defy the State of Emergency regulations by marching to parliament in Cape Town to present a petition to P.W. Botha, then the Chairman of the State Security Council and State President who had racialistically and undemocratically elected White legislature. The petition defiantly notified the government of the intention to "explore every possible avenue for continuing the activities which you have prohibited other bodies from undertaking" (**Document 13.2**).

The procession to Parliament took place on Monday 29 February 1988 following a "service of witness and protest" at St. George's Cathedral. It disruptively ended with the arrest of twenty-five church leaders who were led by Archbishop Desmond Tutu and had included Moulana Farid Esack of the Call of Islam. More than 150 members of the clergy and laity who persisted on marching on after the arrest of the leaders, those who were at the front of the march were violently attacked with a police water cannon, arrested and ferried to Caledon Square police station. After several hours all were released on an official warning that charges are being framed against them.

Following the disrupted march to parliament an unprecedented flurry of furiously worded correspondence between Botha's office, Desmond Tutu and Frank Chikane followed. There was a clear determination from church leaders that despite the vilification of their mission by the state-controlled media and security apparatus, they were prepared to stand for the truth and face the consequences of proclaiming that the country could no longer bear the conflict wrought by the injustices of apartheid.[131]

The events of February 1988 opened a new chapter in the history of South Africa. With the silencing of the political organisations which had voiced the aspirations of the oppressed, and the pervasive repressive campaign unleashed against all anti-regime activity since the declaration of the State of Emergency in July 1985, the church found itself as the only remaining channel for the articulation of the aspirations of the oppressed.

Three seminal realisations dawned. The first, was needing to get beyond the violence/non-violence ethics debate and to focus on effective non-violent action to end apartheid. The second, was that the apartheid regime's show of force 'represent[ed] a desperate attempt by weak people to hold on to power in the face of an ever-increasing determination by the oppressed of our country to bring about justice, democracy and peace" (**Document 13.1**). Thirdly, the church leadership now readily recognised that the struggle activities which had been prohibited "are central to the proclamation of the gospel in our country" and that they would take forward the campaigns from where the restricted organisations had been forced to leave them (**Document 13.1**).

Perceptively, it was reckoned that this fresh protest movement initiated around the moral convictions of ecclesiastical head figures needed to be extended to the whole of the Christian community. To this end, a historic National Convocation of Churches was convened in Johannesburg on 30–31 May 1988. The meeting brought together members of many denominations and faiths from all levels of the religious groupings. Each church sent five representatives which included clergy, women and youth activists to the Convocation.

According to an official report, the Convocation's aim "was to bring an end to the apartheid system by putting pressure on the South Africa regime to abandon apartheid and participate in a negotiated settlement to establish a just, non-racial and democratic society where all will be treated equally before the law".[132] The Standing for the Truth Campaign was launched at the convocation. A National Committee was set up and assigned to catalyse the formation of regional committees. The single purpose of the campaign was to have the whole church in South Africa mobilised and organised into effective programmes of non-violent actions against the apartheid system and National Party rule.

On the night of 31 August 1988, as the programme of the Standing for the Truth Campaign rolled on, Khotso House, which was not only the head office of the SACC but had tenanted a number of UDF affiliated and other community organisations, was bombed and destroyed. Four weeks later, Khanya House, offices of the Southern African Bishops Conference were damaged in an arson and limpet mine attack. There were no doubts as to who the perpetrators were. (The then Minister of Law and Order, Adrian Vlok confessed at the subsequent Truth and Reconciliation Commission in 1996 that the police carried these acts under his command, including the 1987 bombing of COSATU House).[133]

Unshaken, at the beginning of 1989 the Standing for the Truth Campaign in collaboration with an amalgam of UDF-affiliated organisations which had by now re-profiled themselves 'the Mass Democratic Movement' launched the Mass Defiance Campaign. As if the bombing of the offices of church ecumenical offices was not enough, in May 1989 an attempt was made on the life of Frank Chikane. His clothes had been peppered with a chemical warfare agent.[134]

Through this 1989 Mass Defiance Campaign, South Africa witnessed an unprecedented period of protests and defiance of not only apartheid laws, but also the repressive restrictions that were continuously being put in place to muzzle political opposition to the government. The resultant state of widespread social unrest, coupled with the biting effects of international financial sanctions and a United Nations enforced arms embargo, threw the Botha regime into terminal crisis. P.W. Botha was forced by his National Party colleagues to resign, and F.W. De Klerk was appointed as Head of State on 18 August 1989.

By the time De Klerk assumed office, and the National Party tried hard to assume a semblance of legislative authority by passing, for example, the Foreign Funding Act, the intensity of the mass defiance campaign could not be ignored. Segregated group areas laws became redundant as Black people moved into White residential spaces in the main cities. 'Whites only' beaches were invaded, hospitals were forced to treat who ever required their services without racial discrimination, and eventually, marches were permitted during the latter part of 1989. There is no doubt that this explosion of people's power, in addition to other international and reginal political and military events, ultimately drove the apartheid government to the negotiating table with the hitherto demonised liberation organisations.

Sometime during January 1990 President De Klerk issued a public invitation to church leaders to meet with him for a dialogue. Suspecting that the meeting would be used for propaganda purposes to snuff the momentum of the defiance campaign, the SACC issued a press statement rejecting the invitation, pointing to the list of outstanding demands that have been presented to government over the long past period without any fruitful response (**Document D13.3**). They reiterated these demands in this press statement of 31 January 1990, closing it with an exhortation to De Klerk to "Let my People go". They did not know that two days from thence, on 2 February 1990, F.W. De Klerk would in his State of the Nation address in Parliament do exactly what was on their statement: Unbanned the liberation movements and all political organisations, announced the release of Nelson Mandela from prison and the commencement of negotiations for a democratic and non-racial constitutional dispensation.

D13.1 Statement by the Leaders of South African Churches, 25 February 1988

We, the undersigned leaders of South African churches, held an emergency meeting in Khotso House, Johannesburg today to discuss the crisis in our country which was created yesterday by the South African government when it banned the operations of 17 of our people's organisations, prohibited many activities of the Congress of South African Trade Unions and restricted 18 of our leaders.

1. *Implications of the restrictions*
We believe the restrictions represent a desperate attempt by weak people to hold onto power in the face of an ever-increasing determination by the oppressed of our country to bring justice, democracy and peace. The government's drastic and brutal action removes all effective means open to our people of working for true change by peaceful means, and if there is violent reaction to its action, this government must take full responsibility.

The ban on the activities of the 17 organisations is a blow directed at the heart of the Church's mission in South Africa.
Firstly, the organisations which have been banned are the organisations of and for our people.

Secondly, the activities which have been prohibited are central to the proclamation of the Gospel in our country. We must make it quite clear that, no matter what the consequences, we will continue as a matter of course to campaign for the release of prisoners, to call for clemency for those under sentence of death, to call for unbanning of our political organisations, to call for negotiations involving the true leaders of our country to bring about a transfer of power from a minority to all of the people of our country, to commemorate those who have died in what the state calls " riots", and to call upon the international community to apply pressure to force the government to the negotiating table.

Our mandate to carry out these activities comes from God and no man and no government will stop us. If the state wants to act against the Church of God in this country for proclaiming the Gospel, then so be it.

Thirdly, at least one prominent church leader known to us has been banned and house arrested in terms of yesterday's regulations. Dr. Simon Gqubule, principal of the Methodist Church's John Wesley College, has been restricted to the Maritzburg district and house arrested from 6 pm to 5 am. We know Dr. Gqubule to be a man dedicated to justice and peace in our country and we condemn the restrictions on him – as we condemn the restrictions placed on all our other leaders – in the strongest terms we can muster.

We find it particularly horrifying that the government restricted two leaders – in the persons of Mrs Albertina Sisulu and Mr Archie Gumede – who were until yesterday tireless workers for the cause of peace in two of the most desperate crisis areas in our land. Mrs Sisulu has been struggling to bring peace between opposing groups in KTC, Cape Town. It is widely acknowledged that Mr Gumede had been a key advocate for peace in the fighting in Maritzburg.

We believe the time has come to state the truth clearly as we see it: from the government's banning of these two leaders, from its harassment of peacemakers in KTC, from its detention of leaders in Martizburg and from its failure to arrest people against whom there is clear evidence of murder and assault, we must conclude that the authorities are deliberately obstructing peace in our country and encouraging violence among our people. Their purpose is to use surrogate forces to smash effective opposition to their heretical policy of apartheid, and to ensure as far as possible that it is the blood of black people, and not of white people, that is spilled in pursuance of their aim.

2. *A Call for Action*

In response to the current crisis, we feel we must address primarily the oppressed in our land, for it is they who will decide in the final analysis when apartheid is going to be abolished.

We urge the oppressed to intensify the struggle for justice and peace in accordance with the Gospel and we encourage them not to lose hope, for victory against evil in this world is guaranteed by Our Lord. For our part, we commit ourselves to exploring every possible avenue for continuing to carry out the activities which have been banned insofar as we believe they are mandated by the Gospel.

To the white voters of South Africa, we must say – without too much hope of being heard – that you are being deceived by the government. Your fellow South Africans want nothing more than to live in a just and peaceful country. Your position is becoming untenable and we believe that you must dissociate yourself from this government. Apartheid is a heresy, you can't reform a heresy, and if you are to assure your future, you must now pull out of 'white politics' and join the real struggle for democracy.

We now hope the international community – and especially South Africa's major trading partners – will wake up to the face that this illegitimate government is threatening their interests as well as the lives and security of black and white South Africans. It has shown quite clearly that it has nothing to offer but instability and bloodshed. It must be isolated to force the abandonment of the awful path it has chosen.

In addition, we call on our churches to arrange major services of witness and protest against the restrictions in every areas of the country at 3 pm on Sunday, February 28.

D13.2 Church Leaders' Petition to Parliament, 29 February 1988

[This petition was signed by 25 leaders from all the major Christian denominations associated with the SACC; the Catholic Archbishop of Cape Town, leaders of the African Indigenous Churches, and Moulana Faried Essack of the Call of Islam. The religious leaders were water cannoned and arrested as the procession left St. George's Cathedral on its way to houses of parliament]

Dear Mr State President and Members of Parliament

We, as leaders of a number of South African churches, have come to Parliament today to witness and pray in a time of crisis outside the buildings in which you make important decisions affecting millions of South Africans belonging to churches. In terms of the principles of non-violent direct action, we informed the Government of our intention before coming here. Once we have completed our act of worship outside where you work, we intend returning to St George's Cathedral.

We are deeply distressed, and protest to you in the strongest terms, at the restrictions which were placed last week on the activities of 17 of our people's organisations, on the Congress of South African Trade Unions and on 18 of our leaders.
We believe that the Government, in its actions over recent years but especially by last week's action, has chosen a path for the future which will lead to violence, bloodshed and instability. By imposing such drastic restrictions on organizations which have campaigned peacefully for the end of apartheid, you have removed nearly all effective means open to our people to work for true change by non-violent means. Only yesterday we pleaded publicly with our people not to react to your measures by resorting to

violence, but if some of our people turn to violence, you must take responsibility.

We are particularly horrified at the restrictions you have placed on people and organizations who have been in the forefront of the struggle to bring peace to the strife-torn areas of Pietermaritzburg and KTC in Cape Town. Mr. Archie Gumede, Mr. Willie Hofmeyr and Mrs. Albertina Sisulu are just a few of the many people who are now banned from working for peace. Your actions indicate to us that those of you in government have decided that only violence will keep you in power; that you have chosen the "military option" for our country. It appears to us that you are encouraging the growth of black surrogate forces to split the black community and to smash effective opposition to apartheid, moreover that you are trying to ensure as far as possible that it is the blood of black people and not of white people that is spilled in your struggle to hold onto power.

We regard your restrictions not only as an attack on democratic activity in South Africa but as a blow directed at the heart of the Church's mission in South Africa .The activities which have been prohibited are central to the proclamation of the Gospel in our country and we must make it clear that, no matter the consequences, we will explore every possible avenue continuing the activities which you have prohibited other bodies from undertaking. We will not be stopped from campaigning for the release of prisoners, from calling for the clemency for those under the sentence of death, from calling for the release of political prisoners to negotiate the transfer of power to all the people of our country, from commemorating significant events in the lives of our nation, from commemorating those who have died in what you call "riots", or from calling on the international community to apply pressure to force you to the negotiating table.

Last week many of us issued a statement in which we addressed primarily, the oppressed people of our land for we believe it is they who will decide in the final analysis when apartheid is going to be abolished. We urged them to intensify the struggle for justice and peace and encouraged them not to lose hope for victory against evil in this world is guaranteed by our Lord. Our message also applied to you. Your position is becoming untenable. Your fellow South Africans want nothing more than to live in a just and peaceful country and we urge you – without too much hope of being heard – to turn from the path you have chosen. If those of you in government persist with your current policies, then we urge those of you out of government to withdraw from white politics and to join the real struggle for democracy.

We urge you to take the following action:

- Lift last week's restrictions and end the state of Emergency.
- Unban political organizations, release and remove restrictions on our political leaders, allow exiles to return and free all detainees.
- Enter negotiations for a dispensation in which all can live together in peace, freedom and justice

We have not undertaken this action lightly. We also have no desire to be martyrs. However, the Gospel leaves us no choice but to seek ways of witnessing effectively and clearly to the values of our lord and saviour Jesus Christ and you give us virtually no other effective and peaceful means of doing so.

God Bless you.

D13.3 Statement By The SACC on the State President's Invitation to Churches, 31 January 1990

1. We, the member churches of the SACC, have always been and remain committed to a dialogue and communication.

2. We have a long record of approaching the Government, for instance by sending delegations to Cabinet Ministers, Prime Ministers and State Presidents, by open letters to Government, and through Synod and Church Conference resolutions.

3. Out of this process has come a number of issues, conditions and demands which we have consistently put to the Government. Among things we have called for are:
   - The release of political prisoners, detainees and lifting of restrictions on individuals;
   - The unbanning of all banned organizations;
   - The return of exiles;
   - The repeal of all apartheid laws;
   - The lifting of the State of Emergency;
   - The ending of all forced removals and current forced incorporations of people into homelands.

   At this time, we also call on the Government to desist from its attack on the Wilgespruit Fellowship Centre and to abandon its new Foreign Funding Act.

   All these things we have specified time and time again in our denunciation of apartheid as a heresy.

4. This thus constitutes the outstanding agenda which the churches have already put on the table. We find it difficult to

respond to the State President's public invitation until we see actual movement from the Government on this agenda.

5. Only when we see such movement could we consider a further agenda which would make such a meeting worthwhile.

6. We reiterate our position, that we do not see ourselves as negotiators, but a Voice of God and his people. We urge the Government, once again, to act on the above-mentioned conditions and to begin serious negotiations with the recognized leaders and peoples' organizations to bring about justice and peace in our land.

7. Our own call to the Government is still "Let my people go."

NOTES

[1] M. John Lamola, "Debate on Violence", in, *Hammering Swords into Ploughshares: Essays in Honour of Archbishop Desmond Tutu*, edited by Buti Tlhagale and Itumeleng Mosala (Michigan: Grand Rapids, 1986), p.56-67

[2] M. John Lamola, "Does the Church Lead the Struggle? A Caution," *Sechaba*, July 1988, p.7-11.

[3] See, South African Catholic Bishops Conference, *The Bishops Speak*, 3 vols (Pretoria: SACBC, 1990); and A. Prior (ed), *Catholics in Apartheid Society* (Cape Town: David Phillips, 1982)

[4] *Survey of Race Relations in South Africa, 1961* (Johannesburg: Institute of Race Relations, 1962), p.82

[5] In 1948 the Cape Coloureds enjoyed a qualified right to vote, whereby they could elect four white MPs who represented them in Parliament.

[6] *South Africa 1988/89, Official Yearbook of the Republic of South Africa* (Pretoria: Bureau of Information), p.161

[7] Cited in J. W De Gruchy, *The Church Struggle in South Africa* (Michigan: Eerdemans, 1979), p.56

[8] See, Garth Abraham, *The Catholic Church and Apartheid, 1948-1957*, M.A History Dissertation, University of Natal, Durban, 1984, p8-13

[9] See, Diane Paul, "Darwin, Social Darwinism and Eugenics", in *The Cambridge companion to Darwin*, edited by J. Hodge and G Radick, Gregory (Cambridge: Cambridge University Press, 2006), p.230- 293

[10] G.W.F. Hegel, *Lectures on Philosophy of History*, in Eze, E.C. (ed), *Race and the Enlightenment: A Reader* (Oxford: Blackwell, 1997 [1822]) p.120-142

[11] In, A. Prior (ed), *Catholics in Apartheid Society* (Cape Town: David Phillips, 1982), p.171

[12] See, Garth Abraham, *The Catholic Church and Apartheid, 1948-1957*, p.150

[13] Ibid.

[14] Ibid.

[15] Ibid.

[16] Cited in, South African Institute of Race Relations, *Survey of Race Relations in South Africa, 1955-57* (Johannesburg: SAIRR, 1958), p.7

[17] Ibid.

[18] B.B. Keet, *Suid-Afrika Waarheen* (Stellenbosch: University of Stellenbosch Press, 1955)

[19] See J. J. Venter, 'H.F. Verwoerd: Foundational aspects of his thought', *Koers*, 64, 4 (1999), p.415-441

[20] De Gruchy, *The Church Struggle in South Africa*, p.55

[21] See C.E.W Simpkins, *Reconstructing South African Liberalism* (Johannesburg: South African Institute of Race Relations, 1986), *ad passim*

[22] Steve Biko, "Black Consciousness and the Quest for a True Humanity", in *I Write What I Like*, edited by Aelred Stubbs (Johannesburg, Picador Africa, 2004 [1973]), p.96-108

[23] In South African Institute of Race Relations, *A Survey of Race Relations 1955-56*, p.6

[24] Potgieter, D.J. et al. (eds). *Standard Encyclopaedia of Southern Africa* (Cape Town: NASOU, 1970), p. 378-380.

[25] J. J. Venter, "H.F. Verwoerd: Foundational aspects of his thought", *Koers*, 64, 4 (1999), p.415-442

[26] D. W. Kruger, *South African Parties and Policies* (Cape Town: Human & Rousseau, 1960), p. 386

[27] Ibid. p.419

[28] Ibid. p.426

[29] See, Canon L. *John Collins, Faith under fire* (London: Leslie Frewin, 1966), p.195

[30] See Canon J. Collins, *Faith Under Fire*, p.225

[31] J. Cochrane, "Christian Resistance to Apartheid: Periodisation, Prognosis", in *Christianity Amidst Apartheid*, edited by M. Prozesky (London: Macmillian Press, 1990,), p.81-100

[32] Venter, Verwoerd: Foundational aspects of his thought, p.415-442

[33] South African Institute of Race Relations. *A Survey of Race Relations in South Africa: 1955-56,* (SAIRR, Johannesburg, 1957), p.6

[34] Francis Meli, *South Africa Belongs to Us: A history of the ANC* (Zimbabwe Publishing House: Harare; James Currey: London, 1988), p.81-85
[35] Mary Benson, *South Africa: The Struggle for a Birthright* (London: IDAF, 1985), p.220-234
[36] Benson, *Struggle for Birthright*, p.223
[37] See, J.W De Gruch., *The Church Struggle in South Africa* (Michigan: Wm B. Eerdemans, 1979), *ad passim*
[38] See, G Abraham, *The Catholic Church and Apartheid: 1948-1957*. M.A Dissertation, University of Durban, 1984
[39] A. Prior, (ed)., *Catholics in Apartheid Society* (David Phillip: Cape Town, 1982)
[40] Prior, *Catholics in Apartheid Society*, p.173
[41] Prior, *Catholics in Apartheid Society*, p.177
[42] *Ibid.*
[43] Mary Benson, *South Africa: The Struggle for a Birthright* (London: IDAF,1985) p.234
[44] Benson, *Struggle for Birthright*, p.235
[45] N. Mandela,*The Struggle is my Life* (London: IDAF), p.168
[46] K Luckhardt, and B. Wall, *Organise or Starve: The History of SACTU* (London: Lawrence and Wishardt, 1980), p.364
[47] Mandela, *Struggle is My Life*, p.107
[48] Mandela, *Struggle is My Life*, p.165
[49] Mandela, *Struggle is My Life,* p.166
[50] Mandela, *Struggle is My Life,* p.168
[51] *Pro Veritate*, Vol.4, No.6, July 1965
[52] See, C. Villa-Vicencio, J. W. de Gruchy, (eds), *Resistance and Hope: Essays in Honour of Beyers Naude* (Cape Town: David Phillips, 1985) p.17
[53] Republic of South Africa Department of Statistics, *Census of Manufacturing, 1967-68, 1965-66 and 1963-64*, (Amsterdam: Time-Life International, Netherlands, 1975), p.145
[54] International Defence and Aid Fund, *The Apartheid War Machine* (London: IDAF, 1980), p.10

55 Benson, *Struggle for a Birthright*, p.239
56 See, Stephen Clingman, *Bram Fischer: Afrikaner revolutionary*, (Johannesburg: Jacana Media, 2013), *ad passim*
57 Quoted in, Benson, *Struggle for a Birthright*, p.274
58 Benson, *Struggle for a Birthright*, p.276
59 Ibid.
60 Benson, *Struggle for a Birthright*, p.282
61 www.miningweekly.com/article/Barbeton should be the focus of new gold rush", 14 April 2021
62 See, International Defence Aid Fund, *Akin to Slavery*, (London: IDAF, 1979); Mtutuzeli Matshoba, *Call Me Not a Man* (Johannesburg: Ravan Press)
63 Robert H. Davies, Dan O'Meara. *The Struggle for South Africa: A Reference Guide to Movements, Organizations and Institutions* Vol. 2 (London: Zed Books Limited, 1984), p.419
64 Davies and O'Meara, *The Struggle: Reference Guide*, p.149
65 Ibid.
66 The Woodstock Theses were subsequently published in *South African Outlook*, December 1967, issue
67 See, John de Gruchy and W. B. de Villiers, *The Message in Perspective* (Johannesburg: South African Council of Churches, 1969).
68 *Cape Times* (October 28, 1968), p.1
69 SASO Policy Manifesto, in Sadeet Badat, *Black Man, You Are On Your Own* (Johannesburg: Steve Biko Foundation, 2009), p.55
70 Steve Biko, "We Blacks", in *I write what I Like*, edited by A. Stubbs (Johannesburg: Picador, 1984), pp.29-35 (Originally published 1970)
71 *Black Review* 1972, (Johannesburg: Ravan Press, 1973), p.41
72 See, International Commission of Jurists, *The Trial of Beyers Naude*, (London: Search Press, 1975), p.90
73 See, M.P. Gwala, in *Black Review 1973*, (Durban: Black Community Programmes, 1974), p.170; and Steve Biko, "The Definition of black Consciousness", in *I write what I Like*, edited by A. Stubbs (Johannesburg: Picador, 1984), pp. 52-57 (Originally published 1971)

[74] Steve Biko, *Black Viewpoint,* (Durban: Black Community Probrammes, 1972), p.2

[75] Peter Randall (ed.), *A Taste of Power: The Final SPRO-CAS Report,* (Johannesburg: Ravan Press, 1973); and Peter Randall, "SPRO-CAS Revisited: The Christian Contribution to Political Debate', *Resistance and Hope: South African Essays in Honour of Beyers Naude,* edited by C. Villa Viacencio, C. and J. W De Gruchy (David Philips, Cape Town, 1985), p.165-177

[76] See, M. J. Lamola, "The Thought of Steve Biko as the Historico-Philosophical Base of South African Black Theology" *Journal of Black Theology in South Africa,* 3, 2 (1989), p.1-14

[77] See, Steve Biko, "The Church as seen by a Young Layman", paper delivered at the Conference of Black Minister of Religion of the Black Community Projects (BCP), held at Edendale, Natal in May1972. In, Steve Biko. *I Write What I Like,* edited by A Stubbs, (London: Penguin Books, 1978) p.75-86

[78] James H. Cone, *Black Theology and Black Power* (New York: Seabury Press and Orbis Books, 1969)

[79] See, Basil Moore (ed.), *Black Theology: The South African Voice* (London: Hurst & Co., 1973), *ad passim*

[80] It appeared in: *Pro Veritate* Vol 11, No 11 (1972); and *Black Review,* 1973, p.180.

[81] See, Mokgethi Motlhabi (ed), *Essays on Black Theology* (Johannesburg: Ravan Press and BCP, 1972).

[82] Peter R. Randall, *A Taste of Power* (Johannesburg: Ravan Press, 1973), p.188

[83] See, Allan Boesak, *Farewell to Innocence: A Socio-ethical Study of Black Theology and Black Power* (Maryknoll, N. Y: Orbis, 1977)

[84] Z. Mbali, *The Churches and Racism* (SCM Press, London, 1987), p.160

[85] Ans J. van der Bent, *Breaking Down the Walls* (Geneva: World Council of Churches, 1986) p.37

[86] See, E. Adler, *A Small Beginning* (Geneva: World Council of Churches, 1974) *ad passim*
[87] Adler, *A Small Beginning*, p. 38
[88] D. Thomas, *Councils in the Ecumenical Movement in South Africa 1904-75*, (Johannesburg: South African Council of Churches, 1979) p.74
[89] Thomas, p.76
[90] M. John Lamola, "Debate on Violence", in, *Hammering Swords into Ploughshares: Essays in Honour of Archbishop Desmond Tutu*, edited by Buti Tlhagale and Itumeleng Mosala (Michigan: Grand Rapids, 1986), p.56-67; and, Charles VillaVicencio, *Theology and Violence: The South African Debate*, (Johannesburg: Skotaville Publishers,1987,)
[91] *South African Outlook*, Jan/Feb 1973, p.1
[92] International Commission of Jurists, *The Trial of Beyers Naude*, (London: Search Press, 1975), *ad passim*
[93] Peter R. Randall, *A Taste of Power: The Final SPRO-CAS Report* (Johannesburg: Ravan Press, 1973)
[94] Christopher R. Hill. *Change in South Africa: Blind Alleys or New Directions?* (Lanham: Rowman & Littlefield, 1983), p.150-157
[95] *CI News*, March 1974, p.2
[96] CI News, March 1974, p.6
[97] *Ecunews Bulletin*, 4 June 1975
[98] See, Desmond Tutu, "Black Theology/African Theology - Soul mates or antagonists?" in *Black theology: A Documentary History, 1966-1979*, edited by G.S. Wilmore and J.H. Cone, (Maryknoll, NY: Orbis Books, 1979) p.483-491
[99] *Report of the Eloff Commission of Enquiry on the SACC, RP.74/1983*, (Pretoria: Government Printers)
[100] *The Divine Intention: Desmond Tutu's Testimony to the Eloff Commission* (Johannesburg: SACC, 1982)
[101] *Report of the Eloff Commission of Inquiry on the SACC, RP.74/1983*, (Pretoria: Government Printers) p.431-435
[102] Differentiated from the Lutheran Church (Martin Luther, German, 1483 – 1507) and other protestant (non- Catholic) churches, the theology of

the Reformed tradition churches is formulated upon the teachings of the Swiss French reformer, John Calvin (1509-1564)

[103] See T. Dunbex Moodie, *The rise of Afrikanerdom: Power, Apartheid and the Afrikaner Civil Religion* (Bekerley: University of California Press, 1979)

[104] See, Allan A. Boesak, *Black and Reformed*, (Johannesburg: Skotaville Publishers, 1984)

[105] 'Daughter churches' is the somewhat disparaging phrase used by the NGK to describe the black sections of the Dutch Reformed tradition in South Africa, who are viewed as the products of the missionary responsibility of the exclusively white NGK that refers to itself as the 'mother church'

[106] J.H.P Serfontein, *Apartheid, Change and the NG Kerk*, (Pretoria: Taurus, 1982), p.153-7, 270

[107] N. Smith, F.E O'Brien, Geldenhuys, and P. Meiring (eds), *Storm-Kompas: Opstelle op Soek na 'n Suiwer Koers in die Suid-Afrikaanse Konteks van die Jare Tagtig* (Cape Town: Tafelberg, 1981)

[108] *Status confessionis*, Latin, meaning "that which is foundational for belief and behavior and must be affirmed by professing members of the church."

[109] See, John De Gruchy and Charles Villa-Vicencio (eds), Apartheid *is a Heresy* (Cape Town: David Phillip Publishers, 1983)

[110] Ibid, p.160

[111] *Kerk en Samelewing*: *'n Getuienis van die Nederduitse Gereformeerde Kerk*, (Bloemfontein: NG Sendingpers, 1986).

[112] Serfontein, *Apartheid, Change and the NG Kerk*, p.223

[113] For detailed information concerning the unrest and statistics of people killed and arrested between 1984 and 1986, see Catholic Institute of International Relations, *South Africa in the 1980s*, 2nd edition (London: CIIR, 1986), and South African Institute of Race Relations, SAIRR, *Annual Survey of Race Relations:1986*, (Johannesburg: SAIRR, 1987)

[114] Saint Augustine [AD 413] 2009. *The City of God: Book Five, translated* by Marcus Dods. Peaboy, Mass: Hendrickson Publishing

[115] See, Allan Boesak and Charles Villa-Vicencio (eds), *A Call for an End to Unjust Rule* (Edinburgh: St Andrews Press, 1986), *ad passim*

[116] *The Kairos Document*, 1st Edition (Johannesburg: Institute for Contextual Theology) p.22

[117] For example: Hemson, D, *Foreign Investment and the Reproduction of Racial Capitalism in S.A.*, (London: Anti-Apartheid Movement: 1976); Clarke, S., *The Role of Transnational Corporations in Financing Apartheid.* SEM5/79 (New York: UN Centre Against Apartheid, 1975)

[118] See: World Council of Churches, *PCR Information*, No 3. (Geneva: WCC); World Council of Churches, *Time to Withdraw* (Geneva: WCC, 1973); Van Weansberge, R., *Do We Participate in Apartheid* (Geneva: World Council of Churches, 1975); See also, Catholic Institute for International Relations, *Oil and Apartheid: The Churches' Challenge to Shell and BP* (London: CIIR, 1982).

[119] 'Executive Order 12532'. National Archives of the United States of America.

[120] See Nelson Mandela, *Long Walk to Freedom* (London: Abacus, 1995), p.624-627

[121] NB, *NUSAS talks to the ANC: Report back on meeting between the National Union of South African Students and the African National Congress held from Sunday, 31 March to Tuesday 2 April 1986 in Harare, Zimbabwe.* (Observatory: NUSAS, 1986)

[122] World Council of Churches- Programme to Combat Racism, *The Churches Search for Justice and Peace in Southern Africa, Report, Lusaka 4-7 May 1987* (Geneva: WCC, 1987), p.32

[123] *South African 1983/84, Official Year Book of the Republic of South Africa* (Bureau of Information: Pretoria, 1984), p.788

[124] See *Ecunews*, Vol. 13, No.5, October 1987, p.7

[125] Villa-Vicencio, C. (ed.). *Theology and Violence* (Johannesburg: Skotaville Publishers, 1987)

[126] African National Congress, Message to the People of South Africa from the National Executive Committee on the Occasion of 8 January 1988, *Sechaba*, Vol. 12, Issue 1 (10.01.1988)

[127] Frank Chikane, Address to Church Leaders, 2nd February 1988, in *Emergency Convocation of Churches in South Africa, May 30 & 31, 1988, Preparation Material* (Johannesburg: SACC, 1988), p.2
[128] Ibid.
[129] African National Congress, 1988 January 8th Statement.
[130] Frank Chikane, *The Church's Prophetic Witness Against the Apartheid System in South Africa: 25th February- 8th April 1988* (Johannesburg: South African Council of Churches, 1988), p.2
[131] See Frank Chikane 1988. *The Church's Prophetic Witness Against the Apartheid System in South Africa: 25th February- 8th April 1988,* pp 41, p.57-72
[132] South African Council of Churches, *SACC 1988 National Conference Report* (Johannesburg: SACC), p.157
[133] See *SABC's Truth and Reconciliation Special Report*, Episode 25. www.sabctrc.saha.org.za
[134] Bernand Spong & Cedric Mayson *Come Celebrate: Twenty-five years of the South African Council of Churches, 1968-1993* (Johannesburg: SACC, 1993), p.96, 97

SELECT BIBLIOGRAPHY

Abraham, G., *The Catholic Church and Apartheid, 1948-1957*, M.A History Dissertation, University of Natal, Durban, 1984

Adler, E., *A Small Beginning*, (Geneva: World Council of Churches, 1974)

Badat, *Black Man, You Are on Your Own* (Johannesburg: Steve Biko Foundation, 2009)

Bax, D.S., *A different Gospel: A Critique of the Theology Behind Apartheid* (Johannesburg; Presbyterian Church of Southern Africa, 1979)

Benson, M., *South Africa: The Struggle for a Birthright*. (London: IDAF, 1985)

Biko, S., *I Write What I Like,* edited by Aelred Stubbs (Johannesburg, Picador Africa, 2004)

Boesak, A., *Farewell to Innocence: A Socio-ethical Study of Black Theology and Black Power* (Maryknoll, N. Y: Orbis, 1977)

Boesak, A., *Black and Reformed*, (Johannesburg: Skotaville Publishers, 1984)

Boesak, A., and Villa-Vicencio, C. eds, *A Call for an End to Unjust Rule* (Edinburgh: St Andrews Press, 1986)

Brandt, H. ed., *Outside the Camp: A collection of writings by Wolfram Kistner* (Johannesburg: S.A Council of Churches), 1988)

Canon L. *John Collins, Faith under fire.* (London: Leslie Frewin, 1966)

Catholic Institute of International Relations, *South Africa in the 1980s*, 2nd edition (London: CIIR, 1986), and South African Institute of Race

Relations, SAIRR, *Annual Survey of Race Relations:1986*, (Johannesburg: SAIRR, 1987)

Catholic Institute for International Relations, *Oil and Apartheid: The Churches' Challenge to Shell and BP* (London: CIIR, 1982).

Cawood, L. *The Church and Race Relations in South Africa* (Johannesburg: SA Institute of Race Relations, 1964)

Chikane, F., *The Church's Prophetic Witness Against the Apartheid System in South Africa: 25th February - 8th April 1988* (Johannesburg: South African Council of Churches, 1988)

Clarke, S., *The Role of Transnational Corporations in Financing Apartheid*. SEM5/79 (New York: UN Centre Against Apartheid, 1975)

Clingman, S., *Bram Fischer: Afrikaner Revolutionary*, (Johannesburg: Jacana Media, 2013).

Cloete, G. D and smit, D. J. eds, A Moment of Truth: The Confession of the Dutch Reformed Mission Church (Grand Rapids: Wm B. Eerdmans, 1984)

Prozesky, M., *Christianity Amidst Apartheid*, edited by (London: Macmillian Press, 1990)

Cone, J.H. *Black Theology and Black Power* (New York: Seabury Press and Orbis Books, 1969)

Davies, R.H., and O'Meara, D., *The Struggle for South Africa: A Reference Guide to Movements, Organizations and Institutions*, Vol. 2 (London: Zed Books, 1984)

de Gruchy, J. and De Villiers, W. B., *The Message in Perspective* (Johannesburg: South African Council of Churches, 1969).

de Gruchy, J. W., *The Church Struggle in South Africa*, 2nd Edition (London: Collins, 1986) de Gruchy, J. W., and Villa-Vicencio, C. eds, *Apartheid is a Heresy* (Cape Town: David Phillip , 1983)

de Gruchy, J. W., and Villa-Vicencio, C. eds, *Resistance and Hope: Essays in Honour of Beyers Naude* (Cape Town: David Phillips, 1985)

Elphick, R. and Davenport, R,. *Christianity in South Africa: a political, social and cultural history.* (Cape Town: David Phillip, 1997)

Gerhart, G. M and Glaser, C., *From Protest to Challenge: A Documentary History of African Politics in South Africa, Vol 6, 1980-1990* (Johannesburg: Jacana Media, 2010)

Government of South Africa, *Report of the Eloff Commission of Enquiry on the SACC, RP.74/1983* (Pretoria: Government Printers, 1983)

Govender, S. ed., *Unity and Justice: The Witness of the Belydende Kring* (Johannesburg: Skotaville, 1984)

Hemson, D., *Foreign Investment and the Reproduction of Racial Capitalism in S.A.*, (London: Anti-Apartheid Movement: 1976)

Hill, C.R., *Change in South Africa: Blind Alleys or New Directions?* (Lanham: Rowman & Littlefield, 1983)

Hodge, J. and Radick, G. eds. *The Cambridge Companion to Darwin* (Cambridge: Cambridge University Press, 2006)

International Commission of Jurists, *The Trial of Beyers Naude*, (London: Search Press, 1975)

International Defence and Aid Fund, *The Apartheid War Machine* (London: IDAF, 1980)

Kairos Theologians, *The Kairos Document, A Theological Comment on the Political Crisis in South Africa* (Johannesburg: Institute for Contextual Theology, 1985)

Karis, T. and Gerhart, G. M, *From Protest to Challenge: A Documentary History of African Politics in South Africa Vol.3, 1953-1964*, 2nd Edition (Johannesburg: Jacana Media, 2013)

Karis, T. and Gerhart, G. M and, *From Protest to Challenge: A Documentary History of African Politics in South Africa, Vol 5, 1964-1979*, 2nd Edition (Johannesburg: Jacana Media, 2013)

Keet, B.B., *Suid-Afrika Waarheen* (Stellenbosch: University of Stellenbosch Press, 1955)

Kruger, D. W., *South African Parties and Policies*, (Cape Town: Human & Rousseau, 1960)

Lodge, T., *Black Politics in South Africa Since 1945* (Johannesburg: Ravan Press)

Luckhardt, K. and Wall, B. *Organise or Starve: The History of SACTU* (London: Lawrence and Wishardt, 1980)

Mandela, N. *The Struggle is my Life* (London: IDAF)

Mandela, N., *Long Walk to Freedom* (London: Abacus,1995)

Mbali, Z., *The Churches and Racism*, (SCM Press: London, 1987)

McLeoud, B., *Naude: Prophet to South Africa* (Atlanta: John Knox,1978)

Meli, F., *South Africa Belongs to Us: A history of the ANC* (James Currey: London, 1988)

Moodie, T. B., *The rise of Afrikanerdom: Power, Apartheid and the Afrikaner Civil Religion* (Bekerley: University of California Press, 1979)

Moore, B. ed., *Black Theology: The South African Voice* (London: Hurst & Co., 1973).

Motlhabi, M., ed. *Essays on Black Theology* (Johannesburg: Ravan Press and BCP, 1972).

Nash, M., *Ecumenical Witness in the 1960s* (Johannesburg: SACC, 1975)

N.G Kerk, *Kerk en Samelewing: 'n Getuienis van die Nederduitse Gereformeerde Kerk*, (Bloemfontein: NG Sendingpers, 1986)

Prior, A. ed., *Catholics in Apartheid Society* (Cape Town: David Phillips, 1982)

Randall, P., *A Taste of Power: The Final SPRO-CAS Report*, (Johannesburg: Ravan Press, 1973)

Randall, P., ed., *Not Without Honour: Tribute to Beyers Naude* (Johannesburg: Ravan Press)

Regehr, E., *Perceptions of Apartheid: The Churches and Political Change in South Africa* (Scottdale: Herald Press)

Serfontein, J.H.P., *Apartheid, Change and the NG Kerk* (Pretoria: Taurus, 1982)

Simpkins, C.E.W. *Reconstructing South African Liberalism* (Johannesburg: South African Institute of Race Relations, 1986), *ad passim*

Smith, N., F.E O'Brien, Geldenhuys, and P. Meiring (eds), *Storm-Kompas: Opstelle op Soek na 'n Suiwer Koers in die Suid-Afrikaanse Konteks van die Jare Tagtig* (Cape Town: Tafelberg, 1981)

South African Institute of Race Relations, *Survey of Race Relations in South Africa, 1955-57* (Johannesburg: SAIRR, 1958)

South African Institute of Race Relations, *Survey of Race Relations in South Africa, 1961* (Johannesburg: Institute of Race Relations, 1962)

South African Catholic Bishops Conference, *The Bishops Speak*, 3 vols (Pretoria: SACBC, 1990)

South Africa 1988/89, Official Yearbook of the Republic of South Africa (Pretoria: Bureau of Information), p.161

South African 1983/84, Official Year Book of the Republic of South Africa (Bureau of Information: Pretoria, 1984), p.788

Spong, B., and Mayson, C. *Come Celebrate: Twenty-five years of the South African Council of Churches, 1968-1993* (Johannesburg: SACC, 1993)

Thomas, D., *Councils in the Ecumenical Movement in South Africa 1904-75*, (Johannesburg: South African Council of Churches, 1979)

Tlhagale, B. and Mosala, I., *Hammering Swords into Ploughshares: Essays in Honour of Archbishop Desmond Tutu*, edited by (Michigan: Grand Rapids, 1986)

Tutu, D. "Black Theology/African Theology - Soulmates or Antagonists?" in *Black Theology: A Documentary History, 1966-1979*, edited by G.S. Wilmore and J.H. Cone (Maryknoll, NY: Orbis Books, 1979)

Tutu, D., *The Divine Intention: Testimony to the Eloff Commission* (Johannesburg: SACC, 1982)

Tutu, D., *Hope and Suffering* (Johannesburg: Skotaville, 1984)

Tutu, M. and Sparks, A., *Tutu: The Authorised Portrait* (London: Macmillan, 2011)

Van der Bent, A.J., *Breaking Down the Walls: World Council of Churches Statements and Actions on Racism, 1948-1985* (Geneva: World Council of Churches, 1986)

Van Weansberge, R., *Do We Participate in Apartheid* (Geneva: World Council of Churches, 1975)

Venter, J. J., 'H.F. Verwoerd: Foundational aspects of his thought', *Koers*, 64, 4 (1999), p.415-441

Villa-Vicencio, C. and de Gruchy, J. W. eds., *Resistance and Hope: South African Essays in Honour of Beyers Naude* (David Philips, Cape Town, 1985)

Villa-Vicencio, C. *Theology and Violence: The South African Debate* (Johannesburg: Skotaville, 1987)

Walshe, P., *Church versus State in South Africa: The Case of the Christian Institute* (Maryknoll, N.Y: Orbis)

Wilson, F. *Migrant Labour in South Africa* (Johannesburg: SACC and SPROCAS, 1972)

World Council of Churches *The Churches Search for Justice and Peace in Southern Africa, Report, Lusaka 4-7 May 1987* (Geneva: WCC, 1987)

www.ingramcontent.com/pod-product-compliance
Lightning Source LLC
Chambersburg PA
CBHW032147010526
44111CB00035B/1239